Womanpower Unlimited

Womanpower Unlimited

and the Black Freedom Struggle in Mississippi

TIYI M. MORRIS

The University of Georgia Press   *Athens and London*

© 2015 by the University of Georgia Press

Athens, Georgia 30602

www.ugapress.org

All rights reserved

Set in Minion Pro and Myriad Pro by Graphic Composition, Inc., Bogart, Georgia

Printed and bound by Thomson-Shore

The paper in this book meets the guidelines for permanence and durability
of the Committee on Production Guidelines for Book Longevity of the
Council on Library Resources.

Most University of Georgia Press titles are available from popular e-book vendors.

Printed in the United States of America

19 18 17 16 15 P 5 4 3 2 1

Library of Congress Cataloging-in-Publication Data

Morris, Tiyi Makeda.
   Womanpower Unlimited and the Black freedom struggle in Mississippi /
Tiyi M. Morris.
       pages cm. — (Politics and culture in the twentieth-century South)
   Includes bibliographical references and index.
   ISBN 978-0-8203-4730-1 (hardcover : alkaline paper) —
ISBN 978-0-8203-4731-8 (paperback : alkaline paper) —
ISBN 978-0-8203-4793-6 (ebook)
1. Womanpower Unlimited—History. 2. African American women
political activists—Mississippi—History—20th century. 3. African American
women civil rights workers—Mississippi—History—20th century.
4. African American women—Mississippi—Social conditions—20th century.
5. African Americans—Civil rights—Mississippi—History—20th century.
6. Civil rights movements—Mississippi—History—20th century.
7. Mississippi—Race relations—History—20th century. I. Title.
   E185.93.M6M665 2014
   305.48'89607307620904—dc23   2014023162

British Library Cataloging-in-Publication Data available

FOR KAMARIA, JAMAL, AND RASHAD

AND MY MOTHER.

CONTENTS

ACKNOWLEDGMENTS

This project would not have come to fruition without the guidance, support, and assistance of many individuals and institutions. I must begin by thanking my mother, whose early stories of her activism in the Student Nonviolent Coordinating Committee (SNCC) introduced me to the Black freedom struggle. I was inspired by her courageous activism and awed by her remembrances of working alongside women such as Fannie Lou Hamer, Annie Devine, and Ella Baker. I am indebted to the efforts of my mother; other women activists, both the nationally acclaimed and the relatively unknown; the women whose lives occupy the pages of this book; and all of the civil rights activists of this era, and before, for creating the opportunities to which I now have access.

I am especially thankful and indebted to Merrill Tenney McKewen, who introduced me to Womanpower Unlimited as a doctoral student and trusted that I would have the ability to tell their story.

I would also like to thank many persons for the trajectory of my academic career, beginning with those at my undergraduate institution, Emory University. I am grateful for the mentorship of Rudolph P. Byrd, Mark A. Sanders, and other faculty in the Department of African and African American Studies who set me on the course for a career in the academy in general and toward Black Studies in particular. I am also thankful to the staff of the Multicultural Center, such as Dean Vera Rorie and Sylvester Hopewell, who enhanced my academic experience. In graduate school at Purdue University, my dissertation committee—Vernon J. Williams Jr., Nancy Gabin, Sally Hastings, and James Saunders—provided essential feedback in the early stages of the project and helped me set a course for the future development of the work. With their assistance, I established a solid foundation for the manuscript. Leonard Neufeldt, then director of American Studies, was instrumental in structuring a program that allowed me to pursue my interests in Black women's history and creating an environment that celebrated such "soul sisters" as those who are the subject of this book. I am also grateful for my time at Purdue because I met Kay-len Tucker and Angela Hilton, sister-friends and scholars, whose support has helped sustain me professionally and personally as we matriculated graduate school and beyond.

I am also thankful for the support I received during my first tenure-track position at DePauw University. When I arrived as a Consortium for a Strong Minority Presence (CSMP) dissertation fellow at DePauw, I had the pleasure of working with Anne Fernald, who facilitated a dissertation-writing group with my cohort of CSMP fellows—Raymonda Burgman, Kimberly Ellis, and Matthew Oware. We four, and Estevan Azcona and Anne Choi, who joined us the following year, formed a collective of young scholars and I am grateful for their friendship. I am most appreciative of then Dean Neal Abraham and then President Robert Bottoms, who were instrumental in creating these aforementioned opportunities at DePauw for emerging scholars of color. My colleagues in the History department—Julia Bruggerman, Yung-Chen Chiang, John Dittmer, Mac Dixon-Fyle, David Gellman, Glen Kuecker, John Schlotterbeck, Barbara Steinson, and Barbara Whitehead—as well as those in Women's Studies and Black Studies set the bar high with the environment of collegiality and mentorship they provided.

I am also grateful for the many students I had the pleasure of teaching and mentoring who gave relevance to my historical inquiries, especially those in the last cohort of students I taught at DePauw, including Aretha Butler, Adrienne Cobb, Elesse Dorsey, Amber Valverde, and Ashleigh Watson. Jennifer Hinton, whom I was able to hire as a research assistant with DePauw's Student-Faculty Summer Research Grant, assisted with archival research and editing, and was a model student whose interest in Black women's history served as a constant reminder as to why this research is important.

My colleagues in the Department of African American and African Studies at The Ohio State University (OSU) and those at the Newark Campus have also welcomed me into a supportive environment. In particular, Elizabeth "Sunny" Caldwell and Katherine "Katey" Borland were instrumental in shepherding me through the dark hours of assistant professorship at a Research I university. Thanks to Patrice Dickerson and Julia Watson in OSU's Arts and Sciences Recruitment and Diversity Office for introducing me to and providing the funds for me to participate in the National Center for Faculty Development and Diversity (NCFDD). I must state that Kerry Ann Rocquemore's NCFDD's Faculty Boot Camp was key to my completion of this manuscript and maintaining my sanity. My accountability writing group facilitator, Kathryn Gines, and participants, Lorrie Frasure, Patrisia Macias-Rojas, and Courtney Wright, kept me honest and on track. I am also thankful for the friendship that developed with Patrisia, whose perseverance I admire and whose encouragement as another professor-mom has been priceless.

There are several institutions wherein I have conducted research and resources were made available and I am indebted to the archivists who helped me and supported my research. The Amistad Research Center at Tulane University's amazing staff has provided assistance virtually and on location during my numerous trips over the years. Thank you also to Walter Stern, who provided research assistance while a graduate student at Tulane. The Margaret Walker Alexander National Research Center at Jackson State University, the National Archives for Black Women's History, the Peace Collection at Swarthmore College, the Mississippi Department of Archives and History, Loyola University's Women and Leadership Archives, the Schlesinger Library of the Radcliffe Institute at Harvard University, the Woodruff Library Archives at the Atlanta University Center, the Vermont Historical Society, the General Commission on Archives and History of the United Methodist Church, and the Schomburg Center for Research in Black Culture have provided sources that were integral to my research. I thank everyone at the University of Georgia Press for their work on this project, especially Walter Biggins, John Joerschke, Jason Bennett, Beth Snead, and David E. Des Jardines. I am also grateful for the readers' thoughtful suggestions and Kay Kodner's meticulous copyediting, which have enriched the manuscript.

My work has benefited from the time I spent at summer research institutes, which provided the time and space to develop my research as well as engagement with communities of graduate students, faculty, scholars, and activists that have positively influenced my understandings of the Black freedom struggle and Black women's history and activism. Sekai and James Turner convened a wonderful team of scholars to facilitate the Engendering Africana Studies Workshop at Cornell University. The Multicultural Teaching Scholars program at the University of Missouri–Columbia introduced me to Carol Anderson, Wilma King, K. C. Morrison, Clenora Hudson-Weems, and Julius Thompson, who offered scholarly and professional advice. Two programs—the Future of Minority Studies at Cornell University, organized by Beverly Guy-Sheftall, Chandra Talpade Mohanty, and Satya Mohanty, and the National Endowment for the Humanities African American Struggles for Freedom and Civil Rights Summer Institute at Harvard University, under the direction of

Patricia Sullivan and Waldo Martin—were both influential in my development as a scholar. I am so thankful to Luther Adams and Cheryl Hicks for making the time at Harvard more enlightening and enjoyable. My colleagues at the Fannie Lou Hamer Institute on Citizenship and Democracy at Jackson State University will always hold a special place in my heart. Daphne Chamberlain, Emilye Crosby, Michelle Deardorf, Jeff Kolnick, Leslie McLemore (as well as Russell Wigginton at Rhodes College), and the numerous participants who attended our NEH-sponsored summer workshops renewed my spirit and gave me the energy to continue working on the project.

I am also indebted to Vicki Crawford, whose scholarship on Black women civil rights activists helped lay the foundation for this work, and who shared her personal interviews of Womanpower Unlimited members with me when I was a graduate student. Her encouragement and support in the early stages of my research were instrumental in giving me the confidence to proceed with the project. Since then, friends and colleagues have read parts of the manuscript and offered sound advice for improvement. Thank you, Emilye Crosby, Hasan Kwame Jeffries, Ike Newsum, Walter Rucker, Kimberly Springer, and Yohuru Williams. Thanks also to Cynthia Colas for terrific copyediting. And special thanks to Holly Cowan Shulman for sharing her research and her mother's legacy of Wednesdays in Mississippi and for introducing me, literally, to Dorothy Height.

John Dittmer has been a major influence upon me and I will forever be grateful for his scholarship, mentorship, and friendship. He has, patiently and with great care, read more drafts of this work than anyone, beginning with its embryonic dissertation phase and all of the revisions along the way. His questions (and answers), critiques, and praise have made this a much stronger manuscript.

I am particularly grateful to the families of Womanpower members—Clarie Collins Harvey's cousin, Annette Collins Rollins; A. M. E. Logan's children, Shirley Montague and Willis Logan; and Thelma Sanders's brother William "Bo" Brown—who were so willing to share with me the memories and lives of their loved ones.

There are numerous friends whose companionship and love have sustained me throughout the years. My high school friends Angela Powell, Mhanta Crawford, and Andrea Jones and college buddies Cheryl Turner, Terra and Allison Gay, and Aishah Rashied have embodied the meaning of sisterhood. Thank you for your acceptance and love. And most especially, thank you to

Kimberly Ellis, who has been one of my best friends since we met on our first day of college. My journey through college and graduate school and my career in the academy would not have been the same without her camaraderie, advice, and support. From study groups, editing each other's work, and team teaching to road trips, baby-sitting, and everything in between, Kim has been a constant in my life that has enhanced the person and scholar I am.

I am grateful for the community of "younger" scholars like Emilye Crosby, Wesley Hogan, Hasan Kwame Jeffries, and Robyn C. Spencer, who are also studying the Black freedom struggle and whose friendship, support, and intellectual exchanges I have valued over the years.

My family has provided a lifeline without which I would not have survived. The love and encouragement from my brothers, Omar, Orlando, and Earl, and my sister Jessica's support and friendship, has meant more than I can express. My father, Jesse Morris, has provided an activist legacy of which I am proud and offered an insider's perspective throughout my research. My mother, Euvester Simpson, and my stepfather, Les Range, have supported me in ways too numerous to list. Throughout the years, they have given me the material and emotional support to accomplish my goals. My mother, especially, has been my biggest asset, caring for my children during summer research trips, reading and editing various drafts, serving as a research subject and assistant, and providing me with encouragement when I, all too often, doubted myself. Without her this book would not have been completed. And last, but not least, the family that I have created with Judson L. Jeffries and my children, Rashad, Jamal, and Kamaria, have helped me become more patient, learn to truly appreciate the process, and enjoy life more fully.

ABBREVIATIONS

AEU	American Ethical Union
AFSC	American Friends Service Committee
CDF	Children's Defense Fund
CDGM	Child Development Group of Mississippi
COFO	Council of Federated Organizations
CORE	Congress of Racial Equality
CWO	Council of Women's Organizations
CWU	Church Women United
DST	Delta Sigma Theta Sorority, Inc.
FOC	Fellowship of the Concerned
JNM	Jackson Nonviolent Movement
LWV	League of Women Voters
MCAD	Massachusetts Committee Against Discrimination
MCHR	Mississippi Council on Human Relations
MDAH	Mississippi Department of Archives and History
MFDP	Mississippi Freedom Democratic Party
MIA	Montgomery Improvement Association
MPE	Mississippians for Public Education
MSFCWC	Mississippi State Federation of Colored Women's Clubs
MTA	Mississippi Teachers Association
MWANRC	Margaret Walker Alexander National Research Center
NAACP	National Association for the Advancement of Colored People
NACW	National Association of Colored Women
NANBPWC	National Association of Negro Business and Professional Women's Clubs
NCCW	National Council of Catholic Women
NCJW	National Council of Jewish Women
NCNW	National Council of Negro Women
NFDMA	National Funeral Directors and Morticians Association

NYSEC	New York Society for Ethical Culture
OEO	Office of Economic Opportunity
RCNL	Regional Council of Negro Leadership
SANE	Committee for a Sane Nuclear Policy
SCLC	Southern Christian Leadership Conference
SNCC	Student Non-violent Coordinating Committee
SRC	Southern Regional Council
UCW	United Church Women
VEP	Voter Education Project
VIM	Vermont in Mississippi
WCC	World Council of Churches
WILPF	Women's International League for Peace and Freedom
WIMS	Wednesdays in Mississippi
WPC	Women's Political Council
WSP	Women Strike for Peace
WU	Womanpower Unlimited
YMCA	Young Men's Christian Association
YWCA	Young Women's Christian Association

"Women Are the Humanizers of the Struggle"
Black Women's Legacy of Activism

> Next to God we are indebted to women, first for life itself, and then
> for making it worth living.
> —Mary McLeod Bethune

> What Black women did in the Civil Rights Movement was to
> continue looking at what else we had to do in order for there to be
> another day for our people. The Civil Rights Movement, in that
> respect, is not necessarily this gigantic, unbelievable leap. It is, in
> this light, a continuance.
> —Bernice Johnson Reagon

In June 2012, seventy-seven-year-old Ineva May-Pittman launched her campaign for city councilwoman from the second ward of Jackson, Mississippi. Running on a platform of making government more transparent, meeting the needs of the underserved, and improving education, May-Pittman made her fourth bid for local office, having previously run twice for city council (2001 and 2005) and once for the state senate (2007). While the May 7, 2013 vote did not result in her election, May-Pittman was undeterred by the loss and continued her community activism, knowing that the power to promote social change is not limited to elected officials.

A community activist in Jackson since the 1950s, Ineva May-Pittman knew firsthand the power everyday people can wield. During the 1960s, she was one of a cadre of Black women in Mississippi's capital city who worked tirelessly with the civil rights organization Womanpower Unlimited, often behind the scenes, to ensure Black advancement and equality.[1] In the post–civil rights years, her grassroots activism was instrumental in preserving Smith Robertson,

Jackson's first Black public school, as well as the renaming of the Jackson International Airport to the Jackson–Medgar Wiley Evers International Airport. A decades-long member of the National Association for the Advancement of Colored People (NAACP) and the National Council of Negro Women (NCNW), May-Pittman has remained intimately involved in Jackson's political culture as a regular attendee of city council, school board, and election commission meetings.[2]

The youngest of five children, Ineva May was born on July 6, 1934, in Jayess, Mississippi, to Mary Ella and Jeff May. After her husband's death, Mrs. May moved the family to Jackson to be closer to her sister and to afford her children access to the better educational opportunities available in the city. Prioritizing education later would became a central aspect of May-Pittman's life, leading to both her activism and her professional career. Ineva attended school at Christ Missionary and Industrial College (CM&I) and Lanier High School, graduating from the latter in 1952.[3] Upon graduation, she enrolled at Jackson State College (now Jackson State University). May-Pittman recalled that her teachers required students to attend meetings of the Mississippi Teachers Association (MTA). In one such meeting Melvin Leventhal, a Jewish civil rights attorney, asked teachers to serve as witnesses in a suit against the state charging discrimination against Black teachers. No one came forward. May-Pittman said that incident prompted her desire to become involved in the movement. She decided that if such an opportunity arose when she was a teacher she would not sit silently on the sidelines.

Ineva May received her bachelor of science degree in elementary education from Jackson State College in 1956 and began teaching second grade at Isable Elementary School.[4] She married Joe Pittman with whom she had one son. Along with her teaching, May-Pittman expressed her love for her students by working to create better opportunities for them through political activism. Throughout the 1950s and 1960s she worked through her church and with civil rights and women's organizations to effect change. Women like May-Pittman, while not typically in the spotlight, were central to movement successes in the state and across the South, and they continued their community activism in the post–civil rights years. Through their activism, these women sustained a legacy of Black women's activism that reflects their experiences of intersectionality, incorporates a humanist perspective, and centers on women's empowerment, race uplift, and activist/community mothering.[5]

Scope and Methods

Womanpower Unlimited focuses on one Black women's civil rights organization, Womanpower Unlimited, to illuminate its agency and importance on the local and national levels. It explores how Black women used one of their autonomous organizations to sustain civil rights activism in the community by providing leadership and support work and cultivating a younger generation to continue the struggle. Despite often being marginalized in organizations dominated by Black men and white women, Black women did not allow such discrimination to limit their activism. Instead, they created their own organizations that afforded autonomy and provided safe spaces for their activism. The establishment of separate organizations did not preclude collaboration with Black men and white women but allowed Black women more control over the nature of such relationships. Thus, *Womanpower Unlimited* offers a perspective not only on how Black women worked with the established and often male-dominated civil rights organizations but also on how they themselves envisioned and actualized organizational development.

While recent scholars have begun to fill the void on women's leadership during the civil rights movement, fewer studies have explored Black women's agency in the movement through women's political organizations. Such an analysis allows one to better understand the historical continuity of Black women's experiences of multiple oppressions, the thematic consistency of their activism, and the activist influence from one generation to the next. Examining one organization demonstrates the complexities of women's roles within the movement with respect to gender and class dynamics and how women understood their contributions to Black liberation movements when operating in autonomous women's spaces.

Black women are generally acknowledged as the "backbone" of the civil rights movement and providers of key support, yet their activism is often undervalued. In every "local center" of civil rights activism, there was a woman or group of women who were central to the genesis, development, and continuance of activism in the community. Fannie Lou Hamer in Ruleville, Leesco Guster in Claiborne County, Annie Devine in Canton, Unita Blackwell in Mayersville, and Vera May Pigee in Clarksdale are a few examples from Mississippi.[6] These women engaged in multiple levels of activism. Whether working behind the scenes or on the front lines, they were leaders both in their communities and in the larger civil rights movement.[7] They brought integrity, strength, resources, insights based on their intersectionality, and determination to improve the lives of their family and community members.[8] In Montgomery, Alabama, the Women's Political Council (WPC), Mary Fair Burks, Jo Ann Robinson, Rosa Parks, and the countless women who walked to work each day were the initiators and force behind the success of the 1955 bus boycott.[9] Moreover, the Montgomery Improvement Association (MIA), which is the organization most notably associated with the 1955 Montgomery bus boycott, is greatly indebted to local women throughout the city who created groups in their neighborhoods, such as Georgia Gilmore's "Club from Nowhere," to raise money to support the boycott. These women were, once again, doing the essential yet behind-the-scenes work that was critical to the movement.[10] Historian Christina Greene argues that in North Carolina in the 1940s and 1950s, Black women's organizations—including the Year Round Garden Club, and Little Slam Bridge Club in Durham and the sororities, federated women's clubs, and other local women's groups across the state—sustained the NAACP, thereby "shepherding the movement through a difficult and dangerous period."[11] One group of female activists that was crucial to sustaining the movement in Jackson, Mississippi, was Womanpower Unlimited.

Black Women's Activist Traditions: Theory and Practice

Ineva May-Pittman's activist life is not unlike that of many Black women. In fact, her life is representative of the historical continuum of Black women's activism that extends both before and beyond the pinnacles of social movements that have occurred throughout America's history. Black women have advanced, as articulated by historian Barbara Ransby, "a political tradition that is radical, international, and democratic, with women at its center."[12] While working to combat the racist structures of society, Black women have simultaneously striven to create structures within the community that empower Blacks and nurture the development of their communities. Their racial consciousness and experiences of a multiplicity of oppressions have resulted in constructive paradigms, strategies, and tactics for the betterment of all members of the community. Historian Darlene Clark Hine notes that such "'race women' in local Black communities were even more critical [than race men] to the actual conceptualization and implementation of social welfare programs, the nurturance of oppositional consciousness, and the support of essential institutions."[13] May-

Pittman and other civil rights activists sustained a legacy of Black women's activism in which they have been the vanguard for racial progress and in the fight against white supremacy.

Black women activists viewed themselves as the natural leaders of the struggle because of their "special position" at the intersection of multiple oppressions and as mothers of the race. Black women's position at the intersection of race, gender, and class oppression, among other factors, gave them unique insight into how these oppressions interacted and resulted in multiple forms of subjugation. In her 1892 collection of essays, *A Voice from the South*, Anna Julia Cooper addressed Black women's position, stating that "she is confronted by both a woman question and a race problem, and is as yet an unknown or an unacknowledged factor in both."[14] While continually subjected to dehumanization and marginalization, Black women interpreted these varied forms of repression as advantageous in devising strategies to eliminate all forms of oppression and considered themselves better prepared to create strategies to simultaneously eliminate these multiple oppressions. Cooper further claimed, "Only the BLACK WOMAN can say, 'when and where I enter, in the quiet undisputed dignity of my womanhood, without violence and without suing or special patronage, then and there the whole *Negro race enters with me.*'"[15] This view resulted in liberation strategies that stressed the centrality of women's activism based on the premise that Black women's liberation provided freedom for all oppressed people. These beliefs redefined their experiences in terms of institution building, institutional transformation, and resistance rather than by suppression and marginalization. Black clubwomen believed that the progress of the Black race depended upon the leadership of Black women and that their womanhood provided the stability and strength for Black people as a whole to draw on. Contrary to traditional definitions of leadership that present male authority as natural and give primacy to "masculine" attributes—strength, logic, being unemotional—that women supposedly do not possess, many Black women activists articulated a leadership paradigm derived from their participation in both the private (feminine) and public (masculine) spheres through which they fulfilled traditional notions of womanhood and masculine traits of leadership. My analysis of Womanpower draws on Black women activists' interpretations of their intersectionality as well as Black feminist theories that center intersectionality in understanding Black women's experiences.

The concept of racial uplift Black women employed incorporates two methods of action, inspiring initiative among the dispossessed and encouraging those of means to "lift" the underprivileged.[16] These women empowered Blacks to become active agents in the struggle for freedom and justice and to take responsibility for attaining the things that a racist society denied them. They also believed that racial progress was dependent upon the progress of the entire race, not just one section of it. Therefore, they implored those who had achieved some form of privilege to work to ensure such opportunities were created for Blacks who had not.

Mothering is also central to Black women's activism as both a form of resistance and the genesis of activism. Black women's activism has incorporated (other)mothering as a means of addressing the needs of the Black community to ensure the survival of the race and as resistance to societal attempts to dehumanize and denigrate Blacks.[17] According to Black feminist scholar Patricia Hill Collins, Black women activists "work on behalf of the Black community by expressing ethics of caring and personal accountability . . . [working to help] members of the community . . . attain the self-reliance and independence essential for resistance."[18] While this community mothering, or activist mothering, includes caretaking, sharing of material resources, mentoring, and emotional and psychological nurturance to withstand the blows of racist and sexist oppression, it is not predicated on biological motherhood. Indeed, it has been a way that Black women have used nurturing as a form of resistance for biological children, extended families, and the fictive kin that create communities of children for whom they feel responsible.[19] As activist and educator Bettina Aptheker explains, Black women have continuously used nurturing in an effort to raise a community of children who can withstand and fight against societal oppressions. When this type of nurturing "is done collectively over time it becomes a historically defined resistance."[20] Black women's community mothering should be recognized as a cultural practice that celebrates the significance and empowerment of women for the survival of the race.

Mothering has also prompted Black women's community activism.[21] In many instances, the desire to provide better opportunities for their children and a life free of the oppressions they had experienced was the catalyst for women's community and political activism. Standing up for their children propelled many Black women to the front lines of leadership and allowed them to challenge the oppression that permeated southern Black life.[22] At other times, Black women have been drawn to political activism because of their children's or other relatives' participation. Civil rights activists followed in the footsteps of generations of Black women, from enslaved women to professional women, who engaged in this nurturing as resistance.[23] Womanpower members continued this activism in this twentieth-century struggle for citizenship rights and Black empowerment, fully cognizant of the tradition within which they participated and the important strides made by their predecessors.

Mississippi in the Pre–Civil Rights Era

Before Mississippi garnered the national spotlight with the movement's direct action campaign, Blacks worked in Jackson and communities throughout the state to challenge the oppressive nature that characterized southern Black life and the specifically brutal nature of racism, exploitation, and violent repression in Mississippi.

During the post-Reconstruction era, the Democratic Party, dominated by the planter class of the Mississippi Delta, governed the state. After successfully overthrowing the Republican leadership through terror, coercion, fraud, and violence and "redeeming" the state, they began to restore white racial domination in all its forms.[24] The two-party system collapsed as the Democrats took control of state politics and passed laws that ensured the continuation of white domination that characterized Black southern life. Mississippi's 1890 constitution (the second Mississippi Plan) implemented measures such as residency requirements, poll taxes, registration history, and literacy tests based on the interpretation of the state's constitution—all of which served to "legally" prevent Blacks from voting, effectively eliminating Blacks from politics. Mississippi led the South in reversing the tide of Black progress that Reconstruction had ushered in.

Increased state-sanctioned and vigilante violence in the form of lynching accompanied the legislative restrictions to prevent resistance to white supremacy. Often rationalized by whites as preventing Black men from raping white women, more common reasons for the practice included Black economic success, supposed theft, and infringing on the privileges of whiteness.[25] By 1900, lynching had evolved into the South's most common form of vigilante justice and Mississippi, again, led the South (and the nation) in the number of lynchings.[26] Most often the victims of lynching were young Black men who "appeared to challenge racial boundaries." Black women, however, were not exempt from this practice. In many instances women were subjected to the same kinds of beatings, dismemberments, shootings, burnings, and hangings that characterized the practice. Mob killings were sanctioned by the courts and condoned by many white Mississippians—young and old, rich and poor, male and female—as sometimes thousands gathered to witness such barbarism while enjoying a feast.[27] Through interlocking systems of "legality" and terrorism, whites maintained control and subdued Black political participation.

Segregation, codified through the 1896 case of *Plessy v. Ferguson* that legitimated "separate but equal," developed as another tactic to keep Blacks in their place. "Separate but equal" proved to be a farce in every aspect of both Black and white lives. In addition to a lack of political power and a socioeconomic system of agricultural labor that mimicked slavery, education was far from equitable. Black public schools, which at the turn of the century only received 19 percent of the state's school funds (although Blacks comprised 60 percent of school-aged children), were grossly inadequate. This poor educational system was destined to have far-reaching repercussions for Blacks. As described by historian Neil McMillen, "By limiting the quality and the extent of black education, the white minority could hope to cramp black political aspirations, inhibit black ability to compete economically, and assure an adequate supply of low-wage menial black labor."[28] Jim Crow segregation ensured that Blacks were restricted in every aspect of life, withholding from them the opportunities and the resources to challenge their inferior status.

As a system of domination, the aforementioned forces worked together to separate the races and ensure Black subjugation. The doctrines of white supremacy were incorporated into the law in Mississippi, compelling Blacks to enter the twentieth century in a position only a step above slavery. It was a system of oppression that stifled, yet necessitated, Black activism. Blacks had to mobilize to break the effects of white domination, but they were restricted on all fronts—legally, socially, politically, and economically.

This type of domination began to weaken in the 1930s and 1940s as cotton production, whose profitability was based largely on an exploited Black labor force, began to decline. Cotton's decreasing market value and a diminished need for manual labor due to increased mechanization and use of insecticides hastened the commodity's declining power. As a result, the sociopolitical system that ensured Blacks were a dependent agricultural labor force loosened its grip, providing greater opportunities for Black resistance. The eradication of the cotton-based economy, upon which race relations (and one of the primary reasons for controlling Blacks) had been structured, allowed for positive developments for Blacks. This agricultural shift spawned migration to northern states where Blacks became voting citizens and joined an electorate that facilitated the reorganization of political alliances between North and South.

Northern politicians realized that in order to court the newly established Black voters, they could no longer fully support the southern racial status quo.[29]

Despite the political impotence and economic hardships that characterized life for many Black Mississippians, a few were able to obtain some measure of economic success. A small, financially independent group of entrepreneurs, teachers, doctors, ministers, farmers, and federal employees emerged, supplying a cadre of individuals who initiated progressive social movements with some protection from white economic retaliation. These individuals, some of whom were responsible for the creation of the first Mississippi chapters of the National Association of Colored Women, the NAACP, and the MTA, were activists engaged in civil rights activity before the movement became fully entrenched there. This group of people, along with a generation of war veterans, provided the foundation for the modern civil rights movement to develop in the state.

The local affiliate of the NACW, the Mississippi State Federation of Colored Women's Clubs (MSFCWC), was founded in 1903 at the urging of Ursula J. Wade Foster, a faculty member at Alcorn Agricultural and Mechanical College (Alcorn A & M, now Alcorn State University); Mattie F. Rowan, the first lady of Alcorn A & M; and Lizzie Coleman, an educator from Greenville. Two years after the Southeastern Association of Colored Women's Clubs held its regional meeting in Mississippi, club work in the state swelled, prompting Foster, Rowan, and Coleman to convene a meeting mobilizing six of the state's clubs that formed the collective for the MSFCWC.[30] In accordance with the NACW's motto of "Lifting as We Climb," the MSFCWC organized for the "binding together of our women for social, moral, religious, industrial, and educational betterment, with the fundamental object of raising to the highest plane, home, moral, and civil life."[31] During the first half of the twentieth century, Mississippi clubwomen worked on a variety of fronts—"improving home and family life, combatting illiteracy, education and protection of our youth, providing for cultural, recreational, religious, economic and social needs"—to improve the quality of life for Black Mississippians.[32] While one might characterize these endeavors as merely social activism and typical of middle-class women's traditional roles, this is a gross undervaluation of their work. Given the socioeconomic context of the times, their undertakings were inherently political. They challenged the relegation of Blacks to separate and inferior resources and, in many instances, the denial of services altogether. At the same time, these women supported the Black community through institution building and by confronting the racist political structure that dominated the South.

Like Ursula Foster, many of the organization's leaders were educators and middle-class women. Their involvement was of great importance to women's activism in the state—not only because of the resources the MSFCWC could provide for Black Mississippians but also because, for many middle-class and middle-aged individuals who participated in the movement, this organization was the genesis of their social and political activism. Furthermore, the MS-FCWC laid a foundation for Black women's mobilization in Mississippi. This was instrumental in demonstrating the potential and promoting the necessity of Black women's leadership. A significant contingent of Womanpower members were seasoned activists by the 1960s, having gained leadership experiences through the MSFCWC and its affiliates and witnessed how their activism had improved their communities.

One of the most active of these clubs in Jackson was the Mary Church Terrell Literary Club, organized in 1912 by such prominent women as sisters Maggie Revels Howard (whose husband, Perry W. Howard, was head of the Republican Party in Mississippi) and Ida Revels Redmond (wife of local lawyer, physician, and businessman Sidney D. Redmond). The club, organized to facilitate women's self-improvement through literary and cultural opportunities, soon expanded to address "civic, education and social services" for the community, including support for the state federation's Old Folks Home in Vicksburg and the creation of a Race Relations Day during Negro History Week (an event that Womanpower cosponsored during the 1960s).[33] Black women established similar clubs throughout the state, including the Aimwell Federated Club in Lorman (1903), the Eureka Arts Club in Prentiss (1927), the Laurel Federated Club (1929), and L'Entre Nous Federated Women's Club in Greenwood (1937).[34] These clubs focused on a range of activities that included providing social services and programs for youth education and development, voter registration drives, and addressing other deficiencies that resulted from segregation and discrimination. Moreover, these organizations cultivated a collective of women well versed in race uplift and community organizing by the advent of the 1960s Black freedom struggle. For example, Ruth Oates Hubert and Edna Redmond Lovelace served as presidents of the Terrell Club as well as the MS-FCWC and were members of Womanpower Unlimited, with Hubert serving as chaplain. Lovelace, Womanpower Telephone Committee Chair, was also a National Committeewoman for the Mississippi Black and Tan Party (1948–60) and brought her knowledge of politics to all of the organizations with which she was affiliated.[35]

During the 1940s and 1950s Mississippi witnessed increasing Black activism. The role the United States played in the defense of democracy and freedom abroad, while simultaneously denying its own citizens equal rights and protection, generated greater dissatisfaction, uneasiness, and a sense of urgency among Blacks seeking their "freedom rights."[36] Subsequently, Black political mobilization emerged in a variety of forms. Although the NAACP had had an intermittent presence in Mississippi since the organization of its first branch in Vicksburg in 1918, it did not become a stable organization there until after World War II.[37] As the NAACP expanded in the state, local Blacks created new organizations to promote voter education and registration like the Mississippi Progressive Voters League, "a middle-class, Black civic organization" founded in Jackson in 1946, and the Regional Council of Negro Leadership (RCNL), founded in 1951 in Cleveland, Mississippi.[38] A group comprised primarily of Black male businessmen and veterans, who were relatively free from white economic pressure, led these organizations in mobilizing Black political reform movements.[39] Men like Amzie Moore, Medgar Evers, and Aaron Henry, all of whom were Mississippi natives and World War II veterans, held leadership positions in the NAACP and RCNL.[40]

The 1954 case of *Brown v. Board of Education* prompted Black Mississippians to begin organizing around school desegregation. With the assistance of the NAACP, Blacks in various cities filed petitions for their children's admission to white schools. Meanwhile whites responded by organizing the Citizens' Council almost immediately after the Supreme Court decision. Composed largely of upper-class whites, it sought to prevent integration of any kind—primarily through economic intimidation. It began by printing the names of the petitioners for school integration in the newspaper in Yazoo City, Mississippi, which resulted in many Blacks being fired from their jobs and losing their main source of income. Other measures included the cancellation of insurance policies and the refusal to approve Blacks' loan and credit applications. The Citizens' Council quickly became an extremely influential body in Mississippi politics, holding sway over public and private institutions of higher education, various other organizations, and many local clergymen.[41] Intimidation tactics targeting both Blacks and whites in the 1950s left Mississippi in a state of race relations reminiscent of the post-Reconstruction era.

Amid the increased economic pressures and white retaliation, the fledgling local NAACP branches could not withstand the rising forces of the Citizens' Council. With the lack of federal support for the implementation of the *Brown* decision and the noninterventionist position that states should proceed "with all deliberate speed," school desegregation soon became a non-issue, and activists had to resort to other avenues. Voter registration campaigns experienced a resurgence, also accompanied by white violence and intimidation. The year 1955 ushered in the dreadful fates of Reverend George W. Lee, Lamar Smith, and Emmett Till. All three were murdered by whites, who were either not brought to trial or not convicted. Vigilantism resurfaced to enforce the doctrine and practices of white supremacy, and the legal authorities acquiesced with the philosophy and tactics of that worldview.

Across the South, civil rights activism was making some headway. For example, bus boycotts demonstrated the utility of challenging segregation with nonviolent, direct action. Such campaigns and their successes were in the near future for Mississippi's "closed society." As described by historian James Silver, this was the type of society Mississippians created to maintain white supremacy and obviate any changes in race relations from the time of slavery. It was a society in which violence (or the threat of it) was used relentlessly to ensure the silencing of any who sought to challenge the "prevailing doctrine." Challenges from the outside merely caused members of this type of society to proclaim and enforce their orthodoxy more sternly, resulting in customs becoming even more "inflexible."[42] As a closed society, Mississippi was able to prevent (for a while) the connections that were developing among other southern Black communities. Lawrence Guyot, a native of Pass Christian who emerged as a leader in SNCC, described the conditions in Mississippi in a similar manner, stating, "Mississippi was the epitome of what South Africa longed to be. In Mississippi if you decided to break the rigidly enforced policy of racial segregation and social atrophy, you were immediately identified and destroyed. . . . Mississippi used state money and state power to enforce a rigid policy of apartheid in the most literal sense in every phase of life."[43] Activists from inside and outside the state had to bring all their resources to bear on the state to facilitate even the smallest cracks in this society. Local people, such as those who joined Womanpower Unlimited, were the heart of this struggle.

Intertwined with Womanpower's story is the narrative of Clarie Collins Harvey's life as an organizer. Among the organization's four primary leaders, Harvey emerges as a central figure as its founder and also because of the national and international context she used to frame Womanpower's agenda. The way Harvey organized Womanpower as a movement helps us think differently about women's activism and leadership and demonstrates what she hoped to bring to the civil rights movement through women's activism. Examining this "womanist insurgence" of Harvey's activism affords a better understanding of Womanpower for its own primary work and its work as a facilitator and conduit.[44] Just as sociologist Belinda Robnett describes Black women activists as bridge leaders, Womanpower can be understood as a bridge movement— linking the needs of the community members to civil rights organizations and the needs of the local movement in Mississippi to national organizations and networks of women outside the state.

Chronicling the history of such an organization, however, poses its own unique problems and speaks to a larger concern in the field of Black women's history. Uncovering the story of Womanpower is inherently an effort to render visible some of the numerous women who comprised the organization. The fact that this story has not previously been told speaks, among other things, to the invisibility of certain women in the historical record. This invisibility is a result of Black women being less likely to leave written records of their work for concerns over how their image might be (mis)construed by and in a society that has consistently denigrated Black womanhood. For others, internalized beliefs that their records lacked value have produced the same result.[45]

Scholars have also been more likely to marginalize Black women's experiences and contributions. This invisibility can also be attributed to the fact that perhaps many women did not deem it necessary to document or preserve records of their work because this is simply what Black women did; without fanfare or expecting praise, they took care of their communities. To be sure, there are far greater archival resources on Black women than existed thirty years ago, and scholars have made significant headway in (re)constructing Black women's history. Nevertheless, the process of recounting Black women's experiences remains challenging. To compensate for this invisibility, *Womanpower Unlimited* uses other organizations to reconstruct Womanpower's history while simultaneously demonstrating the organization's effectiveness in connecting organizations outside the state to civil rights activism and providing resources for local organizations.

Harvey moves to the foreground much more easily than other activists because she was the only primary member to preserve a public record of her activism. Her work with national and international women's organizations ensured that her activism was chronicled through other channels. *Womanpower Unlimited* pulls together these pieces of history to convey the story of how a group of Black women activists during the civil rights movement mobilized to continue the community work that has been integral to the survival of African American communities.

Ineva May-Pittman's early work with civil rights and women's organizations shaped her activism and leadership and continued to influence her post–civil rights work aimed at teaching people how to use their collective voice and power to improve their lives and their community. Registering voters and educating them about the political process and how to demand from elected officials the resources they are due as citizens remain integral to her efforts.[46] As is evident through May-Pittman's activism, Womanpower's story does not end with its dissolution as its members continued their activism well into the post–civil rights era leaving an indelible mark, individually and collectively, upon Jackson and the people who worked and lived there.

CHAPTER ONE

"It Was Just Women Who Dared to Dream"
The Emergence of Womanpower Unlimited

This may only be a dream of mine, but I think it can be made real.
—Ella Baker

Clarie Collins Harvey was one of many observers who gathered in the Jackson, Mississippi, courtroom on Friday, May 26, 1961, to witness the first hearing in the trial of the Freedom Riders. Designed by the Congress of Racial Equality (CORE), which was at this point under the leadership of the newly appointed national director, James Farmer, the Freedom Rides began on May 4, 1961, when an integrated group of thirteen activists rode Greyhound and Trailways buses departing from Washington, D.C., to protest the segregated transportation facilities that had been outlawed by *Boynton v. Virginia* (1960). Witnessing the injustice these civil rights activists were subjected to for their defiance of Mississippi segregation laws, Harvey was inspired to initiate a local movement to assist them and further the civil rights movement. Fully aware of the scope and magnitude of the movement developing across the nation, she believed this was the perfect opportunity for women's activism to take center stage in Mississippi.

Although as owner and operator of the Jackson-based Collins Funeral Home Harvey had long been involved in political activities for Black advancement through organizations such as the National Association for the Advancement of Colored People (NAACP) and the Mississippi State Federation of Colored Women's Clubs, the events of this day provided a catalyst for new directions in her activism. A middle-aged woman, Harvey was raised in the collectivist community of Southern Blacks (extended biological and fictive kin, neighbors, and friend networks working together to support and care for each other). She was immediately struck by how the local police physically treated the civil rights activists, especially the young women, who she later recalled were cold and shivering because they were not allowed access to their clothing after being arrested. Therefore, her first response was reflective of a "mother's instinct"—to employ practical strategies to assist and sustain the activists in the journey on which they had embarked.[1]

When the first Freedom Riders arrived in Jackson, the Methodist Church was holding its annual conference in Waveland, Mississippi. The presiding bishop, Charles F. Golden, learned that ministers of the Methodist Church were detained in this group, and he sent a delegation from the conference to Jackson for the first hearing "to observe the trial and report back to the conference what the needs were and what Methodists could do to help the situation."[2] Reverend A. E. Mays of Anderson Methodist Church and Reverend S. L. Webb of Central United Methodist Church, along with Clarie Collins Harvey, then the secretary of the General Board of Christian Social Concerns, comprised this delegation.[3] Harvey believed that she was chosen to be a member of the delegation because of her long-standing membership on the board (she had served since 1952) and her "interest and participation nationally" concerning such issues.[4]

The delegation learned that the Freedom Riders would not be posting bail. Instead, they had decided to serve their sentences while they appealed the ruling. The majority would spend up to thirty-nine days at Parchman Prison, the maximum time they could serve and still appeal the decision.[5] Upon learning that the Freedom Riders were to remain in jail, Harvey and Aurelia Young, a music professor at Jackson State College and wife of civil rights attorney Jack Young Jr., sent clothes to the jail that night. Knowing that these activists needed continuing material and emotional support during their stay in Mississippi, "the divine inspiration and revelation of how these needs might be met came to [Harvey] on . . . Saturday night."[6] On the next day, Sunday, May 27, 1961, Harvey sent out a call through the local churches to solicit money, clothing, and necessary personal items for the civil rights activists. In a 1965 interview, Harvey recalled that "if they were going to remain [incarcerated in Jackson], they were going to have continuing needs and that people within the community, for whom they were making this witness, should have some responsibility for seeing that these needs would be met."[7] Local Black churches—Central United Methodist, Anderson Methodist, Mount Helm Baptist, New Hope Baptist, Pratt Methodist, Pearl Street AME, and Farish Street Baptist—donated $145.71

in response to Harvey's call. While not a huge sum, this amount far exceeded the $25 Harvey anticipated collecting on such short notice.[8] She took this as an indication that Jackson women were ready to support the emerging wave of civil rights activism.[9] She hoped to harness this enthusiasm so that women in Mississippi could organize more effectively to support the civil rights movement and improve their communities. On Monday, May 29, 1961, capitalizing on the overwhelming response she had received, Harvey convened a meeting at her home church, Central United Methodist, under the auspices of the Interdenominational Ministerial Alliance of Jackson. And out of this meeting, Womanpower Unlimited (WU) was born.[10]

Harvey began the meeting with a devotional. Then, following a report of the Freedom Riders' treatment at the hands of law enforcement officials and their subsequent trial, she explained the purpose of the meeting: "to develop a Citizen's Committee as it applies to the Freedom Riders." Surmising the work ahead of them, those in attendance declared, "Money is needed!—Local interest is needed. It would help to discount the saying 'These are outside agitators.'"[11] The attendees realized that supporting the Freedom Riders necessitated both material assistance, which required money, and emotional support, which required strength of character and fortitude. They needed not only to publicly challenge the status quo but also to withstand the pressure and intimidation that accompanied such a position. WU wanted to embrace the Freedom Riders to ensure they knew they were part of the local Black community. This gesture was common among activists and reflected the extended family networks that existed in the Black community, as well as its sense of appreciation for the so-called outside agitators. According to Mrs. Carson H. Beckwith, whose letter was read at a Womanpower meeting, a similar organization existed in Charlotte, North Carolina, of which she was a member. "We are a nameless group of about eight women," she stated, who "mothered students in every way we could."[12] The initial officers selected to lead the organization were Mrs. Clarie Collins Harvey, chair; Mrs. A. M. E. Logan, executive director; Mrs. Dorothy Bogans, secretary; and Mrs. Cleother Mason, treasurer.[13]

In the tradition of nineteenth-century Black activists like Zilpha Elaw and Sojourner Truth, who attributed their work to divine inspiration, Harvey said that she was "called" to organize women for the purpose of assisting those who had undertaken God's work of achieving social justice. Like many women participants in the Black freedom struggle who were rooted in a strong religious faith and tradition, Harvey's religious beliefs propelled her to activism and provided legitimacy for her work. She attributed these efforts to the social orientation of the Methodist Church, which teaches that one must demonstrate one's belief not merely by professing that one is a Christian but by effecting change in society "so that people don't have to live in poverty . . . segregation, degradation, and oppression."[14] Harvey also believed that women were inherently suited to fulfill such a purpose. Accordingly, she stated that the name "Womanpower Unlimited" gave reference to "the inner, divine power of each woman, as all women work together for peace among the peoples of a given community, nation, and in the world. This power is unlimited because it is God's power. . . . Using this power within us, we can help to make life what it should be for any people at any time and in any place."[15] Faith and a belief in justice, grounded in religious morality, were what many women relied on as a source of strength to persevere.

In her discussion of enslaved women's ability to persevere, historian Deborah Gray White dispels the myth of the inherently strong Black woman, arguing that their "strength had to be cultivated. It came no more naturally to them than to anyone. . . . If they seemed exceptionally strong it was partly because they often functioned in groups and derived their strength from numbers."[16] This strength is often misrepresented as an innate characteristic of Black women, something that they are somehow predisposed to at birth. Believing in this, White argues, diminishes the courageousness of Black women and the reality of pain and struggle they faced in undertaking these endeavors. Black women during the 1960s engaged in similar efforts of community building and support, believing that this was their responsibility—their calling. Joann Christian Mants, a civil rights activist from Albany, Georgia, confirms this belief, stating, "We were reared with a calling, in the way that preachers are called. I do believe our commitment to the uplift of our community is our calling; it is part of what we must do."[17] Dorothy Height similarly remarked, "Black women at their best come from a kind of base in faith. If you didn't have it, you'd be discouraged."[18] Harvey admitted having had thoughts of leaving Mississippi to escape the harshness of life in the South. In a 1971 article, Harvey acknowledged, "I thought about leaving, but then I realized I couldn't. I saw that I must get involved totally, seeking God's will for our community."[19] Racial responsibility, strength, and religious faith kept Harvey and other Blacks rooted in the community and willing to fight for change.

Early Civil Rights Activity in Mississippi

The response of the Jackson community, and Black women specifically, represented decades of the ebb and flow of repression and resistance that had been occurring in the state. By 1961, generations of free Blacks had resisted the post-Reconstruction measures (sharecropping, convict leasing, disenfranchisement, and segregation) implemented to maintain Black subservience to whites through social, economic, and political repression.

As the fifties turned into the sixties, direct action protest demonstrations continued with sit-ins. At this time of growing civil rights activity in other Southern states, Black Mississippians were making piecemeal progress. Medgar Evers had become a central figure in the Mississippi movement. He was effective at mobilizing both younger and older generations of Blacks. A Mississippi native, Evers dropped out of high school to serve his country during World War II. Upon returning to Mississippi, Evers, along with his brother, Charles, and four other veterans, registered to vote (but were unable to actually vote) in their hometown of Decatur. This event marked the beginning of his career as a civil rights activist. By the time he began his education at Alcorn A & M, Evers was a member of the NAACP. When his later work as an insurance salesman showed him the poverty-stricken life of Delta Blacks, his involvement with the NAACP increased and he began organizing branches across the region. In 1954 Evers became Mississippi's first NAACP field secretary. While working with the NAACP, Evers also worked with the Regional Council of Negro Leadership and for a time with the Southern Christian Leadership Conference (SCLC). His activities were essential to civil rights activism in Mississippi. They ranged from assisting the impoverished and those suffering economic retaliation from whites to getting people safely out of the state and generating local leadership. Evers had a good rapport with young people. He organized many youth chapters and expressed a willingness to build coalitions with other organizations (a practice the governing body of the NAACP was uneasy with). Because of his determination for the civil rights struggle to succeed and his affinity for young people, Evers understood the impatience of youth activists and thus became an advocate of their direct action protests earlier than other NAACP leaders.[20] Ultimately, Evers laid much of the groundwork for the success of increased civil rights activism in Mississippi.

The president of the NAACP state chapter, C. R. Darden, stifled the organization's youth members, who were inspired by student sit-ins in other states.

Although youth members engaged in direct action, it was the 1960 Biloxi "wade-in" that captured the state's attention. In that event, Dr. Gilbert Mason led two groups of Blacks on April 14 and April 24 to swim at the segregated "public" beach. The initial group was forced to leave, but spared any violence. The second group of swimmers was brutally attacked by local whites while the county police watched. That adults were supporting direct action in the state caught the attention of the NAACP's national office. The NAACP officially adopted this new strategy of direct action in April 1961 when it began to officially support student activism in this phase of the movement. The NAACP was, in fact, adopting the students' tactics. On March 27, 1961, nine students from Tougaloo College conducted a sit-in at the downtown Jackson public library.[21] Using earlier sit-ins in other locales as a guide, the students carefully planned their demonstration by undergoing training in nonviolent protest and contacting the press. Arrested and detained for more than twenty-four hours, the group that became known as the "Tougaloo 9" generated support from their peers at Jackson State College as well as older members of the Black community. The violence that ensued at their trial made national headlines and solidified the new wave of civil rights activism that had taken hold in Mississippi. Attempts to desegregate other public facilities began in Jackson and in other cities. This activity, though, coincided with and was overshadowed by the arrival of the Freedom Riders. Their journey included stops in Maryland, Virginia, Georgia, Alabama, and Mississippi, with New Orleans as the final destination. It was the Freedom Riders' stop in Mississippi that thrust the state head-first into the heart of the movement.

With the social, political, and economic constraints designed to ensure white supremacy, Mississippi was indeed a "closed society." This system of domination was the very force that necessitated the gradually increasing Black protests in Mississippi. Progress for Blacks was slow and was resisted on all fronts through both violent and "legal" measures, even as the civil rights movement began to achieve major successes across the South. The Freedom Riders pushed Mississippi into the spotlight of civil rights activism, increasing indigenous activism in the state and securing a position of prominence in the movement that it held for the next few years. And Black women stepped forth to ensure that the struggle in Mississippi was successful.

The Freedom Riders were embraced by a community of women dedicated to advancing the Black freedom struggle by ministering to the needs of the protesters. Womanpower members attended to the physical, material, and emotional needs of the activists to ensure the manageability and success of their efforts. A long journey ensued, however, before the Freedom Riders reached this community of support.

The Freedom Riders Come to Town

The Freedom Riders began their journey south from Washington, D.C., in two buses on May 4, 1961.[22] They experienced sporadic harassment and violence during stops in Virginia, North Carolina, and South Carolina. During stops in both Macon and Atlanta, Georgia, the Riders were able to use the terminal facilities with no incidents of violence. Both this moderate success and the resistance they encountered increased their exposure in the media—positively and negatively. As news of the Freedom Riders spread and generated support for their efforts, whites who opposed integration began a resistance movement, making the trek more difficult as they traveled farther south into Alabama.

Travel through the Deep South was dangerous, to say the least. The group's experiences in Alabama resulted in the iconic image of a burned-out bus near Anniston, now ingrained in the minds of many Americans when they think of the Freedom Riders. The Alabama leg of the trip was characterized by brutal beatings that left some activists with permanent damage, prompting bus drivers to refuse to transport them. Some members of the group decided to conclude the Rides with a flight to New Orleans.

Although CORE decided that the flight to New Orleans would end the Freedom Rides, members of SNCC maintained that they would not give in to repression, and they recruited students to continue the Riders' original itinerary. In light of the negative publicity President John F. Kennedy was receiving in the international press concerning the violence in Birmingham, and given his fear that continued Rides would result in increased racial violence requiring federal intervention, Attorney General Robert F. Kennedy insisted upon a "cooling-off" period to minimize direct action protest. President Kennedy had taken a noninterventionist stance regarding civil rights activism and did not want to use federal power to achieve the desegregation of public facilities. The students, however, resisted the attempted silencing by vicious racists or by a federal administration that expressed little concern for their protection. Through the efforts of SNCC leader Diane Nash, ten students from Nashville, Tennessee, provided the first response and mobilized to continue the demonstration. After further violence and the threat of federal intervention, Alabama

Governor John Patterson declared martial law in Montgomery and sent in the National Guard to restore order.[23]

Accompanied by the National Guardsmen and reporters, the Freedom Riders departed Montgomery and journeyed to Mississippi. The state's governor Ross Barnett secured "order," with the assurance that the federal government would not intervene, and had the activists arrested upon arrival. They were charged with "inciting to riot, breach of the peace, and failure to obey a police officer."[24]

Upon the arrival of the first bus in Jackson, the Freedom Riders attempted to use the "white" facilities and were arrested. Riders on the second bus that arrived hours later were also arrested. In accordance with the agreement made by President Kennedy not to send in federal troops if local officials maintained order, Jackson police swiftly transported the Freedom Riders to the city jail. Despite Robert Kennedy's continued requests for a "cooling-off period," numerous volunteers traveled to Montgomery to participate in the Rides to Mississippi. With the leadership of a Freedom Riders Coordinating Committee composed of representatives from SNCC, CORE, and the SCLC, more than three hundred activists from across the country traveled to Mississippi as Freedom Riders and were subsequently arrested. Many local Black residents also participated in this effort to desegregate the Jackson bus terminals and were arrested with the Freedom Riders. This influx of civil rights activists into the state of Mississippi caused a dramatic shift that altered the course of the movement as well as the future of the state.

In the weeks following the arrest and sentencing of the Freedom Riders, Womanpower Unlimited amassed many resources for them. They collected toiletries and money to buy small items such as shower shoes, soap, candy, and magazines for the protesters. Local ministers delivered these items as they and the lawyers were the only people allowed to visit the jail. As a result, many Freedom Riders never met the Womanpower members or knew of their support until after their release from prison. Freedom Rider Sandra Nixon, a native of New Orleans, stated that some of the jailers even sold the female Freedom Riders the items Womanpower had left for them. Though Nixon did not have the opportunity to meet or thank Womanpower members in person, she was grateful for their kindness and concern.[25]

Some of the activists did have the opportunity to interact with members of Womanpower upon their release from Parchman Prison. The women secured transportation for the Freedom Riders, provided them with places to bathe and clean clothes, and prepared food for them. Womanpower also provided free beauty and barber services to the Freedom Riders and helped them make arrangements to return home. With funds donated from the local Black community, the organization did everything within its means to take care of the Riders' physical needs and to counter the emotional distress they suffered during their incarceration.

That Womanpower was successful in achieving its goals is apparent in the testimony of many Freedom Riders who attribute their endurance to the WU women. Joan Trumpauer Mulholland, a Freedom Rider from Virginia who was one of the first white students to attend Tougaloo College and was active in the student movement in Jackson during her tenure at Tougaloo from 1961 to 1964, vividly recalled Womanpower's contributions. In reference to material items, Mulholland stated that the ladies of Womanpower "were like angels supplying us with just little simple necessities," and though they were not Freedom Riders "they were doing really equally important things to support us." Mulholland continued that Womanpower was "great for the morale; things like this really helped people keep going. And if you were having a rough time, to see that somebody cared—they knew and thought about you—that was outstanding."[26] The women's actions clearly conveyed to the young people the emotional connection that prompted Harvey to take action at the first hearings. WU employed activist mothering and nurtured the resistance of Freedom Riders through psychological and physical expressions of love.

In a collection of firsthand accounts of the Freedom Riders, Louise Inghram wrote that Womanpower "did as much as was possible to make jail more bearable. . . . In short, they tried to do whatever was necessary to help us feel and look like human beings again. Their relationship to us, white and Negro, when we were in jail, gave the lie to the slanders in the press that the Southern Negro was 'hostile' to the Freedom Riders."[27]

Shirley Smith, a Freedom Rider from New York, provided a similar account, explaining in detail how instrumental Womanpower was to her survival:

> [In the Mississippi State Penitentiary] I went through a grueling experience—a rough body examination by the jailers, meager food and water, and was placed in maximum security. Prison conditions were especially filthy so packets of sanitary supplies, and a bar of soap were received gratefully from a group called *Womanpower Unlimited*. . . .
>
> It was a strange feeling to be released and walk out all alone. A black man approached me and asked if I were Shirley Smith. He represented *Womanpower Unlimited* and took me to a nearby Negro church. There were women waiting for

me with clean clothes and a place to wash and warm food. I was taken then to a beauty shop where a black operator washed my hair—a blessing beyond description. Any one of these persons could have gotten into trouble, but in their wonderful communication system which is theirs I was cared for until I boarded the plane for home.

So you see why I want to thank Clarie Harvey and *Womanpower Unlimited* on my own behalf and on behalf of other young people who needed some Mississippi citizen to take the risk of kindness for an outsider.[28]

Freedom Riders collectively believed that Womanpower's support was indispensable to their sanity and endurance.

Activist mothering guided the WU women's actions, just as it was the impetus behind Harvey's response to the Freedom Riders' initial arrest. Whether biological mothers or not, Womanpower members knew that the activists needed mental and physical support to persevere. They mobilized to provide this in Jackson, taking on a role akin to that played by other Black women in the civil rights movement and indeed by Black women throughout American history. They were intentional and explicit in their efforts to claim the Freedom Riders as their own, in part because many of the Freedom Riders were young enough to be their children, and they felt a responsibility to take care of them.

In a letter dated September 15, 1961, twenty-two-year-old Freedom Rider David Loring Richards wrote to Womanpower expressing his "gratitude to all of you, for the wonderful work you've done in aiding the Freedom Riders. . . . I would especially like to thank Mrs. [Susie] Noel, in whose home I stayed, during my return to Jackson for arraignment. . . . I feel there's no way I can thank all of you enough."[29] Womanpower's initial civil rights work, while in a supportive role, was indispensable to the Freedom Riders. They were engaging in work that was integral to the success of the movement as a whole. Furthermore, Black women did not see supportive work as subordinate to the more visible positions of being on the front lines but, as Mulholland stated, as "equally important" supportive work.[30] Diane Nash echoes this sentiment, stating, "For me [Womanpower] provided me with a sense of security and stability because to know that they were solidly in agreement with what we were doing represented a reinforcement. That was important."[31] Thus, Harvey and Womanpower were content working behind the scenes and mothering these young activists because they knew that what they could contribute in this regard was vital.

CHAPTER TWO

"You Could Just See Things Being Accomplished"
The Women Who Built the Movement

Negro women are the real active forces—the organizers and workers—in all the institutions and organizations of the Negro people.
—Claudia Jones

[Black women] are people builders, carriers of cultural traditions,
key to the formation and continuance of culture.
—Bernice Johnson Reagon

While Womanpower Unlimited grew to encompass over three hundred women
nationwide, it was a Jackson-based organization that sustained the civil rights
movement in Mississippi. As with any group, there were a few instrumental
people who were primarily responsible for the group's operation: Clarie Collins Harvey, A. M. E. Logan, Thelma Sanders, and Jessie Mosley. Because of
their prior civil rights activism in Mississippi through organizations like the
NAACP and the MSFCWC, these women were able to make Womanpower a
successful endeavor. They had organizational experience and a familiarity with
each other that enabled an effective working relationship. Just a month before
Womanpower's organizing meeting, Logan, Harvey, and Sanders collaborated
on a Woman's Day Program at the Masonic Temple, serving as mistress of ceremony, presenter of the occasion, and introducer of the guest speaker, respectively.[1] Furthermore, their economic independence afforded them an opportunity to openly support the movement that many other middle-class Blacks
lacked.

Historian Charles Payne highlights a couple of key factors that prompted
people to movement participation, including "knowledge of the wider world,
such as comes from . . . travel . . . [and] a degree of economic independence."[2]
Clarie Collins Harvey, the visionary at the heart of the organization, possessed

both of these traits. The only child of Mrs. Mary Augusta (Rayford) and the Reverend Malachi C. Collins, Emma Augusta Clarie Collins was born on November 27, 1916, in Meridian, Mississippi, one of the manufacturing hubs of the South. Located approximately ninety miles east of Jackson, close to the Mississippi/Alabama border, Meridian was the largest city in Mississippi at the time of Clarie's birth.[3]

Her mother, Mary Collins, a native of Lauderdale County, Mississippi, was born in 1887, the second of the three children of Missouri Emma Walker and Bryan Henry Rayford. Mary's father, along with her maternal grandfather, George A. Walker, and uncle, Arch Walker, founded a grocery and mercantile partnership in 1893 in Meridian, providing her with the economic advantages to obtain a first-rate education. After completing high school in Meridian, Mary attended the Tuskegee and Hampton Institutes. She obtained employment at two historic institutions in Meridian. She taught at Wechsler Junior High School, the first brick public school for Blacks in the state built with public funds, and she became Mississippi's first Black public librarian at the Andrew Carnegie Negro Library.[4]

Malachi Collins, a native of Crystal Springs, Mississippi, was born in 1879, the second child of landowners and farmers Tempie and Isaac Collins. He attended Rust College, receiving his bachelor's degree in 1909, and became a math professor there after pursuing graduate studies at the University of Chicago.[5] Collins became an ordained minister in 1912 and, although he never pastored a church, he served as a lay delegate to five Methodist General Conferences during the subsequent two decades. He and Mary Rayford wed in 1914. During the year of Clarie's birth, Reverend Collins left a teaching position at the Haven Institute (formerly Meridian Academy) to establish, with E. W. Hall, the Hall and Collins Funeral Home, the first Black funeral and insurance business in Hattiesburg, further cementing a model of entrepreneurship for Clarie to emulate. At the same time, business ownership provided young Clarie with a practical lesson in self-defense. When Hall and Collins opened their business, the local white undertaker circulated handbills to Blacks that read, "Don't patronize those niggers, we can give you better service."[6] Threats and intimidation accompanied this notice and escalated to the point that Hall and Collins took turns providing an armed watch at the establishment. Despite attempts to shut them down, the business thrived, and in 1924 Collins purchased the G. F. Frazier Undertaking Company in Jackson, of which he was the sole proprietor until he and Mary established a partnership.[7]

An only child, young Clarie lived a privileged life in the predominately white town of Meridian. Her parents wanted to have twelve children. Not blessed in that respect, Clarie received the love and attention intended for a dozen. Being the daughter of business owners afforded her educational opportunities uncommon to the masses of Southern Blacks. In addition, as the child of a librarian, she was of course encouraged to develop a love for reading. After the family relocated to Jackson, Clarie attended primary school at Smith Robertson and high school at Tougaloo College.[8] Upon the completion of her studies at Tougaloo (high school in 1933 and her freshman year of college), Clarie enrolled at Spelman College in Atlanta, Georgia, graduating with a bachelor's degree in economics in 1937. Although she initially pursued a premed curriculum intending to pursue a career in medicine, she settled on a major that would prepare her for the ownership of her parents' funeral home. Clarie also studied mortuary technique at the Indiana College of Mortuary Science in Indianapolis, where, thanks to the premed courses at Spelman, she excelled and surpassed many of her male classmates.[9] After receiving a certificate in that program, she continued her education by earning in 1950 a master's degree in personnel administration from Columbia University in New York. She studied at the Union Theological Seminary as well as at New York University's Graduate School of Business Administration.[10]

Clarie followed in the footsteps of her parents, who were both committed to political and social activism through the Methodist Church and various civic organizations and were pioneers in the state. In addition to his various church activities, Reverend Collins was one of the founders of the Jackson NAACP.[11] Mrs. Collins served as the only woman on the Central United Methodist Church's board of trustees from 1939 to 1967.[12] She held memberships in numerous organizations including the Mississippi State Federation of Colored Women's Clubs (board member), the Jackson branches of the NAACP and YWCA, and the Mary Church Terrell Literary Club, of which she was vice president. Clarie later became involved in all of these organizations as well.

According to Harvey, "the seeds of freedom and independence and all that [had been] passed down to [me]."[13] Harvey was acutely aware that she was sustaining a generational legacy of activism. She realized that her work was part of a larger tradition of Black women's activism. In a 1964 essay titled "Civil Rights and the American Negro," Harvey wrote, "Negro women have had an historic part in the freedom struggle; Sojourner Truth, Harriet Tubman, and others remain with us in memory as heroines from the days of slavery."[14] She pursued civil rights activism with the inspiration and guidance of her mother and collective foremothers.

Harvey's diverse organizational experience helped develop her leadership skills and prepared her to create Womanpower's unique structure. Through her activism in the male-dominated NAACP and Methodist church organizations, Harvey learned the formal procedures for running meetings and how to manage an organization effectively. She witnessed the exclusion of women and knew they needed a forum where their energies could be fully utilized. And through the women's organizations, she learned that their productivity was often diminished when they became too engaged in purely social activities.[15] As a result, she created a political movement in which women could use their fullest leadership and activist skills, leaving the social activities for other forums. Harvey empowered her peers to engage in social activism and simultaneously cultivated a new generation of leaders. Like Ella Baker, Harvey understood the vital role of youth in the movement and mentored young leaders within her community.[16] Dora Wilson, a Tougaloo student at the time, explained her influence: "She would say, I want you to grab the reins of this and get ahead of this and know that you can effect change; you can make the decision. . . . She, too saw herself as moving out of holding the reins [of leadership]. She's thinking, I need to think about who is coming along behind me."[17] Harvey had been active in the YWCA and the Youth chapter of the NAACP and supported youth leaders in the same way she was nurtured as a young adult. Her parents and community nurtured and encouraged her activism, and she did the same for the next generation.

Harvey's early years of activism were devoted to Christian work through the Methodist Church and the YWCA. She explained that her introduction to social activism came through her experiences in the church, recalling, "I was trained in human dignity and to work with people. I think that my great social concerns came through my exposure to the . . . United Methodist Church, where specific issues came up. One had to deal with specific issues such as housing, education and racism in its varied manifestations [the practical issues of the day-to-day quality of life for Black people]."[18] Her international travels emerged as an outgrowth of her desire to learn about and work with people. In 1939, at the age of twenty-three, as a representative of the national student YWCA (she served as president of the Spelman chapter her senior year), Harvey attended a World Christian Conference in Amsterdam, Holland, "to mobilize youth to witness to the reality of the Christian community."[19]

This trip was significant not only because it was her inaugural international trip but also because she met the man she would marry four years later, Martin L. Harvey Jr. Five years her senior, Martin grew up in the community of Hempstead in Long Island, New York. He, too, was the child of a minister: Martin Harvey Sr. presided over A. M. E. Zion, the largest Black church in the area.[20] His mother, Rosa Monroe Harvey, "ran an employment agency and Negro beauty shop."[21] Like Clarie, Martin had led a life of privilege and opportunity and spent his youth involved in ecumenical activities. He received his bachelor's degree in religious education from New York University (NYU) in 1934, and a master's in personnel administration in 1941. In 1936, Martin became the first Black president of the Christian Youth Movement of North America. He emerged early on as a leader within the YMCA on the local level, serving first as a member of the Junior Board and then as a delegate to the New York State Youth Council, of which he would eventually become president. Upon graduation from NYU, he became president of the Youth Section for the Department of Christian Education for the A. M. E. Zion Church. In this capacity, in 1939, Martin led a 300-member Methodist delegation to the Amsterdam conference.

In many ways, Martin Harvey was the perfect complement to Clarie Collins, something she recognized soon after their first meeting in Berlin (after getting over how short he was—five feet, six inches).[22] By the time she returned home from the conference, she knew she had found a true partner in life, explaining, "I terminated my engagement, for now I knew that I wished to share my life with someone whose interests were in people instead of being in material things."[23] After a four-year courtship, during which they both obtained graduate or professional degrees, Martin continued to travel the world in service to ecumenical and student-focused missions, and Clarie helped run her family's funeral home. They wed in August 1943.

The following year, Martin Harvey took a position as dean of Student Affairs at Southern University in Baton Rouge, where he spent the remainder of his career and life. The couple set up a home there from which Clarie Harvey commuted to Jackson. By the 1960s she typically spent two weeks per month at each residence. Their ecumenical activities were a central aspect of both their individual lives and their relationship, and Martin fully supported Clarie in her business and activist endeavors. Said Harvey, "Martin encouraged me in our business management [and] in my participation as a representative on four different boards and agencies of the Methodist (later the United Methodist) Church."[24] Harvey had found a partner who respected and encouraged her work.

Earlier than she had anticipated, Harvey joined her mother to fulfill the role of business leader after her father's untimely death during her trip to Amsterdam in 1939. The entrepreneurial spirit embedded in Harvey's family and her perception of the family business as a way to serve the community eased her adaptation to life as a businesswoman. Squarely within the tradition of Black entrepreneurs in general and undertakers specifically, Harvey followed a path of institution building and racial uplift that was guided by a sincere Christian belief of service to others. In her study of the ways in which "black funeral directors used their business capital and prestige as local community leaders to fight the indignities of racial segregation," historian Suzanne E. Smith explains that "as entrepreneurs in a largely segregated trade, funeral directors were usually among the few black individuals in any town or city who were economically independent and not beholden to the local white power structure. For these reasons, African American funeral directors . . . often found themselves serving the living as much as they buried the dead."[25] Harvey was fully aware of the privileges and opportunities business ownership afforded her, as well as the responsibility to the community that made her business successful. She understood how her business challenged the white supremacist attitudes of the segregated South and that her success threatened the status quo while serving as a model and inspiration for other Blacks.

In addition to running the business, Harvey became fully involved in the leadership of the profession, succeeding her father as secretary of the Executive Committee of the Mississippi Funeral Directors and Morticians Association, a position she held until 1965. In 1956, she became the Governor of Region VI for the National Funeral Directors and Morticians Association (NFDMA).[26] She was an associate editor for the organization's monthly journal, *The National Funeral Director and Embalmer*, and author of the publication's "Management Clinic Corner" column. Harvey was a trailblazer and, in 1955, she received the NFDMA's inaugural "Woman of the Year Award" acknowledging her service to the profession.[27]

Her activism spread beyond the religious and business realms and included participation in the peace movement and in local women's organizations. Her life experiences as a business owner and social activist were multifaceted. Thus, by the time the Freedom Riders arrived in Jackson, Harvey was well prepared to organize the movement. She hoped to generate in other women the spirit of service and activism that had guided her life. Additionally, as the civil rights movement had begun to gather momentum in Mississippi, she envisioned it as the perfect opportunity for women to become more actively involved in the efforts to attain rights for Blacks. Often marginalized in organizations dominated by men, Harvey created a "safe space" for women to contribute in their own ways to the movement in Jackson.

The connections she developed nationally through her previous activism helped Womanpower's growth. In the first two months of the organization's existence, when its focus was solely on the Freedom Riders, Harvey secured monetary support from contacts in the Methodist Church, including Irma Kinkel of Wisconsin, who served on the General and Conference boards of Christian Social Concerns, and Carl Soule of the Methodist Board for World Peace, Methodist General Board of Christian Social Concerns.[28] Locally, she used her professional contacts to secure a donation from the Mississippi Funeral Directors. All aspects of Harvey's life were influenced by her desire to improve the lives of those in need and create a better society for all.

One of the first women Harvey contacted regarding the organization of Womanpower Unlimited was A. M. E. Logan. Both were involved in the Jackson branch of the NAACP, but they were primarily acquainted through Logan's husband's work as an independent contractor for Harvey. Harvey traveled frequently for business and during her absences she often relayed information for Mr. Logan to Mrs. Logan. As a result, Harvey came to know her as a professional, competent, and reliable woman.[29] Based on this personal interaction and knowledge of her community activism, Harvey believed that Logan would be an asset to the organization.

A. M. E. (Marshall) Logan was born on August 19, 1914 in Myles, Mississippi, in Copiah County, to Mrs. Nellie (Rembert) and the Reverend John Collins Marshall.[30] She grew up in Carpenter, Mississippi, about an hour southwest of Jackson, where the Marshalls were farmers and Mrs. Marshall a homemaker. Unlike Harvey, A. M. E. hailed from a large family, the eighth of twelve children. She was named for the African Methodist Episcopal Church of which her father was a minister. Growing up under the influence of her independent and strong-willed father, A. M. E. followed closely in his footsteps. In a 1986 interview, Logan stated, "My daddy wasn't afraid of nothing . . . he wasn't a mean man, he was a kind person and a very religious person, but he never took second step for nobody, I don't care who you were and I guess I got that from him. And I've never been afraid of nothing. . . . My daddy was a very independent person."[31] Her father nurtured her independent spirit and she believed that independence was part of her destiny. Named after the church founded by Richard Allen and Absalom Jones in protest of their mistreatment by white Methodists, Logan believed that she had to present herself in the spirit of her namesake, especially because the forces that brought about the creation of the church were still at play in the lives of Blacks. Moreover, she stated that her being named in the church's honor imbued her with an inherent sense of freedom.[32] Even though she only had a ninth-grade education, she never limited herself by the dictates of segregation. She, too, was very involved in the African Methodist Episcopal Church, "serv[ing] as superintendent of the Sunday school and every office in the church except the Minister."[33]

In 1932, while still a teenager, A. M. E. married Style Logan, a native of Lorman, Mississippi. They initially settled in Carpenter where the two opened a grocery store together and started a family. Logan also worked as a beautician, laying an early foundation for the entrepreneurial life they would lead in Jackson and following her father's expectations that she and her siblings "be a real man or woman. . . . Be independent; learn something that you could do that you wouldn't have to work under white people."[34]

In the early 1940s the Logans moved to Jackson with their three children, and in 1944 they built a house on Biloxi Street near Jackson State College. Like most Black neighborhoods, theirs represented the economic diversity of the Black community, with teachers, maids, professors, and everyone in between residing in the same general area. The Logans spent the rest of their lives in that home, which in the sixties became a regular overnight stop for activists coming into the state. After moving to the capital city, Logan worked for a period as a cashier at William's Grocery Store on the corner of Lynch and Dalton streets and also at J. P. Campbell College, an AME-funded and all-Black-controlled institution that provided educational opportunities for Blacks from the elementary to collegiate levels.[35] In the fifties, she found similar work at her husband's employer, the Illinois Central Railroad Station. Her youngest son, Willis, recalled that his mother began opening their home to Blacks traveling through Mississippi during this period. Often Blacks who had migrated to Chicago or other northern cities returned to the state for visits, sometimes arriving in Jackson on the last train without transportation to their final destination or anywhere to spend the night. Logan offered the weary travelers a place to lay their heads and some of them became lifelong family friends.[36] Those who knew her said that she always offered assistance to anyone in need. Alferdteen

Harrison, a retired history professor at Jackson State, aptly described Logan as someone who never met a stranger.[37] The selflessness and caregiving she exhibited toward Blacks expanded exponentially when she joined Womanpower Unlimited and the civil rights movement gained momentum in Mississippi.

In the late 1950s, Logan left the railroad to become a traveling salesperson and franchise manager for A. W. Curtis, a distributor of the Michigan-based George Washington Carver cosmetics. Her office was located at the Masonic Temple on Lynch Street, the primary facility for civil rights meetings in Jackson.[38] Dedicated in 1955, the building also housed Medgar Evers's office, and it soon became the hub of local civil rights activities. Working in this location and catering to a Black clientele gave Logan the opportunity to build personal, professional, and activist relationships with relative ease. She and her family developed a close working and personal relationship with Evers. Willis Logan, for example, delivered the newspaper to Evers's office on his paper route, and he became president of the West Jackson Youth Council of the NAACP. Logan allowed the staff of the Council of Federated Organizations (COFO) to use her office until they were able to secure their own.[39] Mr. Logan, who was a carpenter by trade, established his own contracting business and the two were again entrepreneurs and economically independent. In the mid-1960s, Mr. Logan lost some business from white clients because of their joining the school desegregation lawsuit. Blacks comprised the majority of his clientele, and his business survived despite those losses.

The Logans became registered voters shortly after moving to Jackson. When the NAACP was reorganized in the 1950s, Logan was the only woman present at the initial meeting. She contributed significantly to the door-to-door canvassing that built the Jackson branch's membership. She played an instrumental role in establishing the Jackson chapter of the SCLC. Around 1961, James Bevel and John Ross met with Harvey to begin planning, and Harvey invited Logan to join them. Logan then volunteered to house Bevel and Ross when they returned to undertake the initial organizing efforts. The activists used her residence for the initial SCLC meeting and appointed her secretary.[40] Logan also served as hostess for Martin Luther King Jr. when he visited the city. As the story goes, he so enjoyed the cake she made the first time she met him that, every time he came to Jackson, he asked her to make him a cake.[41] Civil rights organizing became a prominent component of her life. While Mr. Logan, a quiet and reserved man, was not as visible as Mrs. Logan, he was involved in the NAACP and fully supported his wife's activism and the movement as a whole.

Logan was a full-time activist in addition to being a working mother. She was heavily involved in her church, the AME-affiliated Campbell College, the Masonic Order, and her neighborhood association prior to joining Womanpower. Her daughter, Shirley Montague, recalled that during the 1950s her mother led a petition to build a wider street to ensure the safety of her family and neighbors and to challenge the inadequate funding and services allocated for Black communities.[42] This prior mobilizing experience was instrumental to Womanpower's success. By the 1960s, when her youngest son Willis was a high-schooler and the only child at home, Logan's parenting began anew. She became "mother" to hundreds of young organizers who stayed at her house and affectionately called her "Mom" as well as those who attended meetings at her home. As for her biological children, she encouraged and nurtured their civil rights activism as well, instilling in them the same type of independence that she had learned from her father. This was especially true for Willis, who was a youth leader as the movement reached its climax in Mississippi while he was a student at Jim Hill High School.

In recalling the meeting to organize Womanpower Unlimited at Central United Methodist Church, Logan stated, "Mrs. Harvey said she had one person in mind and she didn't want that woman to refuse. All types of people were there—PhDs, lawyers, teachers, and ministers and I wasn't thinking anything about it at the time that she was talking about me. . . .[And she said] that's Mrs. A. M. E. Logan and I was just knocked off my feet because I'm just an insignificant person in comparison to the [others]."[43] Logan accepted a position as executive director/administrative secretary of Womanpower Unlimited, thereby taking responsibility for executing and overseeing the daily tasks of the organization as Harvey's business and church commitments necessitated extensive travel.[44] Harvey recalled that "every morning for a month, the first call I would make in the morning was to A. M. E. Logan."[45] She was central to the overall functioning of Womanpower.

Logan's peripatetic experience became an added bonus for both the organization and civil rights activists. As a saleswoman, she traveled in a sixty-mile radius of Jackson to many rural areas, developing relationships with individuals who were useful contacts for organizing in those communities (and canvassing for voter registration for the NAACP). Logan recalled that, because she owned a car, she was repeatedly called upon to transport activists around town. This proved to be an asset for WU's voter registration project. Thomas Gaither, a CORE field secretary stationed in Jackson to manage the arrival and release of the Freedom Riders, remarked that Logan "extend[ed] this entire movement out into the Mississippi countryside . . . she would actually bring back the items from people in the Mississippi countryside who wanted to contribute to the movement, but were otherwise fearful of really connecting with the movement, but they could connect with the movement through Mrs. Logan."[46]

Logan's participation in the movement became an integral part of her life. She utilized all possible avenues to support other activists and generate support to advance the cause of Womanpower and the larger civil rights movement. In a 2001 interview, Logan said, "I worked with . . . Womanpower Unlimited, SCLC, SNCC, CORE, NAACP; all of them. All five of them. Didn't make me no difference 'cause see, the thing about it, we were all working for one common goal, for civil rights. Your own rights, you know?"[47] Echoing Harvey's sentiments of forty years earlier that Womanpower needed "to get *every*woman supporting the movements for freedom and good through: 1. Prayer . . . 2. Giving [of] one's self, one's service [and] one's finance—money [and] 3. Special Action as needed in cooperation with NAACP, Interdenom[inational] Alliance, Progressive Voter's League, YWCA, etc." Logan's comments underscore the collaborative nature and flexible associations of Womanpower's efforts that reflected Black women's organizing tradition as well as the strategic leadership of local leaders, regardless of gender.[48]

Womanpower's goals transcended organizational differences and strategies and made connections among various groups of people. The organization uniformly supported other civil rights organizations working in the state, from the NAACP to the Student Nonviolent Coordinating Committee (SNCC), because members realized that the success of the overall goals of the movement was more important than the politics of certain leaders or organizations. As historian Françoise Hamlin explains in her analysis of local civil rights activists in Clarksdale, Mississippi, local leaders often utilized "flexible associations" that allowed them to "mov[e] between organizations as circumstances demanded."[49] This strategy was beneficial and accessible to the indigenous community leaders who often operated outside the spotlight and confines of national organizations such as the NAACP. It resulted in the optimal use of movement resources and provided access to larger numbers of potential recruits. Historian Barbara Ransby describes Ella Baker's varied political alliances similarly, stating, "Although Baker had a definite worldview, which she articulated, enacted, and defended, there was fluidity and flexibility in the positions she took and the alliances she formed."[50] Womanpower members in general possessed a likeminded approach that afforded them the ability to hold overlapping associations with multiple organizations in an effort to, like Baker, build "a movement rather than any one organization."[51] Resulting from their experience of negotiating the margins, what scholar Kimberly Springer refers to as *interstitial politics*, Black women frequently embodied a position that bridged organizations and/or allowed them to "straddle organizational divides."[52] Womanpower employed this strategy to generate the broadest possible support for civil rights workers in the state. WU reflected the coalition building that Black women activists desired, demonstrating that they were movement-oriented rather than organization-oriented.

Womanpower's vice chair Thelma Sanders, another prominent businesswoman, was the youngest of this core group. Recognized by *Ebony* magazine as one of the nation's best-dressed women, Sanders was more than just another pretty face.[53] She was born Thelma Caldwell in Tougaloo, Mississippi, in 1924. The daughter of Bessie (Britton) and Charles Caldwell, Thelma was the oldest of her mother's seven children. As Bessie's marriage to Charles was short-lived and she was only a teenager when Thelma was born, Thelma was raised primarily by her maternal grandparents, Carrie (Agee) and Henry Britton. Thelma had a kind and generous nature that, as her brother recalled, was evident even in childhood. When she was around twelve or thirteen, a neighbor's house was destroyed by fire. A little girl in the family was one of Thelma's playmates, and when Thelma learned that all of their possessions were destroyed, she volunteered to give her two of her dresses, which were half of the dresses she owned.[54] This is indicative of the selflessness and generosity she offered her community as an adult.

Thelma Caldwell attended Tougaloo College, obtaining her bachelor's degree in home economics in 1946. She likely pursued this degree under the influence of her grandmother, who was an exceptional homemaker.[55] After completing her studies at Tougaloo, Ms. Caldwell began teaching home economics in Neshoba County, close to where her grandmother's people were from. In the summers she taught at Lanier High School in Jackson, where she secured a full-time job. One of her requirements for students in her course was that they prepare a formal dinner for the principal, Isaiah Sumner ("I. S.") Sanders, to demonstrate what they had learned. The story goes that the principal was so impressed by the meal, he called Ms. Caldwell to inquire about how she had acquired such superb cooking skills, to which she replied that if he really wanted to taste some delectable cooking, he needed to taste her grandmother's food.

Thus began Principal Sanders's visits to Mrs. Britton's house and his courtship of Ms. Caldwell. Although thirty-nine years her senior, I. S. was persistent and Thelma eventually fell for him. The two were married in 1949.

A native of Hinds County, I. S. Sanders was born on September 27, 1885, to Reverend and Mrs. Thomas Sanders. Like Thelma, he completed his high school and college education at Tougaloo, earning his bachelor's degree in 1910.[56] After teaching at Yazoo City High School and serving as the assistant principal, he joined the faculty and became the first dean of Alcorn College, a position he held until 1935. During this time, he earned his master's degree from the University of Chicago in English language and literature. He eventually left Alcorn to serve as principal of Lanier High School in Jackson, where he remained until his retirement in 1956.[57] Mr. Sanders, a well-known and respected community leader, was a staunch advocate for Black equality. His economic stability and standing in the community provided Mrs. Sanders with the security to pursue her business and activist endeavors.

Incensed by the discrimination Blacks experienced while shopping in white stores, Thelma Sanders opened a clothing business to serve Black women. In 1950, Sanders Boutique opened its doors at 507 North Farish Street in downtown Jackson (next door to Collins Funeral Home). Sanders recalled that on an earlier shopping trip with her husband, she decided to test the policy that Blacks could not try clothing on—that instead the clerk would try it on for you—a practice she says was not in place prior to 1950. After being refused by the clerk and manager, Sanders "decided then and there, that day, why couldn't I have a store? Why couldn't I have clothes like this and we'd have a place for our own people to try on and we wouldn't have to worry about this discrimination here in Jackson."[58] Because she was often subjected to discrimination by local businesses and sales representatives, Sanders conducted much of the purchasing for her store directly from manufacturers in major cities outside the state. As the owner of a business that serviced the Black community almost exclusively, Sanders was in a position of economic independence that allowed her to openly support civil rights activities. She had little fear of economic retaliation because few of her business transactions involved local whites, and her excellent reputation as a businesswoman afforded her several institutional networks.

Her product line included millinery, lingerie, jewelry, handbags, and accessories. As her business grew, Sanders relocated to a larger location (still in the heart of the Black community on Farish Street) and expanded her products to include a full line of women's clothing and hats as well as a beauty shop. Aside from offering Black women respect in their purchasing, Sanders believed that her business was important for offering employment opportunities to "young ladies as sales clerks, or bookkeepers."[59] She used her business for philanthropic opportunities. For example, Sanders brought the Ebony Fashion Fair to the state to raise money for civic organizations such as the United Negro College Fund, the Urban League, and the National Association of Negro Business and Professional Women's Clubs, as well as her alma mater, Tougaloo College.[60]

Prior to her association with Womanpower Unlimited, Sanders was actively involved in NAACP and civil rights activities in Jackson. She eagerly responded when Harvey called upon her to support Womanpower. She opened her home and her business to the Freedom Riders, providing them with food, a place to stay, and free access to the services of her beauty salon. Sanders was open in her support of the Freedom Riders, as proven by an incident she relayed to Harvey. Sanders recalled being questioned from one of her wholesalers about the clothing that she was purchasing, which was inferior in quality and in much greater quantity than her usual orders. He then asked her point-blank if the items were for the Freedom Riders. Sanders replied in the affirmative, followed by, "What about it?" The retailer responded, "I just want to tell you more power to you. There are a lot of people who are proud of what you women are doing and if you will come to me personally any time that you want anything I will give you not only your business discount but an additional discount."[61] Despite possible repercussions, Sanders proclaimed her civil rights activism and support for the Freedom Riders. Her activism did not go unnoticed. In October 1964, vigilantes dynamited the Sanderses' car, destroying it along with the windows on one side of their house.[62] Sanders remained steadfast in the face of this type of intimidation and did not let it deter her commitment to the struggle.

Jessie Mosley, who served as treasurer for the majority of the organization's existence, was the only member of this core group who was not a native of Mississippi. Jessie Bryant was born in Houston, Texas, on November 30, 1903, the only child of Emma and William Bryant.[63] Her parents traveled extensively, and young Jessie had the opportunity to live in cities all over the state including Waco, Fort Worth, and Dallas. While attending Jarvis Christian College in Hawkins, Texas, she met Oklahoman Charles Clint Mosley, whom she married in 1926. Jessie Mosley graduated from Jarvis with a bachelor of science degree in 1942, and the couple moved to Edwards, Mississippi, to work at Southern Christian Institute—Charles as dean of students and Jessie as a teacher.[64] During this time Mosley published a book titled *The Negro in Mississippi*. This was an early step in her efforts to recover the history of African Americans, and she perceived this as part of her struggle for equality, ensuring that Black history was recorded and taught and that Blacks were acknowledged for their contributions to this nation. Mosley went on to establish the Negro in Mississippi Historical Society in 1963 (with Womanpower member Ruth O. Hubert as a charter member) and led preservation efforts for the historic Smith Robertson School, the first public school for African Americans in the city.

The Mosleys resided in Edwards for nearly a decade before moving to Jackson in 1951. Mr. Mosley joined the faculty of Jackson State in the Education Department, and Mrs. Mosley gained employment at the Marino Branch YWCA on Farish Street as director of the teen programs. The "Branch Y" (colored YWCA) was a cornerstone of the Black community, providing social services, education, and recreational resources. Working at the Y brought Mosley into contact with many of the politically active Black women in Jackson, such as the Y's director and charter member, Lillie Bell Walker Jones (who was also I. S. Sanders's niece), and Clarie Collins Harvey, who served on the board of directors. Not surprisingly, many of the prominent federated clubwomen, such as Ruth O. Hubert and Edna R. Lovelace, were affiliated with the Y. Thus, Mosley was immediately connected to a key segment of the city's Black leadership. She was active in the MSFCWC and chaired the organization's Junior and Young Women's Department in the 1950s.[65]

Like Thelma Sanders, Mosley was incensed by the discrimination Blacks faced in the downtown stores and opened a "shoe salon," Mosley's Shoe Store, in the Masonic Temple on Lynch Street.[66] She, too, used her business resources to take care of the Freedom Riders, providing some of them with shoes.[67]

While all of these women were veteran activists at the time of their involvement with Womanpower, their positions of economic independence were of equal importance. Relying solely on the patronage of Black Mississippians and largely on suppliers outside the state, Harvey, Logan, Sanders, and Mosley were less concerned about economic retaliation from whites. Unlike teachers and other middle-class professionals whose activism was often prevented or stifled by their white employers, self-employment provided these women a degree of freedom that encouraged their unreserved and open support of the movement. Most Womanpower members were not hesitant about supporting the movement. Unlike the middle-class teachers, professionals, and ministers whom NAACP field secretary Medgar Evers described as individuals "who won't be hurt by belonging to the organization, but who won't give us 50 cents for fear of losing face with the white man," Womanpower members worked to mobilize this segment of the population to take action.[68] In reference to Harvey's activism as a middle-class woman, Lawrence Guyot stated, "she did a lot of open organizing and gave legitimacy to organizing the Black middle-class of which she was certainly a respected and a staunch member. She was able to give legitimacy to the right to dissent. . . . Mrs. Harvey was the sort of link who had been involved when it was dangerous; [she] could bring in [and] give legitimacy to a lot of the people who had not been involved."[69] Through their leadership and activism as well as active encouragement, these women were able to bring many previously uninvolved Blacks into the ranks of civil rights activism.

Without a doubt Harvey, the visionary behind the organization, was its driving ideological force. Her national and international travels and affiliations, combined with her religious and social activism, cultivated a perspective that was inaccessible to many Black women at that time. Harvey seems to have taken what she deemed the best from those experiences and added to that what she thought was lacking in creating Womanpower Unlimited. She imbued the organization with her hopes for Black advancement and implored other women to join in her efforts to bring about social justice.

Organizational Philosophies

With the unwavering dedication of Logan, Sanders, and Mosley, Womanpower set forth an agenda aimed at creating a "beloved community" in which freedom, justice, and equality existed indiscriminately among humankind.[70] As stated in a 1963 self-published history of the organization, Womanpower's vision and purpose were multifaceted:

> To help create the atmosphere, the institutions, and traditions that make freedom and peace possible. We are all women working together for a peaceful world and wholesome community life. Mississippi must be a better place to live and work because of our efforts.
>   We mean by freedom:
> - the right to speak and organize, to think and write, to work and play, to register and vote as we choose without intervention from those who would keep us silent slaves; the right to be different from the crowd; the right to walk alone and unafraid with God guiding our path;

- the right to initiate and participate in peaceful protests and petitions of grievances against arbitrary and unjust laws; the right to support, in whatever way we can, those others who protest also; for the right to oppose an unconstitutional law is deep in our moral and legal tradition;
- the right to coordinate our activities with and to be a part of peace movements. . . .

Where there are no movements or organized efforts to bring about such freedoms, we shall take the initiative. Where efforts in these directions exist, we shall attempt to stimulate more creative and effective action and to cooperate in achieving abundant life for all of us by lending our "womanpower."[71]

Embracing nonviolence and direct action, WU members envisioned themselves providing both the leadership and the support work necessary to achieve the movement's goals. Recognizing the necessity of both for sustaining the movement, these women did not give primacy to one over the other. Instead, they believed they could best serve the movement by providing whatever was necessary at any given time. The dichotomous thinking that exists in our society (rational vs. emotional, white vs. Black, man vs. woman, leadership vs. support), typically privileging one category over another, has not defined Black women's experiences. Living simultaneously in the margins and at the intersection of multiple "otherized" identities, many Black women have embraced multiple roles in their pursuit of justice. Black women's activism often incorporates a reinterpretation of what is valuable. This reinterpretation has allowed women to embrace behind-the-scenes work and deem it equal in importance to more visible, typically male-dominated leadership roles. Womanpower's incorporation of leadership and support work demonstrates their political acumen to determine what was best to advance the movement's larger goals in any given situation. Members positioned themselves to work both independently of and in collaboration with existing organizations. They were fully aware of the benefits of building coalitions in the struggle against oppression and of assisting others committed to pursuing the goals of peace and freedom locally, nationally, and internationally.

WU's organizational structure reflected a leadership style like that of Ella Baker, Fannie Lou Hamer, Victoria Gray Adams, Vera Pigee, and other Black women civil rights activists—one in which there is no desire for celebrity. Its focus was instead on representing the masses, cultivating leadership among women, and supporting causes with similar goals of freedom and justice. Baker,

Hamer, Adams, Pigee, Harvey, and Womanpower members nurtured and mentored youth activists, providing young women with a model of womanhood that was not defined by traditional gender roles. Harvey described her efforts to promote leadership as both an activist and a businesswoman thus: "One of the contributions I have tried to make to the community . . . as well as in my business interests too, is to develop leadership. . . . In the community I try to do it within the framework of the women's movement, in that other women learn to accept leadership roles and carry them out and perform them well, and do it—because this is the way I feel that a community grows—not just with one person doing everything, but many people being trained and learned to do things."[72] Like Ella Baker, who professed that "strong people don't need strong leaders," Harvey believed that everyone had the capacity for leadership, and she challenged the exclusion that women faced with respect to leadership opportunities.

WU members were fully aware of the male-dominated society in which they lived, and they understood that the exclusion of women's voices limited organizations' and movements' effectiveness. Historically, Black women have had to claim a space that was not intended for them. In the patriarchal American society, the public sphere has traditionally been male space, and, although socioeconomic factors often necessitated that Black women participate in the workforce, thereby contradicting the dichotomy between private and public, Black women have found themselves hindered by this ideology. Additionally, the "respectable" spaces and roles for women in American society have often been "reserved" for white middle-class women. Many members of the Black community, particularly the middle class, have embraced traditional gender roles in employing a "politics of respectability" in working for Black inclusion. This strategy has restricted women's agency in activist circles. For example, while working with the Fellowship of Reconciliation in 1947, Ella Baker, Pauli Murray, and Natalie Mormon helped plan the Journey of Reconciliation, holding some of the planning meetings at Mormon's residence. This was intended as a direct action response to *Morgan v. Commonwealth of Virginia* (1946).[73] All three women, seasoned activists by this time, assumed they would participate in the protest, but they were "overruled by the group, who felt that the trip would be too dangerous for women."[74] Likewise, scholars examining the construction of the public personas of Mamie Till Bradley Mobley (Emmett Till's mother) and Rosa Parks have noted that their male peers urged them to embrace a "politics of respectability" (which they likely agreed with given its political efficacy) and to tolerate being silenced as well. Historian Ruth Feldstein observed, "From the outset, her weakness, even hysteria, and her need to defer to men confirmed her femininity and her religiosity and were vehicles for asserting [Mamie Till Mobley's] 'authenticity' as an American woman and mother."[75] While part of this persona made the assertion of justice for her son Emmett more palatable for white Americans, it embodied the typically male view of the deferential female—a striking irony in the context of women's increasingly powerful place in the movement.

Similarly, describing the mass meeting held at Holt Street Baptist Church the night the Montgomery Improvement Association was formed (a meeting neither Rosa Parks nor Jo Ann Robinson attended), historian Danielle McGuire noted that Reverend E. N. French informed Parks that she did not need to speak but merely be presented to the crowd. She continued that "because Reverend French and the ministers leading the mass meeting that night silenced Parks, they turned her into the kind of woman she wasn't: a quiet victim and solemn symbol."[76] Even Black men who were fighting for freedom and equality for Blacks engaged in behavior that limited Black women's agency.

By the 1960s the sands were shifting—SNCC birthed a new generation of Black women activists whose "politics of respectability" did not mean deferring to male authority. As SNCC activist Bernice Johnson Reagon explained, "One of the things that happened to me through SNCC was [that] my whole world was expanded in terms of what I could do as a person. I'm describing an unleashing of my potential as an empowered human being. I never experienced being held back. I only experienced being challenged and searching within myself to see if I had the courage to do what came up in my mind."[77] As political successors to the 1947 Journey of Reconciliation, the 1961 Freedom Riders provided a clear illustration of this shift in women's activity. Not only were women active participants, but Diane Nash, who had been mentored by Ella Baker, ensured that the Rides did not end prematurely in Alabama due to violence. And the older generation of women leaders—Harvey, Hamer, Adams, Pigee, and many others—were finding and asserting their voices. This is not to suggest that gender politics were no longer relevant by the 1960s. Women activists, however, were far less willing to be constrained by gender politics than in the past and Womanpower Unlimited made this clear.

Flexibility was equally important to the organization's modus operandi. As described in its statement of purpose, Womanpower asserted, "We are a movement—without membership, without dues—open to all women who wish to develop their leadership abilities and to make a significant contribution to the good life beyond their homes, local churches, and club groups."[78] Womanpower's stance was both unique and advantageous because it took women out of their traditional spheres of influence and allowed them to place their emphasis on action. Harvey explained that they chose to function "as a movement so that we could be flexible and so that we could move immediately, rather than waiting for a board to convene and to make decisions and all the rest of it. We felt that we needed a relatively free group in the community that could just act, if some action needed to be taken."[79] This position opposed the hierarchical, bureaucratic leadership structure that frequently kept women on the periphery of organizations, and simultaneously it provided the flexibility to instantly address the needs of the larger movement. Womanpower had the momentum to engender, nurture, and propel ideas and action; the breadth and flexibility to employ multiple strategies; and the freedom to evolve without abandoning its core values. This is a characteristically Black feminist position. In discussing the features of Black feminist thought, sociologist Patricia Hill Collins writes, "Neither Black feminist thought as a critical social theory nor Black feminist practice can be static; as social conditions change, so must the knowledge and practices designed to resist them."[80] In this respect, WU positioned itself to remain "dynamic and changing," recognizing that its efficacy was predicated on keeping pace with the movement's evolution. Womanpower emerged as a women's movement within the Black freedom struggle.

In their classic study of protest movements, Frances Fox Piven and Richard Cloward asserted that movement organizers often fail because they direct too much of their energy to creating and sustaining "formally structured organizations" rather than developing the energy that emerges among the populace during incidents of unrest. They contended that this failure partially results "from the doctrinal commitment to the development of mass-based permanent organization, for organization-building activities tended to draw people away from the streets and into the meeting rooms."[81] Womanpower was able to avoid such ineffectiveness by addressing the issue of functionality at its inception. Aware of the limitations that can accompany permanency, Harvey developed a structure that accommodated the rapid changes in the movement's strategies and goals. This line of thought evidences the hope that permeated the movement—that they would be successful in their endeavors to open the closed society and create a beloved community and, therefore, that an organization based on accomplishing those goals would no longer be necessary.

Harvey emphasized that Womanpower's existence was predicated on productivity and change, not entertainment. Theirs was a movement of women promoting activism, and their commitment to assisting the freedom struggle was their raison d'être. Womanpower sought to bring women out of their traditional spheres of activity (the home and the church) and into an arena in which they could affect broader change. Harvey wanted to ensure that members of the group, especially women in her own economic position, addressed quality of life issues within the larger community. She admitted being frustrated by women of her own socioeconomic class who devoted time and energy to organizations like the Links (a service organization for professional women that Harvey believed was largely a way of showcasing the fact that they had "arrived"), when the majority of the Black community faced so many social and economic concerns. She described her early association with the group, recalling, "[My friends] wanted me to be a part of the Links. . . . And, I met with them for a while, and . . . I couldn't go on with it. . . . To me this is just wasted time, energy and money, you know, and all the rest of it. And I'm very critical of my friends, who can think only of themselves and pushing themselves . . . because I think this thing has got to be broad based, you know, if we are to get far."[82] Womanpower members regarded a cessation of their activism as tantamount to ending their work altogether. Harvey's identification with the masses supports the assertions of several scholars who argue Black women are able to transcend differences of location and identify with one another. Duchess Harris, for example, posits that women born into middle-class entrepreneurial families, like those of Clarie Collins Harvey and Gloria Richardson (in Maryland), had a firsthand view of Black poverty because their businesses catered solely to Blacks.[83] These types of experiences imbued Black women activists with the responsibility of incorporating economic justice into their efforts of race uplift.

Organizational Structure

Although Womanpower was a movement that could act spontaneously, it did have structure. It consisted of a group of highly organized persons whose vision was to support the movement, develop women as leaders in civil rights activism, and provide opportunities for social, political, and spiritual elevation in order to meet the needs of the community. Womanpower Unlimited was comprised of an executive board, committees, and a general membership body. By August 1961, permanent officers were selected and the initial four officers evolved into an executive board (at times called the executive council or steering committee) that included recording and corresponding secretaries, treasurers, chaplains (and assistants), pianists, parliamentarians, news editors, and publicity directors.[84] Womanpower established committees for voter registration, membership, hospitality, prayer fellowship, programming, finance, research, and telephone, with new ones being created as needed and whose chairs also comprised the executive board.[85] The membership and publicity committees were charged with responsibilities of increasing and documenting membership; advertising meetings, news, and programs; and assisting the news editor with publishing *Woo*, the monthly newsletter.[86] Some committees were unique to the organization. The hospitality committee, likely one of the first committees Womanpower established given the decision to take care of the Freedom Riders once they were released from prison, made housing and food arrangements for civil rights activists and speakers coming to Jackson. Vice chair Thelma Sanders headed this committee; she was a natural choice as she had previously taught home economics and, according to her brother, was the best hostess in the state of Mississippi. The telephone committee was designed to disseminate information quickly. It was actually a chain of communication through which committee chairs contacted certain women who each had another group of women to contact. This allowed for a quick and efficient distribution of information to members.

Using a traditional civil rights organizing forum, Womanpower typically held its bimonthly (by 1963 these had become monthly) meetings at local churches. In addition to the Central United Methodist Church, the site of the initial organizing meeting, Womanpower used the Farish Street Baptist Church, the Pearl Street AME Church, and the Mount Helm Baptist Church (with each church represented by Womanpower membership), as well as J. P. Campbell College, as meeting locations. These venues gave credence to the organization in the eyes of community members and created interdenominational alliances.

The spectrum of general public meetings included forums where community members could voice their opinions, information sessions where they could learn about the activities of other civil rights organizations working in the state, workshops on nonviolence, and discussions about peace activism.[87] For example, in April 1964, Womanpower invited representatives from COFO to speak about the campaigns of Victoria Gray for the Senate and James M.

Houston for the House of Representatives for the third Congressional District (which includes the central part of the state where Jackson is located).[88] Harvey proposed that they collectively decide if and how to support these campaigns as an organization. The minutes of the officers' meetings and agendas of the general meetings indicate that Womanpower actively sought to collaborate with the other civil rights organizations and were reciprocally contacted as a resource. It was not uncommon to have a representative from COFO or the Jackson Nonviolent Movement (JNM) attend a Womanpower meeting. Additionally, other organizations regularly relied upon the efforts of the hospitality committee as they requested housing assistance for activists coming to the state.[89]

Women brought their neighbors, church members, and relatives into the organization to create a local membership body, which at its apex of approximately 125 included women of all classes and professions.[90] Their levels of activism varied greatly. Some were schoolteachers who feared losing their jobs, so they chose to donate money anonymously and attended meetings irregularly. Others like Aura Gary, who served as membership chair and was employed at St. Dominic's Hospital under the supervision of a "devout Christian" who supported her activism, did not worry about white economic retaliation.[91] And still others were homemakers, professors, ministers' wives, domestic workers, nurses, secretaries, and beauticians. Regardless of economic class, most members were middle-aged and were not burdened by the responsibilities of caring for young children. Additionally, like Clarie Collins Harvey, A. M. E. Logan, Thelma Sanders, and Jessie Mosley, many of these women had previous organizational experiences, whether through their church, sorority, the MSFCWC, or the NAACP. Womanpower created a "safe space" for these women to become agents of social change. Safe spaces—whether they be organizations, physical locations (like beauty parlors), or space carved out within existing institutions (like women's groups within the church)—are places where Black women can find their voice and freely express it without the fear of being penalized, ostracized, or subjugated. As described by sociologist Patricia Hill Collins and historian Darlene Clark Hine, they are spaces where Black women have been able to become empowered through self-definition and the development of a culture of resistance.[92] Within the safe space created by Womanpower, women contributed in numerous ways to the Black freedom struggle.

National affiliation with Womanpower through its Chain of Friendship increased its numbers to over three hundred women committed to social change and working to effect it specifically in Mississippi. From this national network of white women allies, who were contacts primarily from Harvey's travels, Womanpower solicited assistance for the civil rights struggle in Mississippi. Womanpower specifically asked these allies to offer:

1. Your prayers.
2. Your finance to the NAACP, to Womanpower Unlimited and other civil rights groups.
3. Your influence on government for civil rights and peace legislation.
4. Your influence on the industry operating in Mississippi to give on-the-job training and upgrade Negroes in jobs.
5. Your influence on chain stores here to employ Negroes on all levels.
6. Your influence with national and international groups where you hold membership and which operate also in Mississippi, to join this Chain of Friendship in creating a climate of goodwill in which social change can come easily and painlessly.
7. Encouragement of your Mississippi Jewish and Caucasian friends to become a part of this Chain of Friendship and work unceasingly within the Mississippi white community for positive social change.[93]

This collective was extremely beneficial in raising the consciousness of Americans outside of the state and generating much-needed support for civil rights projects in Mississippi. As the list above specifies, the responsibilities of these Friends were not limited to money; they were expected to be active as well. Similar to the Friends of SNCC, which engaged in fundraising, sometimes through concerts or other events, collecting supplies, disseminating organizational literature, and letter writing, Womanpower's Friends were expected to use their resources and influence to help sustain the movement and promote change in their circles that would impact the South.[94] Unlike Friends of SNCC, however, which had formal groups on campuses and in major cities throughout the country, some of whom were paid staff members, Womanpower's Chain was just that. They were typically individual women connected to the Mississippi freedom struggle through Womanpower Unlimited, who personally wrote letters, sent donations, and/or disseminated information about Womanpower and other civil rights organizations and solicited financial support from the local and national organizations in which they held memberships.

The requests to Friends underscored the need for assistance on a variety of levels and illustrated many of the ways that American racism negatively impacted Blacks—from political and economic discrimination to de facto segregation. It emphasized the interconnectedness among movements for social justice. Womanpower members knew that opening the closed society required work on the part of local whites, and they implored northern whites to support the movement by encouraging their southern white associates to ban discriminatory practices in their businesses and to support legislative changes.

Fay Honey Knopp was a prototypical Friend, a member of Womanpower's Chain and a convert to the Quaker faith. Harvey met Knopp, a native of Connecticut, during the Women Strike for Peace pilgrimage to Geneva in 1962. On the trip back to the United States, they discussed the Black protests in the South and the violent retaliation by whites. Believing that working for peace should include focusing on one's own community, the two women discussed how Knopp could contribute. Harvey began sending her articles and other information about the movement and civil rights organizations in the state. Eventually, Knopp decided to go to Mississippi to work in the white community. Harvey supplied her with names of local whites, some sympathetic and some not so sympathetic. But Knopp spoke to whoever was necessary to create connections of likeminded people within the white community, convert whites who were opposed to Black equality, and create bridges between the Black and white communities. She made three trips to Mississippi between 1964 and 1965.[95] As Knopp explained in a report from one of her Mississippi trips, "it was a brief, though earnest, effort to practice a deep ministry of listening and presence in the tense community of Jackson, Mississippi. In seeking out white, female moderates in the community, we hoped that our support and contact might in some way contribute to the unity and strength of such women and perhaps ultimately, through its own dynamic, lead to the building of an integrated sense of purpose between *all* concerned women in Jackson, black and white."[96] In addition to her trips to the state, Knopp sent clothing and other items to Rosie Redmond for Womanpower's clothing project.[97] She was the kind of active and engaged woman WU wanted to bring into the movement.

Additionally, the Chain of Friendship was a manifestation of a traditional organizing strategy by Black women to engage in interracial coalitions. Womanpower continued the efforts of earlier activists who attempted to work with white activists in support of women's suffrage, with the YWCA, and with the Council of Interracial Cooperation, and it "believed that the contribution of women, both Black and White, was essential to racial harmony."[98] In spite of the tenuousness of such alliances in the past, Womanpower encouraged alliances with white women's organizations like United Church Women and Women Strike for Peace to increase support for the civil rights movement and to fulfill their humanist agenda based on the belief that the activism of both races was necessary to improve race relations. The Chain of Friendship was a way to get white women outside the South involved in and committed to issues of racial injustice. This strategy was also pursued as a way to eventually gain the support of local white women, through the encouragement of their northern white friends.

The Chain of Friendship bolstered other projects through consciousness raising, connecting people outside of the South to the movement, and promoting the belief that it is a responsibility of citizenship to address injustices. Whether these Friends came to Mississippi or not, Womanpower's Chain of Friendship was designed to undermine the stigma of "outside agitators" and generate national support for the Black freedom struggle.

Womanpower's configuration demonstrates the influence of members' previous organizational experience in other ways. Two aspects of the organization—the pianist and the Chain of Friendship—were also features of the MS-FCWC to which Harvey and many other WU members belonged. The assistant pianist, Aurelia Young, was a music professor who had helped establish the bachelor's program in music at Jackson State. Ruth O. Hubert, Womanpower's chaplain, was a founder of the Harmonia Music Club, a MSFCWC affiliate established "to promote and encourage public appreciation for music."[99] The MSFCWC itself had a Department (Committee) of Fine Arts and Literature, demonstrating the importance of music. The MSFCWC's Chain of Friendship consisted of the youth clubs and clubs created to visit and run errands for the sick and elderly. WU members incorporated aspects of a national organization that they thought would fit well with their program.

Just as Womanpower Unlimited represents a continuation of Black women's activism from previous generations, its members were not alone in continuing this legacy. While some of them, Harvey in particular, were unique with respect to their experiences and resources, in general they were not unlike many other Black women throughout the South during the mid-twentieth century who were putting their livelihoods and lives at risk for the sake of freedom and justice.

Womanpower is unique in that it was an explicitly political organization with the leadership of independent women who, as business and community leaders, challenged women's traditional roles long before the civil rights movement took shape in Mississippi. They worked overtly and covertly through religious, professional, and civic organizations to advance civil rights and enhance the quality of life for Blacks. Women from all positions of life, such as Maddye Lyne Henry (domestic worker); Vera, Verna Lee, and Orthella Polk (sisters and students at Jackson State College); Blanche Brown (seamstress); Aurelia Young (professor at Jackson State College); Lula Belle Forte (owner of Lulabelle's Fashion Center); and Daisy Reddix (first lady of Jackson State College) joined the ranks of Womanpower Unlimited to help Mississippi become a beloved community.[100]

During the first two months of its existence, Womanpower raised close to $700 to support the Freedom Riders, with donations coming from across the state and even the nation.[101] Members encouraged those who attended WU meetings to "flood Freedom Riders with letters and cards," and they organized a system to take care of the activists, physically and emotionally.[102] Thus they began a seven-year existence of sustaining the Black freedom struggle in Mississippi through nurturing resistance among activists, offering innovative leadership to achieve the movement's goals, and providing novel ways to enhance the quality of life for Black Mississippians.

Members of Womanpower were in tune with Black women's specific needs and structured the organization to reflect these needs. Many male leaders of the era marginalized women. This was evident in the cases of men who were active in civil rights organizations yet believed that their wives should not be involved, as well as ministers who presided over largely female congregations yet maintained a hierarchy of leadership composed primarily of men. Additionally, the threat of economic retaliation from whites prevented the involvement of some women whose families depended upon their financial support. Womanpower recognized how women's marginalization due to their gender or tenuous economic status affected their ability to become involved in the movement. Members were aware of how these forms of oppression interacted to affect Black women's lives, and they created a "safe space" for women to address and work to subvert these obstacles. Womanpower empowered women by bringing them out of their "homes, local churches, and club groups" and encouraging and teaching them how to become agents of change within their communities and the larger society. Womanpower members created a forum that welcomed and encouraged Black women's participation on all levels, covertly and overtly.

Womanpower members who were not hindered by their economic position were aware of their unique status as economically independent, "comfortable," or securely employed, and they used this to the advantage of their communities. They did not distance themselves from the hardships other Blacks faced simply because they had achieved economic success. Instead they advocated group survival and, like their activist predecessors, worked to create opportunities for all members of the community to live as full citizens. This affluence proved to be a tremendous advantage for the organization itself. As business owners and/or others who were economically privileged, some members were well suited to contribute necessary resources. Unlike other civil rights organizations such as the NAACP and SNCC, WU had no paid staff, and the resources provided to this wholly volunteer organization were critical. Harvey's and Sanders's businesses were used as places to hold meetings and disseminate information, while Harvey also provided office supplies. A. M. E. Logan, whose work as a salesperson required that she own a car, served as a key provider of transportation for civil rights activists, as did member Ineva May-Pittman.[103] Logan commented that she drove for the movement so much that she wore out a brand-new station wagon.[104]

Harvey, Logan, Sanders, and Mosley were key to generating participation, particularly among middle-class Blacks in Jackson, who were hesitant about becoming involved in the movement. Operating businesses in the two primary Black business districts, the Farish Street and Lynch Street corridors, which became two of the central organizing locations for the movement, placed all of these women in the center of Black life.[105] Additionally, all of them were involved in their respective churches and, consequently, had connections to many Blacks that spanned socioeconomic backgrounds. These connections allowed them to enlist the support of numerous people, regardless of class, and added many new recruits to the movement. They brought legitimacy to movement participation for the Black middle class, and their visibility in the community positioned Womanpower to set an example of race uplift that was embraced and emulated by Black women throughout the city.

Thelma Sanders's dynamited car, 1964. Courtesy of William "Bo" Brown.

Clarie Collins Harvey's wedding, 1939. Photograph by Beadle Studios. Courtesy of the Clarie Collins Harvey Collection, Amistad Research Center, Tulane University.

Clarie Collins Harvey. Photograph by Horrell Photography. Courtesy of the Clarie Collins Harvey Collection, Amistad Research Center, Tulane University.

Mary Augusta Collins, Annette Collins Rollins, Clarie Collins Harvey, late 1960s, Los Angeles, California. Courtesy of Annette Collins Rollins.

A. M. E. Logan, ca. 1960s. Courtesy
of Shirley Logan Montague.

A. M. E. Logan at street-renaming ceremony in her honor, 2010, Jackson, Mississippi.
Photograph by Daphne Chamberlain. Courtesy of Daphne Chamberlain.

Thelma Sanders, 1969. Courtesy of William "Bo" Brown.

Sanders Boutique, early 1970s. Courtesy of William "Bo" Brown.

Thelma and I. S. Sanders, 1975. Courtesy of William "Bo" Brown.

Inside Sanders Boutique, 1975. Courtesy of William "Bo" Brown.

Womanpower Unlimited. *Left to right*: Clarie Collins Harvey, Thelma Sanders, Artishia W. Jordan, A. M. E. Logan, Ruth O. Hubert, R. Arline Young, fall 1961. Courtesy of the Clarie Collins Harvey Collection, Amistad Research Center, Tulane University.

Jane Schutt speaking at the Civil Rights Advisory Board's Police Brutality Hearings, Jackson, Mississippi, January 1962. Image capture by Paul Naughton, WLBT Newsfilm Collection. Courtesy of the Mississippi Department of Archives and History.

Claire Collins Harvey (*right*) seeing Dora Wilson off for her trip to The Hague to attend the Multinational Peace Rally and Demonstration as a representative of Womanpower Unlimited and Women Strike for Peace, May 1964. Courtesy of Dora Wilson.

Clarie Collins Harvey, Francis Herring, Nancy Mamis, and Selma Sparks in Accra, Ghana, representing Women Strike for Peace at the World without the Bomb Conference, 1962. Courtesy of the Clarie Collins Harvey Collection, Amistad Research Center, Tulane University.

Women Strike for Peace Vatican Pilgrimage, April 24, 1963. Clarie Collins Harvey and Therese Casgrain. Courtesy of Virginia Naeve.

Ineva May-Pittman, Jackson City Council Meeting, May 2013. Photograph by Jay Johnson. Courtesy of Jay Johnson.

Meeting with Gov. Ray Mabus (seated) during The Box Project Twenty-Fifth Anniversary Celebration. *Left to right*: Nancy Normen, executive director; Odell Durham, field consultant; Rosie Redmond Holden, Womanpower member; Jean Griffen; Jean's daughter; Mamie Harper; Amy Parsons; Diane Parsons; Betty Harper; Baby Harper; and Virginia Naeve, Box Project founder. 1988. Courtesy of Virginia Naeve.

CHAPTER THREE

"'Cause I Love My People"
Sustaining the People and the Movement

Many a heroine of whom the world will never hear has thus
sacrificed her life to her race amid surroundings and in the face of
privations which only martyrs can bear.
—Mary Church Terrell

And survival is the greatest gift of love. Sometimes, for Black
mothers, it is the only gift possible.
—Audre Lorde

The year 1961 marked the beginning of a new phase of civil rights activism
in Jackson. The courage and determination of the Freedom Riders generated
broad support for the civil rights movement. These young pioneers helped
catalyze local Black women activists as they incubated a brand-new organization that galvanized the base and marshaled further resources: Womanpower
Unlimited. Its founding members supported other civil rights organizations
and projects and simultaneously created their own while establishing a nationwide network of movement supporters.

Although Womanpower initially organized itself around the narrowly defined mission of meeting the Freedom Riders' most immediate needs, its activism soon expanded to other initiatives, including voter registration and school
desegregation. Womanpower members employed activist mothering and
women's empowerment to sustain the developing movement, working in conjunction with other emerging movements and organizations in Jackson such as
the Jackson Nonviolent Movement (JNM), another organization that grew out
of the Freedom Rides; the Council of Federated Organizations; and the Jackson
Movement, spearheaded by John Salter and Medgar Evers. They filled the gaps

created by the quickly evolving and expanding movement and asserted their leadership in initiatives they deemed central to Black advancement.

Organized primarily by SNCC activists, the Jackson Nonviolent Movement capitalized on the increasing desire for activism among youth by focusing on direct action protests in the capital city. Local youth had begun their own direct action campaigns by the summer of 1961. For example, members of the NAACP Youth Council and College chapter, one of whom was Logan's fifteen-year-old son Willis, were arrested in June for a sit-in at the city zoo.[1] Diane Nash, James Bevel, and Bernard Lafayette, all of whom were central to the Nashville sit-ins, remained in Jackson following the Freedom Rides to develop and lead the JNM. The group challenged segregation and integrated public facilities through nonviolent direct action protests and participation in boycotts of the segregated state fair and buses.[2] Capitalizing on the desire of local high school and college students to become more involved in direct action, both the JNM and the Jackson Movement were built upon the willingness of Black youth to openly challenge the city's segregationist policies and disrespectful treatment of Blacks. Womanpower members worked with the JNM from its inception in July 1961 until its dissolution in the summer of 1962 disseminating information about the boycotts, encouraging participation among their peers, promoting voter registration, and sponsoring workshops on nonviolence.[3]

In February 1962, Bob Moses of SNCC, Tom Gaither of CORE, and Aaron Henry and Medgar Evers of the NAACP reorganized the Council of Federated Organizations to unify state and national civil rights groups; local ones, such as county voters leagues, that were emerging throughout Mississippi; and social and fraternal organizations.[4] State NAACP leaders created the initial COFO the previous year as a cover for a meeting concerning the release of the Freedom Riders, with Governor Ross Barnett, who was not keen on the NAACP.[5] The revived COFO, for which Henry served as president, Moses as program director, and Dave Dennis (CORE) as assistant director, created a collaborative base that was necessary for a successful movement in Mississippi. To a degree, it minimized the competition for geographical strength and support from the masses that existed among the major civil rights organizations. Although the SCLC and the state NAACP were also members of COFO, SNCC and CORE were the most influential in the organization.

In its capacity as an umbrella organization, COFO's efforts included organizing voter registration campaigns, the Freedom Vote in the fall of 1963, and the Mississippi Summer Project (Freedom Summer) in 1964. COFO began its work in Mississippi with a focus on voter registration and with financial support from the Voter Education Project (VEP) of the Southern Regional Council.[6] The Voter Education Project grew out of the Kennedy administration's attempt to foster a "cooling-off" period following the chaos of the Freedom Rides. President Kennedy hoped to direct civil rights activity toward an issue that he believed would generate less confrontation and violence—voter registration. By endorsing voter registration, the Kennedy administration believed it could support civil rights without losing the southern white support necessary for its foreign policy. Through meetings with administration officials, civil rights groups, and representatives from major foundations, including the Taconic Fund and the Field Foundation, the VEP was founded to help fund nonpartisan voter education and registration efforts of civil rights groups. Additionally, the VEP was designed to investigate problems encountered by Blacks attempting voter registration. Although the civil rights activists were suspicious of the administration's true intentions, they were nevertheless prepared to undertake voter registration efforts and welcomed additional funding from other sources. Wiley Branton, a Black attorney from Arkansas who worked on the Little Rock desegregation case, was the first director of the VEP.[7] SNCC was responsible for organizing four of Mississippi's five congressional districts, including District 3, where Jackson was located; CORE coordinated efforts in District 4.

Before it disbanded in the summer of 1965, COFO relied heavily on the support of Womanpower Unlimited. While technically a member, given COFO's desire to include all civil rights organizations working in the state, Womanpower initially was not involved in any planning or decision-making capacity with COFO.

The Jackson Movement began in the fall of 1962, on the heels of the JNM's cessation. Writer M. J. O'Brien aptly describes it as "the confluence of varied forces and personalities that by synchronistic convergence found themselves pushing in the same direction for social change."[8] Drawing largely on youth support, the movement was spearheaded by Medgar Evers of the NAACP and John Salter, adviser to the North Jackson Youth Council and a sociology professor at Tougaloo. In the months preceding the emergence of the Jackson Movement, Evers had been responding increasingly more positively to NAACP youth members' desires for increased direct action, in spite of the national organization's resistance to such efforts. Meanwhile, Salter's students had recruited him to advise the Jackson Youth Council. In the fall of 1961, during his first semester at Tougaloo, the twentysomething Salter was approached after class by one of his students, Colia Lidell, the NAACP Youth Council president, with a request that he speak at their next community meeting. Salter accepted the invitation. Soon after this community meeting Lidell asked Salter to serve as the Youth Council's adviser, to which he consented as well.[9] At the start of the next academic year, the Jackson Movement began its efforts in earnest to attack segregation in the state's capital head-on.

Between the summer of 1961 and the summer of 1964, each of these local movements relied upon each other and was mutually reinforcing of the other's projects, which built support in various segments of the Jackson community. This cross-section of Black support was key to sustaining the local movement. During this period, Womanpower collaborated with these movements and implemented their own independent projects for Black advancement.

After the Freedom Rides, Womanpower Unlimited immediately directed its energy toward voter education, registration, and participation, one of the priorities of the movement in Mississippi, and then to the Jackson Movement's boycott campaigns.[10] Politics was an area that warranted mass efforts because Blacks continued to encounter the problems of discrimination that had existed in the early decades of the century.

Getting Out the Vote

Voter registration had always been a program that could draw broad support from a variety of individuals.[11] Black activists saw the vote as a necessary key to freedom, inclusion, and the actualization of Blacks' attainment of full citizenship rights. As argued by Dr. Martin Luther King Jr. and others, "the achievement of such other goals as school integration, decent housing, job opportunities, and integrated public transportation was closely tied to the Negro masses' having the right to vote."[12] Voting would allow Blacks to influence the legislative branch of the state government, theoretically resulting in improved conditions and opportunities for Blacks.

This approach was not an unfamiliar strategy for women activists. Black women have a solid history of political activism that includes suffrage issues that extend beyond the simple act of voting. In an examination of Reconstruction-era politics in the South, historian Elsa Barkley Brown noted that Black women's political history does not focus solely on the "legally granted franchise" but is much more implicit, involving a variety of participation in both internal and external political arenas. She argued that despite their disfranchisement, Black women had the power to affect the vote and political decisions. Although their participation in political meetings may not have always been welcome, Black women maintained an active presence even when the issue of women's suffrage was not the topic of discussion. Furthermore, Brown asserted that in many Black communities, both women and men understood men's voting rights as a collective possession.[13] Brown demonstrated Black women's longstanding interest in the Black vote. Prior to the national enfranchisement of women with the passage of the Nineteenth Amendment in 1920, Black women were active voters in states such as New York, Colorado, and Illinois and were aggressively involved in the fight for their suffrage. Particularly through the established order of the National Association of Colored Women, "Black women organized voter-education clubs, gathered and presented petitions, voted in those states where they had the franchise, and were effective in political campaigns."[14] Despite the political limitations imposed upon them, Black women sought all available means to assert their opinions in politics, for they believed that political activism was a key source of empowerment.

Black women activists, like those in the NACW and WU, perceived the vote to be advantageous in protecting their rights as both women and Blacks. They alleged that voting would lead to an end to Black women's sexual exploitation, foster advances in education, and provide protection for Black labor. Moreover, they believed that the vote would lead to improvements for the Black community as a whole.[15] These earlier generations of activists knew they had a responsibility to act in accordance with the best interests of the race and believed that they had previously done so. Anna Julia Cooper captured this idea in 1892 when commenting on Black women's commitment to race uplift. She wrote, "Her voice, too, has always been heard in clear, unfaltering tones, ringing the changes on those deeper interests which make for permanent good. She is always sound and orthodox on questions affecting the well-being of her race. . . . It is largely our women in the South to-day who keep the black men solid in the Republican party."[16] Cooper and many of her contemporaries believed that Black women, who tended to act in accordance with the best interests of the race, provided the solid foundation necessary for racial progress.

In addition to joining (or in some cases attempting to join) organizations such as the National American Woman Suffrage Association and the League of Women Voters, Black women created their own organizations and their own means of educating women and generating political participation. By the 1900s, there were Black suffrage clubs and state suffrage societies in all regions of the country, from Tuskegee to Los Angeles and from Montana to New York.[17] Through these collective associations, Black women added a strong force to the suffrage movement and to political campaigns, asserting their voice and demanding to be heard.[18]

The ratification of the Nineteenth Amendment gave impetus to Black women's desire for increased opportunity, and they easily incorporated the task of electoral politics into their agenda. Consistent with attempts to exclude them from the Nineteenth Amendment, however, Black women were subjected to discrimination aimed at disfranchising them immediately after its ratification. In the South especially, Black women attempting to register and vote faced blatant discrimination. For example, in Columbia, South Carolina, property tax receipts worth at least $300 were declared mandatory in order for Black women to register to vote. Similar tactics were employed in other southern states, and despite assistance from the NAACP and appeals for assistance from white women's organizations like the National Women's Party, Black women were successfully disenfranchised within a decade of the passage of the Nineteenth Amendment.[19] This discrimination only increased Black women's political activism.

The connection between the NACW and voting was further cemented when the Republican National Committee enlisted outgoing president Hallie Q. Brown to direct its voter drive among Black women in 1924.[20] This maneuver connected Calvin Coolidge and the Republican National Committee to the political consciousness of thousands of Black women and placed these women on the front lines of partisan politics. Although politicians such as Coolidge may not have been genuinely concerned with Black women's issues, they realized the power that Black women voters held and wanted to position themselves to benefit from it.[21] Along with improved access to the American political process came increased involvement as "Black women's Republican clubs sprang up everywhere—led by clubwomen already in the vanguard of the civic and political affairs of their communities."[22] Clarie Collins Harvey continued this tradition by working to maintain a connection between Black women and political affairs.

Voter registration and electoral politics were certainly nothing new to Harvey, who had long been aware of the potential power of choice and representation held by the vote; it was a lesson she learned from her mother, Mary Collins. In a 1955 letter to the members of the Mississippi State Federation of Colored Women's Clubs, Mary Collins, then chair of the Department of Civics, reported, "many club members are not exercising their privilege of voting. In a broadcast following our Gubernatorial election, you perhaps heard the commentator say that the Negro Voters did not bother themselves about going to the polls. *Let this not be said about us again.* The ballot is our greatest weapon. Let us use it!!!"[23] Harvey followed in her mother's footsteps and advocated similar beliefs about empowerment through her organizational affiliations. It was not until her organization of Womanpower Unlimited that she was able to establish a full-fledged program to address issues with respect to the Black vote, a tool that she believed was severely underutilized.

Womanpower coordinated its voter registration efforts with other civil rights organizations and maintained an independent initiative funded by the Voter Education Project. In the fall of 1961, WU began its collaborative efforts with the Jackson Progressive Voters' League, a nonpartisan group organized in the late 1940s to encourage and assist Blacks in becoming registered voters. With the assistance of the Voters' League, whose secretary was Womanpower's director of publicity, Essie Randall, WU conducted weekly voter registration/education workshops at the Farish Street Baptist Church and reactivated certain precincts.[24] These classes were essential to the voter registration effort. In addition to providing potential voters with instructions on how to fill out the registration form, the workshops informed Blacks that voting was an act of American citizenship that they rightfully possessed and were being unjustly denied. These organizations hoped to convey the potential power and opportunity that voting could afford their communities.

This collaborative endeavor soon resulted in the establishment of the Jackson Voter Education Coordinating Committee, which served to create a single plan for Black voter education and registration in the greater Jackson area. In January 1962, this Coordinating Committee, comprised of Womanpower Unlimited, the Voters' League, and the NAACP, among others, opened an office at 538½ North Farish Street, staffed by Evelyn L. King from 9:30 a.m. to 9:00 p.m. Hoping to reach larger numbers of Blacks by pooling their resources, the Coordinating Committee sought to educate Blacks on the importance of the vote and its proper use. Furthermore, through workshops, they instructed people on how to complete registration forms, how to interpret the constitution (as required by the infamous question 19 on the Voter Registration Form, which asked applicants to write a "reasonable interpretation [the meaning] of the Section of the Constitution of Mississippi which you have just copied"), and trained others to assist in these efforts. The office served as a location where people could pay their two-dollar poll tax so they would not have to go to the sheriff's office to do so.[25] By the end of the organization's second month, it had collected poll taxes for just over three hundred people.[26]

By the spring of 1962, Womanpower considered that its work with the Voters' League and the Coordinating Committee had equipped it with the knowledge and practical experience necessary to undertake its own program of voter registration directed primarily at women. The organization applied to the Voter Education Project for $1,250 to support its endeavor, which included hiring someone "to organize and train women in Hinds County communities for registering and voting."[27] The VEP awarded Womanpower a grant of $1,000 for a three-month period beginning August 1, 1962. By August they had opened a Voter Education Office in Womanpower's office in the Masonic Temple, replacing the Coordinating Committee's office that closed in July.[28] As stated in Womanpower's final report to the VEP, "the unique goal of this special project was to create an awareness among women for social action in the community especially as it relates to registering and voting."[29] Harvey argued that WU would be best suited for such an undertaking "because of fear or other reasons, many women prefer not to identify with major organizations as NAACP, CORE, Non-Violent Movements. For them, Womanpower Unlimited offers an opportunity for social expression without stigma."[30] Harvey's remarks highlight the safe space for Black women that she envisioned Womanpower Unlimited providing.

The method employed for Womanpower's voter registration campaign was to contact prominent community women and enlist their support in organizing a group of women to whom Womanpower representatives could speak. They initially hired Carolyn Tyler to coordinate this effort. Tyler was a native Mississippian born in Jackson in 1937. After high school, Tyler enrolled at J. P. Campbell College and earned a degree in business and secretarial science. After college, she worked as Reverend R. L. T. Smith's office manager for his campaign and as the women's voter registration chair with the NAACP, working closely with Medgar Evers. With this experience, coupled with the fact that A. M. E. Logan was her mentor through the church, Tyler was an ideal person to oversee Womanpower's voter registration project.[31]

Unfortunately, after working in this capacity for one week, Tyler resigned to take a permanent position at Tougaloo College, while volunteering her secretarial services to WU on weekends. During her brief time in the position she organized the office, made contact with nineteen women, attended two conferences, and produced literature on the project and Womanpower Unlimited. This is indicative of the level of work undertaken by Womanpower members. Tyler's position remained vacant for just ten days until A. M. E. Logan, Womanpower's administrative secretary, accepted the responsibility. Logan was ideally suited for the job, particularly given her comfort level with its travel and networking requirements. Under Logan's direction, Womanpower set up units in Jackson and surrounding areas (Clinton, Bolton, Crystal Springs, Canton, Brandon, Hazlehurst, and Gluckstadt) to carry out the program of organization, education, registration, and voting. By using local communities' established organizations, such as churches, civic clubs, and neighborhood groups, this process reached large numbers of women and received the endorsement of community leaders, giving it more credence.

Logan arranged meetings at women's homes and encouraged them to undertake informal voter registration efforts in their neighborhoods. With these small collectives, Womanpower used established networks to encourage registration among acquaintances and friends. Logan personally kept in contact with many of the women involved. This proved particularly valuable in efforts to keep track of persons who were able to register. Whenever possible, Womanpower reported newly registered voters at their monthly meetings.

Larger audiences were made possible with the assistance of local churches. After attending a church service and presenting Womanpower's program for voter education and registration, Logan was often invited back to conduct a class. For example, as detailed in her October/November Field Report, on November 4, 1962, Logan attended services at Buckhorn M. B. Church in Canton, Mississippi, and spoke on Womanpower and voter registration. Later that afternoon, she addressed the congregation at Mount Pleasant M. B. Church in Gluckstadt. She was invited back that Wednesday to conduct a class on voter registration, and seventy-five to eighty people, ironically mostly men, attended.[32] By using a traditional civil rights strategy of organizing through the church, Womanpower spread the word about its philosophy and educated the community about the political process. As the project coordinator, Logan engaged in door-to-door canvassing, called people to encourage and remind them to register, and physically took people to register.[33]

Logan organized five Womanpower Units, four of which were in Jackson. Unit 1 was organized at the home of Essie Martin, with Annie Moore elected as chair. Unit 2, whose slogan was "Act Now," was organized at the home of Eva Bruhson. Earnestine Chess eventually took over this unit after the original chair, "Mrs. Knights would no longer have anything to do with WU because of fear."[34] Bessie Thomas and Rinda Warmack chaired Units 3 and 4, respectively. A Mrs. Johnson chaired the fifth unit that was organized in Gluckstadt with the assistance of Mrs. M. G. and Reverend Haughton.[35] Units held regular meetings that Logan typically attended to discuss voter registration and examine registration forms. Those present at meetings made commitments to try to register, shared their experiences, and pledged to encourage neighbors to register. Unit chairs followed up on individuals' promises to register, convened meetings, organized classes to instruct people on the registration process, and urged women to address "community problems."[36]

Womanpower Unlimited sponsored workshops for the general public. On September 8, 1962, WU held a daylong Voter Registration Workshop at the Masonic Temple. Harvey began the workshop at 9:30 a.m. with an opening statement that was followed by sessions on "Qualification for registration," "The registration process," "The poll tax," "Techniques of registration and poll tax payment," "The election process," and "Recent developments and suggestions for action." Harvey, Logan, and attorney William Higgs made the closing statements.[37] WU provided an extensive discussion of all aspects of the registration process to demystify it as much as possible, thereby empowering people to embrace their citizenship rights. As records of the final session indicate, they encouraged participation in the electoral process as one part of the movement's multipronged approach toward obtaining inclusion and equality for Blacks.

Despite Logan's efficiency as an organizer, Womanpower's voter education project did not always experience smooth sailing. In one instance, she noted that Elizabeth Powell of Crystal Springs was interested in hosting a meeting at her home but was unable to because of her husband.[38] While Logan's report does not provide details about the nature of Mr. Powell's resistance to such a meeting at his house, fear of losing his job is a likely reason. Undeterred by this setback, Logan eventually spoke at a late October meeting of the Crystal Springs Christmas Savings Club, garnering enthusiastic support.[39] On another occasion, Logan reported that one contact in Edwards rescinded an offer to hold a meeting at her house "because someone had told the law that she was coming to Jackson to learn how to teach others to register (she was, in fact, attending the Baptist seminary), and was called in question about this."[40] Womanpower operated in a climate of fear and intimidation that at times hindered its progress.

Mississippi was notorious for its resistance to Black enfranchisement. In addition to the "legal" measures such as poll tax requirements that restricted voter registration, Blacks had to contend with the harassment and brutality of white registrars, who were brazen in their outright refusal to register Blacks and use of violence (or the threat of it) to turn potential registrants away. Attempting to register in Jackson did not pose the same threats as it did for Blacks living in areas like Sunflower and Holmes Counties where individuals (and sometimes their relatives) were routinely fired from their jobs, beaten, or had shots fired into their houses. In the capital city, though, police brutality was a reality. It was not uncommon for individuals to be harassed for supposed affiliation with civil rights organizations. For example, Cornelius M. Johnson and a few of his friends were accosted by police while walking home one evening. He was accused of belonging to CORE or the NAACP and was slapped, arrested, and fined for mischief. His mother too was taken to the jail and fined for "interfering with the law" for attempting to defend her son.[41] Incidents like these prompted Medgar Evers to conclude that "police brutality had become the order of the day in Mississippi."[42] This climate of violence and possible economic retaliation was enough to keep many Blacks away from the courthouse.

Womanpower's voting rights campaign included more tangible services. Members worked on Reverend R. L. T. Smith's campaign during his 1962 bid for Congress. They played numerous roles, such as "speakers, as committee members, as fund raisers, as telephone chain contacts, as office workers, as poll watchers, and otherwise," expanding women's opportunities for leadership and activism.[43] Womanpower members assisted in taking people to register, making group transportation available to those in need and simultaneously "strengthening morale," thereby lessening common fears of the process or consequences of registration.[44]

Consistent with its philosophy of promoting women's activism for the betterment of the community, the nation, and the world, Womanpower encouraged women's participation as agents of influence in their own families' activism. When Harvey made her presentation to the Southern Regional Council, she argued that "women were the key to the voting issue, because the mother in the home not only could vote herself, but she could encourage her husband to vote, she certainly could teach her children the importance of citizenship; and so on the basis of this they granted us the funds."[45] Echoing the sentiments of Anna Julia Cooper and club women nearly seventy-five years earlier, Harvey emphasized that the perceived innately superior morality of women and the political influence Black women had within their households could yield positive results for Black political activism. Womanpower believed that stimulating women, who could positively use their "God-given powers of persuasion," would positively affect the registration and voting experiences of women themselves as well as their families.[46] Members' efforts capitalized on the resources available to them as women targeting a woman-dominated audience, for example, by organizing babysitting services and setting up telephone chains to disseminate information.

Womanpower reached approximately six hundred people through its Voter Education program, extending its work into December, two months longer than the funding provided by the VEP would last. Members ensured that people's poll taxes were paid and cited some instances of voter registration success, as in the case of Clarence Watson, who registered after two previous unsuccessful attempts.[47] Overall, the actual numbers of Black persons who registered and voted as a result of their efforts were relatively low. Neither Womanpower Unlimited nor the VEP believed these low numbers diminished the efforts of this essential, yet arduous, grassroots organizing strategy as it laid the groundwork for later voter registration campaigns and provided knowledge on how to educate Black communities about actualizing their citizenship rights through participation in electoral politics. Despite the information that they received in voter education classes, many Blacks still feared registering or remained apathetic—some fearing failure of passing the test and wanted to avoid being humiliated in that manner, particularly because of Question 19, which asked the applicant to interpret a section of the Mississippi state constitution chosen by the registrar. Others were unsure of the impact their vote could actually have on their lives. Additionally, Blacks who attempted to register were frequently discriminated against and intimidated, keeping the numbers low. Willie Brown, for instance, explained to Logan that on his first attempt to register, "he was treated so badly that he had not gone back again."[48] Efforts were further hampered by "innumerable fall revivals in the churches," which detracted from their audiences at times; people's desire not to be associated with the NAACP; the mistaken belief that WU's project was another NAACP program; and fallout from the "Meredith situation" (James Meredith's integration of the University of Mississippi).[49] Such setbacks did not prevent Womanpower from believing its efforts in voter registration were successful and worthwhile. In a 1965 interview, Harvey stated:

Now I wish I could report that we had howling success, we had absolutely numerically, statistically—we had a very limited amount of success, but we did accomplish this: we did give people courage and we got them thinking about registering and voting so somebody would be able to report a year later that they were able to get so many registered people. If we had not been able to get this spade work, really hard dirty spade work done, of getting people to see why they should register, the good results others had would not have been possible. . . . And so this was our particular contribution in that area.[50]

Although they did not achieve one of their stated goals of registering a significant portion of Blacks, they recognized how their activities added to the momentum of the movement and were in that sense a success. The Womanpower Units did not disband when the project ended, but were designed to continue their voter education efforts. Comparatively speaking, WU's registration numbers were consistent with other organizations in the state, and its perspective on success not being measured solely by these numbers was similar to the VEP's. The Second Annual Report of the Voter Education Project stated that Mississippi "presents more resistance to would-be Negro voters than any other state and offers more intimidation and violence to Negroes than all the others combined." The report continued that, despite the fact that the number of Black voters across the state of Mississippi was smaller than the number of those from small cities in other southern states, the $50,000 spent on voter registration efforts was successful in helping "to develop educational programs which will be most effective in providing voters with the knowledge and will to register."[51] Similarly, the types of efforts displayed by community women may not be viewed as successful endeavors on the surface. These activities within local communities should not be judged solely on quantitative measures of achieving a set goal but rather by their contributions to advancing the movement. By using the latter criterion one can conclude that Womanpower successfully contributed to this aspect of the movement by helping to eliminate some of the apathy and fear that prevented many from attempting to register.

If people were at least willing to attend the workshops or create a forum for Womanpower to address voting issues, they assisted the movement in raising people's consciousness, a precondition for movement participation and continuance. Womanpower's efforts changed more people's consciousness and, as a consequence, their behavior soon followed, giving momentum to the movement.

The Jackson Movement and the Council of Women's Organizations

One of the Jackson Movement's major projects was a boycott of downtown businesses. On the second anniversary of its founding, WU established the Council of Women's Organizations (CWO) to assist with this selective buying campaign. Womanpower reported that approximately two dozen organizations worked through the CWO to support the campaign, under the motto "sacrifice," until stores treated customers with respect through using courtesy titles and equal employment opportunities.[52] These were definitely issues that concerned Womanpower members as both Thelma Sanders and Jessie Mosley were entrepreneurs whose businesses were established in part as a response to this kind of discrimination.

Begun in earnest in late November 1962, at the beginning of the Christmas buying season, the boycott of downtown businesses was combined with picketing and door-to-door canvassing.[53] John Salter approached WU in December and asked members to help disseminate information about the boycott by calling prominent local residents, including public school teachers. Teachers were a particularly difficult group to reach because they feared losing their jobs.[54] Hazel Whitney, first lady of the Farish Street Baptist Church, recalled that "when we asked that they would stop going downtown, our biggest problem was with teachers."[55] Educators with the outspokenness of Gladys Noel Bates, who fifteen years earlier had brought suit against the state for equalization of Blacks' and whites' salaries, were atypical. Womanpower and other boycott supporters worked diligently to obtain the participation of this segment of the community. One strategy used to prevent teachers from breaking the boycott was to subject them to a barrage of telephone calls asking why they had crossed the picket line. WU member Ineva May-Pittman explained that teachers' names and phone numbers were given out at mass meetings, and the women made a schedule of who would call them every hour throughout the day and night to ask why they were shopping at the stores downtown. This proved effective in garnering participation by some members of the community.[56] And while gaining the support of teachers was difficult, Womanpower did have some success with women like Ineva May-Pittman, Mildred Williams, Pearl Draine, and Dorothy Stewart. These women demonstrate the diversity of Black women's experiences and the varied levels of participation among Womanpower members while simultaneously revealing the activist mothering that was common among women civil rights activists. Their activism reveals the commitment to race uplift that guided many Black women's activism.

Mildred Williams, a native of Grenada, Mississippi, was born in the 1920s, the daughter of a teacher and missionary worker and an artisan. Williams received her bachelor's degree from Jackson State College. During her tenure at the Tuskegee Institute, where she obtained her master's degree, she trained to be a Jeanes supervisor.[57] Her teaching career led her to rural Mississippi places such as Corinth, Greenville, and Oktibbeha County, where she served as Jeanes supervisor from 1947 to 1959.[58] Applying the Jeanes approach, Williams embraced a holistic pedagogy with her students, expressing concern for their well-being both inside and outside of the classroom. The Mississippi Department of Education hired Williams in 1961 as the first Black Assistant Supervisor of Elementary Education, and shortly thereafter promoted her to Supervisor of Early Childhood Education for the state. Because of her public visibility, Williams was cautious about openly displaying her civil rights activism. Her primary contribution to Womanpower came in the form of monetary donations, and she attended meetings when possible.[59] She was already connected to some of the women through her membership in the Mary Church Terrell Club. Like other Black middle-class members of Womanpower, she was keenly aware of her connection to the Black community and the Black freedom struggle, despite the unique class privilege she held.

Pearl Montgomery Draine was an educator who developed a more overt relationship with Womanpower. She was born in 1926 in Lexington, Mississippi, to sharecroppers Cora (Mayfield) and George Montgomery.[60] Despite the fact that the white landowner on whose farm her family worked told her that she could not attend school year-round because the cotton needed to be picked, her parents supported her quest for knowledge. She enrolled in Saints Industrial and Literary School in Lexington and worked her way through school. Upon graduation, Draine enrolled at Jackson State College, obtaining her bachelor's degree in education and social services in 1949. She became a teacher while continuing her own education, obtaining two master's degrees from Indiana University and one from the University of Missouri at Columbia. Her husband, Roosevelt Draine, whom she married in 1946, opened Draine Refrigeration in 1950. Pearl Draine taught elementary school in the Jackson Public School system, holding that job for seventeen years before resigning in 1966 to work full-time with the Child Development Group of Mississippi, an offshoot of the Head Start programs. When the Freedom Riders came to town, the Draines opened their home as well as their property across the street for the civil rights activists.[61] Undeterred by the possibility of losing her job, Draine overtly supported Womanpower and the movement. She was at least in part motivated by her own childhood experiences of poverty, discrimination, and white attempts to limit her opportunities.

Dorothy Stewart was younger than Williams and Draine and many other Womanpower members. Born Dorothy May Thompson in Vicksburg in 1938, she was the daughter of Mabel, a housekeeper and domestic worker, and K. D. Thompson, a laborer and millworker. She grew up in the Jackson suburb of Clinton. After graduating from Holy Ghost Catholic High School, Dorothy Thompson attended Jackson State. A month after obtaining her bachelor's degree in history and social studies education in May 1960, she married Peter H. Stewart. The following year, she embarked upon her teaching career at Lanier High School in the Jackson Public School system. Stewart recalled that her earliest involvement in the movement was inspired by her neighbors on Ash Street, Womanpower members Geneva Blalock and Francis Britton (the wife of civil rights activist and Jackson physician Dr. A. B. Britton), who encouraged her to get involved. Her work with youth through the YWCA alongside Lillie Bell Jones provided a natural segue to working with this group of women.[62]

Notwithstanding the hesitancy of many teachers, the Council of Women's Organizations (CWO) effectively mobilized support with the involvement of women like these. These women were central to efforts to recruit other teachers and gave legitimacy to movement activism. Salter emphasized Harvey's and the CWO's role: "Her important business and professional contacts in the Black community were of great value within our very broad array of boycott support forces which, although mostly stemming from, and centered on Jackson, also included surrounding rural counties and potential shoppers in those settings. Her fine efforts in that general contact vein were one of the major strains in the [CWO]. . . . She displayed much enduring courage indeed as she ran many risks, over those very tough and sanguinary years, for the Cause."[63] Womanpower members also offered instrumental support to Medgar Evers. Just as they offered emotional and spiritual sustenance to activists from outside the state, they provided similar assistance to local leaders. Salter recalls that many teachers who lived in Evers's neighborhood "would scarcely talk to him—they were scared to death to even see him" for fear that associating with him would result in the loss of their jobs.[64] Yet, among the leadership of Womanpower, he found confidants, comrades, and friends. Shirley Montague, A. M. E. Logan's daughter, recalled that Medgar Evers took her to the courthouse to register to vote.[65] And, according to Salter, Harvey, who provided the service for his funeral, "was a very important support person all the way through for [Evers]."[66]

The boycott continued with subdued support from activists both within and outside the state. Internally, many CORE and SNCC workers were slow to support it because of their skepticism of Salter (whose Native American heritage was mistaken for white) or because of their involvement in other civil rights projects already underway. The national NAACP's hesitancy to endorse direct action was the reason behind its lackluster support. This all changed in May 1963, when the SCLC began to garner national and international attention for Project-C in Birmingham.[67] To avoid being overshadowed by the SCLC, the NAACP offered its full resources to the Jackson boycott and in doing so inspired greater support from local activists. Unfortunately, the New York leaders of the NAACP who converged on Mississippi interrupted the movement's momentum by assuming the leadership of the Jackson Movement and, along with conservative, local ministers, displacing both Salter and Evers. After Evers's assassination, demonstrations were halted to negotiate with the mayor. In addition, scholar Steven D. Classen explains that "in the days following the murder and Evers's funeral, 'go slow' forces with the NAACP and the Kennedy administration employed successful strategies to curtail the movement's sustained confrontation campaigns."[68] The conservative local leadership agreed to the mayor's "concessions," which included none of the Jackson Movement's major demands and which the mayor failed to follow through on.[69]

At an NAACP mass meeting in June 1963, Harvey was scheduled to report on the selective buying campaign. She was one of twelve speakers for the evening and was, for not the first time, the only woman on the program.[70] Although the selective buying campaign officially ended that month, Womanpower continued to urge people not to patronize downtown businesses well into the fall.[71] Womanpower's Council of Women's Organizations provided a model of sacrifice for the community to follow. Its members offered instrumental support for the campaign, demonstrating an allegiance not to specific organizations but to the movement itself—a position that would have served other civil rights organizations well.

By the end of June, the Movement's momentum had decreased drastically. Saddened by Evers's death and demoralized by the ministers' "compromise," many workers departed Jackson to work in other parts of the state. Salter, too, left Jackson for North Carolina to work with the Southern Conference Educational Fund. The Jackson Movement resumed in the fall, although much subdued, as Tougaloo students attempted to integrate local churches; assisted with COFO's Freedom Vote; and recommended the boycott during the Christmas buying season. The Jackson Movement officially came to a close in July 1964, with the implementation of the Civil Rights Act of 1964, and energies were directed toward the movement's next major undertaking—the Mississippi Summer Project.[72]

Freedom Summer

As 1964 and 1965 were the zenith of civil rights activism in Mississippi, Womanpower activists responded accordingly. While developing its own programs, Womanpower continued to provide considerable assistance for the activities of other civil rights organizations. One such project was Freedom Summer in 1964, which brought hundreds of volunteers to the state who required housing and other support. Learning from the experience with the Freedom Riders, Womanpower Unlimited was aware of the positive impact that moral and material support (no matter how minimal) had on civil rights activists. They declared, "visitors working here in the Jackson community MUST feel our support of their efforts."[73] Womanpower members felt an obligation to sustain the civil rights workers in their state because they knew that, by doing so, they were sustaining the movement. Although not involved in organizing for the Summer Project, Womanpower contributed in a variety of ways, from disseminating information to housing workers.

Freedom Summer was designed with the primary goals of bringing national attention to the state, getting people registered to vote, and organizing Freedom Schools and community centers.[74] In so doing, civil rights activists hoped to focus attention on the plight of Blacks in Mississippi and to engender federal intervention for their protection and proper inclusion in America's political, economic, and social systems. In addition to campaigning for voter registration and political education, Freedom Summer organizers hoped to solicit support for the newly formed Mississippi Freedom Democratic Party (MFDP), an independent organization founded to provide an alternative to the standard Jim Crow Democratic gatherings and to challenge the all-white Democratic Party delegation. Freedom Schools, the brainchild of SNCC activist Charles Cobb, were designed to improve the education of rural Black youth and raise their political consciousness by administering a curriculum focused on basic educational material as well as Black history. The community centers provided some of the basic needs of Blacks that had been ignored by social services, such as job training and prenatal care programs, as well as extracurricular activities for students. Consistent with its reputation for conducting grassroots operations, as the primary organizer of Freedom Summer through COFO, SNCC drew on the support of other organizations and individuals and commenced a program to organize, educate, and empower Black Mississippians.

Womanpower leaders regarded their exclusion from the planning as a definite oversight on COFO's part. In a report to the U.S. Commission on Civil Rights, Harvey noted that "a better job might have been done, from our viewpoint of housing, feeding, schools, etc., had COFO in its initial planning and continued programming included some of the Womanpower Unlimited ladies and other women and men of the community."[75] This was likely an innocent oversight by the organizers, as COFO did not engage in much organizing in Jackson. In fact, some of the planners were from outside the state and simply did not know that the organization existed. Surely the NAACP would have known about Womanpower, but its leadership was not centrally involved in the planning process either.[76] Once plans were fully in place, COFO reached out to Womanpower for assistance in several ways and Womanpower offered the project its full support. Between April and June 1964, Womanpower held meetings that COFO members attended "for the purpose of helping us learn something of the nature of the project so that we might know personally some of those responsible for its planning and implementation and that they might know us and further to determine some of the needs that WU might assist in fulfilling."[77] The Summer Project appealed to Womanpower because its primary foci were initiatives that Womanpower had worked on, such as voter registration and community development. The reliance on interracial cooperation was a likely bonus for Womanpower because it too was a strategy its leaders believed was integral to effecting change.

A significant portion of the volunteers for the Summer Project was recruited from predominantly white colleges and universities across the country. The use of these students was fundamental to accomplishing the goal of gaining national coverage. As explained by the CORE director for Mississippi and assistant project coordinator, Dave Dennis, "if we had brought in a thousand blacks, the country would have watched them slaughtered without doing anything about it. Bring a thousand whites and the country is going to react . . . to protect. . . . If there were gonna take some deaths to do it, the death of a white college student would bring on more attention to what was going on than for a black college student getting it. That's cold, but that was also in another sense speaking the language of this country."[78] Whites were sought after for "strategy impact." Yes, volunteers were needed, but white volunteers provided a special edge. As the "sons and daughters of America," they were sure to provoke a national response.

Another reason that the majority of volunteers were white students is because they were just that, volunteers. Volunteering required that one be able to financially support oneself through the summer and provide one's own transportation to and from Mississippi, along with money for housing and possibly bail. As most of the white volunteers were upper-middle-class college students, the issue of money was not a major concern for them.

With sponsorship from the National Council of Churches, COFO held two-week-long training sessions at Western College for Women in Oxford, Ohio, where volunteers learned about nonviolence and were warned about the dangerous summer they would face in Mississippi. COFO invited WU members A. M. E. Logan, Ineva May-Pittman, and Marcia Hall to assist in this training and educate volunteers about the conditions in Mississippi and also about the movement.[79] The volunteers were informed that they would lack certain rights in Mississippi and that they were risking their lives. Most frighteningly, they were told that there was no federal police force to offer protection and that the FBI merely served as an investigative branch of law enforcement. In light of the "disappearance" of James Chaney, Mickey Schwerner, and Andrew Goodman, the second group of volunteers was prepared for the possibility of death.

Hundreds of people, both Black and white, sojourned to and emerged from within Mississippi to reach the grassroots communities and uplift the masses of people who had been neglected, dispossessed, and disconnected. They were joined together by the common goal of fighting for consciousness raising among Blacks, fostering democracy, and fighting for quality of life issues. Civil rights workers sought to uplift Black Mississippians from an essentially "slave type existence" to a life where they had "a decent house, a decent education, a decent job and [those] kinds of things [they] did not have."[80]

Womanpower made significant contributions of housing and food to support the Freedom Summer volunteers. Rosie Redmond, who succeeded Thelma Sanders in chairing WU's Housing and Hospitality Committee, and said she joined Womanpower "'cause I love my people and I wanted to see them get what belonged to them," coordinated these services.[81] The group continued its efforts of subsidizing local housing by supplying material for four Freedom Houses in Jackson, which provided cost-free housing for civil rights volunteers. Womanpower members raised funds and mobilized donations to furnish the Freedom Houses and stock them with linens and food. They provided accommodations in their own homes and sought additional space from friends. Jane Schutt, for example, provided housing for Howard Romaine, a native of Louisiana and recent college graduate, and other volunteers for the White Folks Project, the Biloxi-based component of the Mississippi Summer Project that focused on organizing in white communities. In these homes, volunteers received comfort, support, and encouragement for their activism. Romaine recalled that staying at Schutt's house was like being at home and that "she was like some aunt or godmother."[82] Again, propelled by a commitment to activist mothering, Womanpower members expressed a genuine sense of caring for the volunteers and attempted to provide them with the physical and emotional sustenance to withstand the brutality of challenging Jim Crow Mississippi.

Feeding the activists was another responsibility Womanpower assumed. Initially, "hot meals were served to the project workers at the COFO office during June and July."[83] Monetary and food donations from Jacksonians as well as from members of the Womanpower Chain of Friendship outside the state funded this operation. In July, Womanpower established a formal Community Food Project in partnership with Reverend S. L. Whitney, pastor of the Farish Street Baptist Church, where meals were served daily. Approximately eighty-five people per day were served until the end of August.[84] The approximately fifty COFO staff and volunteers in Jackson, who coordinated the Summer Project out of the headquarters on Lynch Street, engaged in voter registration, and staffed the city's Freedom School, likely comprised the majority of those being fed at the church. In addition to the COFO workers, other local activists took advantage of the Food Program, including attorneys in town working with the National Lawyers Guild and the NAACP Legal Defense Fund to defend the movement workers; and members of the Medical Committee for Human Rights, organized by a group of doctors in June to provide and/or pay for medical care for activists in the state and work to improve the quality and care available to Blacks.[85] Womanpower encouraged community involvement in this program by requesting that individuals and organizations volunteer to sponsor certain days.[86] This served the dual purpose of sharing the financial and "womanpower" costs as well as providing an opportunity for community members to interact with the civil rights workers. Womanpower supplied the Freedom Houses and Freedom Schools with snacks, breakfast foods, and fresh fruit. This was of particular importance to Harvey, who practiced a holistic lifestyle of healthy eating and exercise. In recalling her caretaking of the

Freedom Riders, A. M. E. Logan remembered cooking for the young people who otherwise would have been eating "cheese and crackers" or other "little junk."[87] Providing the activists healthy and nutritious meals was a priority for the women, as they envisioned this as a component of their nurturing as a form of resistance.

The Chain of Friendship was key for raising money to support these programs. Local organizations, neighborhood associations, and allies from outside the state generated funds. Members "Mrs Rosie Mitchell and Mrs Young secured $60 on August 13, 1964 from the Veterans' Administration Employees and Neighbors on Randall Street" for Womanpower.[88] And Virginia Naeve, whom Harvey had met in 1962 while traveling to Geneva, Switzerland, with Women Strike for Peace, had been collaborating with her on civil rights issues and generated an abundance of resources for Freedom Summer workers. Naeve hosted a Civil Rights Fair at her Connecticut home in July for which admission was food or clothing or items for auction. Proceeds were intended for "Tuition assistance for Negro students; help for a farming cooperative in a depressed area; help for a Community Center which houses a Freedom School, library, sewing center, etc.; [and] help for a cooperative sandal-making project in a depressed area."[89] At the end of the day, Naeve had raised approximately $1,100 and collected enough clothes for 250 boxes, which she had visitors mail — visitors to the Naeve residence often left with a wrapped and addressed box that they were asked to take financial responsibility for mailing.[90] Because of her relationship with Harvey, Naeve was well informed about material needs within the movement. She sent packages to families and to specific activists. In one letter to Harvey, Naeve recounted that they "made up a gigantic box of clothing for Sam Block in Greenwood for school. . . . Also sent him the last $50 we had for a vacation as the N.Y. team of doctors who came down said he had to get away or collapse."[91] Naeve's donations were spread across the state and included the Meridian Community Center (in memory of Chaney, Schwerner, and Goodman); Aaron Henry for the Clarksdale Project Center; the COFO centers in Hattiesburg and Greenwood; the Free Southern Theater; and of course Womanpower Unlimited.[92] The financial assistance supplied by Womanpower's contacts provided a much-needed supplement to the strained COFO resources.

For the Freedom Schools, WU provided library books, school supplies, and transportation for some of the students. One of them, Alice Jackson (Wright), who wrote the oft-cited poem "Mine," stayed with Harvey while she attended the Freedom School.[93] Alice lived adjacent to a cottage Harvey owned at the

Gulfside Assembly in Waveland. Her father was a Methodist minister, and she suspects that her parents' relationship with Harvey developed from years of interactions through church conferences. Alice stayed with "Aunt Clarie" when she came to Waveland and sometimes visited her in Jackson. One trip to visit Harvey happened to be during the summer of 1964, during which Harvey asked Alice if she wanted to attend a Freedom School and she responded affirmatively. This is reflective of the community mothering that Womanpower members engaged in and that often shaped and inspired Black women's activism. For Harvey, especially, who had no biological children, this othermothering was central to her life.

Womanpower's contributions had a profound effect on the activists who benefited from their work, as evidenced in a letter by the COFO staff and volunteers to Womanpower:

> There is a very important way, perhaps the most important way, that the Mississippi Project has been able to be so successful. That is that all of the workers have been made to feel here that you are really glad for us to be here. . . . And a very important sacrifice . . . was made by the people in Jackson who are housing us and by the ladies in the community who fed us this summer every day for six weeks.
>
> We want to say something special to these ladies. . . . They kept us healthy in a very real way, and we are very grateful to them. . . . We will miss much more than the food, much more than the vitamins—and we thank you for the real sense of being cared for that you gave us this summer.[94]

The volunteers knew that their success depended upon the support and willingness of Mississippi residents, and Womanpower was responsible for providing and generating a significant part of that support in Jackson.

Womanpower's contributions to Freedom Summer cannot be overstated, as they provided the basic means of survival for many of those volunteers who carried out the legwork of the project. The Food Project, chaired by Rosie Redmond, continued into the fall for the civil rights workers who remained in the state. It resumed in mid-September at Pratt Methodist Church and continued until funding ran out near the end of October.[95] Womanpower provided the civil rights activists with the motivation and encouragement to continue their work. Just as it had supported the Freedom Riders, its members provided a fellowship of emotional and spiritual support for the civil rights workers who were putting their lives on the line for racial justice in the South. Womanpower's ability to generate resources for this project exemplified its commitment to sustaining the Mississippi movement and its dedication to improving conditions for the local communities.

Education

Education is another channel through which Black women activists have traditionally sought to achieve empowerment and uplift. Emerging from a history of slavery, during which it was legal to keep enslaved Blacks illiterate and uneducated and also common practice to deny free Blacks educational opportunities, many Black people have pursued education as a means of uplift and have sought any and all available means to attain this forbidden fruit. During slavery and after, Black people have been creative and relentless in their pursuit of education through individual as well as collective initiatives. Education was seen as the basis for advancement and providing growth and wisdom that could never be taken away.

In this context, Black Mississippians anxiously awaited access to educational opportunities that were expected to result from the implementation of the 1954 Supreme Court decision *Brown v. Board of Education*, which declared segregated public schools unconstitutional. Both the Black and white communities were split on how to best address the decision, and members of each community were on both sides of the desegregation issue. What was unarguably evident was that Blacks wanted better educational opportunities for their children. Womanpower was dedicated to assisting in this effort.

Although the Supreme Court handed down the *Brown* decision in 1954, its mandate was actually enforced a decade later in Mississippi. In March 1964, U.S. District Court Judge Sidney Mize announced that the school boards in Jackson, Biloxi, and Leake County must make preparations to integrate for the upcoming fall.[96] While school desegregation was a big step for Mississippi, the plan was limited insofar as it only applied to children entering the first grade. Regardless of its limited scope, school integration required a great deal of support from the Black community.

Womanpower chose two avenues to assist with the integration of public schools. First, they participated in efforts to disseminate information about the desegregation plan. Black members engaged in door-to-door canvassing in their neighborhoods to encourage those who had children entering the first grade to send them to integrated schools and to address questions and concerns people had about the school board's plan. They opened their homes to hold meetings concerning school desegregation for interested parents. Womanpower encouraged those who were able to take this monumental step toward securing equality for Blacks, understanding the effort as not just about accessing equality of opportunity but an important gesture of civil rights activism as well.

In September 1964, forty-three first-graders were admitted to previously segregated schools. In order to provide support for these children and their families, Womanpower acted from its activist mothering stance and "adopted" some of these children to facilitate their success in the new and likely hostile environment. As advertised in its newsletter, *Woo*, and memos sent out to numerous individuals and organizations (including clergy, Greek letter organizations, and professional groups), Womanpower sent out a call for support in adopting the families of children that were identified by social workers as needing comprehensive assistance. "In order to support the one child at a desirable performance level," Womanpower asserted, "we will need to support the entire family in a variety of ways. This may mean some new clothing and much used clothing for all the children . . . assistance in 'learning how to cope with their problems,' other material and spiritual assistance."[97] Womanpower wanted to eliminate any barriers to success with the hope that more Black students would have such opportunities in the near future. With this goal in mind, they understood that adopting a holistic approach to each child's life would be most effective. Once again they recognized the importance of administering to the total needs of individuals and enlisted support in addressing all of these areas.

The families of children integrating the schools needed items that ranged from basic necessities, such as clothing and lunch money, to a wheelchair for one father. Womanpower conveyed these needs to those they appealed to for help. They emphasized that academic success would be difficult to achieve if students lacked either the materials required for school or the resources for a decent home life. They hoped to provide a stable foundation from which the children's success could develop.

Womanpower assisted ten families by providing necessary items for all members of the household throughout the school year. This assistance included transportation for the students and extracurricular activities, such as holiday parties for the children and their families. The Christmas party was an especially important event because it provided an occasion for the thirty-nine remaining children and their families to come together socially. It was also an opportunity for the parents to ask questions. For the children, it was a time to receive presents and interact with others in their community, such as volunteers from local Delta Sigma Theta sorority chapters.[98]

On both of these initiatives, Womanpower worked with Jean Fairfax of the American Friends Service Committee (AFSC), a Quaker organization founded in 1917, to address social justice issues. According to historian Charles Bolton, the AFSC, along with Mississippians for Public Education (MPE), a group of moderate, middle-class white women, played a prominent role in keeping public schools open and ensuring desegregation took place.[99] In *Woo*, Fairfax made a special plea to women, stating that "women should support the efforts of these [public] officials but should also find out where present plans need to be supplemented."[100] The AFSC sent clothes to Jackson for distribution to the families of the children integrating the schools, and Womanpower purchased new clothes for some of the students.[101] Womanpower members Edna Lovelace, Rosie Redmond, and Pearl Draine coordinated these efforts. Redmond, the Hospitality Chair, who coordinated WU's clothing distribution program, and Draine, as a teacher, were ideal persons to work on this project. The following academic year, the Jackson public schools integrated the first, second, third, and twelfth grades, and Womanpower offered similar assistance to those children and their families.[102]

The Chain of Friendship was called upon to support this project, and Honey Knopp again assisted Womanpower. In a letter to New York attorney Seymour Herzog thanking him for his contribution, which had been forwarded by Knopp, Harvey explained that his donation would be used to provide "lunch money, clothing and transportation" for one of the children integrating the Jackson public schools.[103] She also asked that he imitate Knopp by joining the Chain of Friendship and becoming a regular contributor.

Most WU members did not have children young enough to benefit directly from this phase of school desegregation; nonetheless, they realized the significance of the decision and worked diligently to provide opportunities for Black children that their own children did not have. They continued their efforts of encouraging Black parents to desegregate and supported the students who did for the remainder of the organization's existence.

Vermont in Mississippi

In another attempt to connect those outside the state to the movement and to improve the conditions of Black Mississippians, Womanpower supported the efforts of Ted and Carol Seaver and the Vermont in Mississippi (VIM) project. Returning to Montpelier, Vermont, in the fall of 1964, after teaching at a Freedom School, Ted Seaver, a high-school English teacher in his mid-twenties, began developing a way to build upon his summer activism. He conceived the idea of moving his family to Jackson for a year to establish a center to be used as a base for community and leadership development. Specifically, the project was designed "1) to help the Negro community there organize a community center and any educational and civic organizations they felt they needed to meet their needs; 2) to help train local leadership that could replace the Seavers as soon as possible; 3) to inspire other groups to undertake similar activities."[104] In essence, they desired to empower the Black Jacksonians in much the same way that SNCC had done throughout the state. Jesse Morris, COFO's office coordinator, asked Harvey to assist Seaver in this endeavor.[105]

In January 1965, Seaver successfully petitioned the Vermont Civil Rights Union to adopt VIM as a project.[106] In June 1965, after a great deal of fundraising on the part of Vermonters, the Seavers headed to Jackson with their two children in tow to work on building the community center while living in a house owned by Pearl Draine. Womanpower members Clarie Harvey, Pearl Draine, and Esther Sampson all served as members of the center's local, biracial advisory board.

Robert Smith Jr., co-owner of Smith Grocery, financed the construction of a building on Booker Street and rented it to VIM for the Medgar Evers Neighborhood Guild. Smith owned the store with his father R. L. T. Smith, who ran for Congress in 1962. Within months, the Guild offered a variety of services for the local community providing programs and resources for all segments of the population. Draine was instrumental to this effort as Seaver's "chief advisor and planner" in addition to conducting the Guild's "training program for mothers and teachers."[107] The building housed the first day care center in the area, provided childcare with a sliding scale fee, and "operated as a cooperative with a board composed of the mothers whose children [were] enrolled."[108] The Guild provided counseling services and meeting space for local organizations, such as the Mississippi Freedom Democratic Party and the American Veterans Committee. It established the Hinds Community Council, a coalition of neighborhood and community groups "established to encourage democratic participation of the poor in the anti-poverty programs."[109] Womanpower used the Guild as a place to hold meetings and collaborated with the Springfield VIM Committee on their camping project. Womanpower also started a theater group for six- to thirteen-year-olds at the Guild.[110]

Out-of-state support for the Guild came from Vermont members of Womanpower's Chain of Friendship. Virginia Naeve and Myrtle Lane (a member of the VIM board of trustees), who were running the Mississippi Box Project, added the Guild to their list of groups in the South to whom donations should be directed.

The Guild maintained operation through the remainder of the decade providing much-needed resources for the community, developing local leadership, and working with initiatives such as the Office of Economic Opportunity's Community Action Programs.

Prayer Fellowship

The Prayer Fellowship Committee coordinated Womanpower's efforts to foster interracial fellowship between Black and white women who were sympathetic to the civil rights movement. Harvey stated that Womanpower "wanted white women who had the courage of their convictions who would be willing to work with us in fellowship and grow together."[111] Jane Schutt, Womanpower's most active white member on the local level, and M. G. Haughton, first lady of Pearl Street AME Church, led this initiative.

Jane Menefee, the oldest of Gertrude and Randolph Menefee's four children, was born in Washington, D.C., on January 2, 1913.[112] After completing her education in the public schools, she attended George Washington University. There she met a civil engineering student, Wallis J. Schutt. The couple married in 1934, and Wallis gained employment in the construction industry, resulting in their moving across the country. Eventually Wallis secured a job with M. T. Reed Construction, which took them, and at that time their three children, to Mississippi. The family settled in Jackson in 1942.[113]

Schutt's early years in Mississippi were occupied with rearing five children and community activities like the Girl Scouts and the PTA. Her interest in ecumenical activities and service to her church, St. Columb's Episcopal Church, led to two nominations for the presidency of United Church Women (UCW) of Mississippi.[114] She declined the position the first time but accepted it in February 1959 after the incumbent was forced to resign after the Fellowship of the Concerned (FOC) discovered that she had ties to the Citizens' Council.[115]

During the first board meeting Schutt presided over, some members declared that the organization needed to "make a public statement clarifying the position of the United Church Women of Mississippi in regard to race relations."[116] The rather vague statement they developed declared their autonomy as a branch of the National Council of Churches that would adhere to "local and state policies," which some interpreted as supporting segregation and some regarded as supporting the national policy of integration.

Shortly after the publication of this statement, Schutt and other leaders of the local UCW were approached to serve as members of the Mississippi Advisory Committee to the U.S. Commission on Civil Rights. Schutt was the only woman to accept the invitation. She joined Murray Cox, a minister from Gulfport, who chaired the committee; Dr. A. D. Beittel, president of Tougaloo College; Admiral Robert Briscoe; and James Allen, a physician from Columbus. They comprised the state's first Advisory Committee, which began meeting in December 1959. Schutt served as chair of the committee beginning in the fall of 1962, following the death of Reverend Cox. The committee served in an advisory capacity to the national commission to provide an opportunity for people at the state level to offer their assessment of civil rights violations and accounts of abuse.[117] Charged solely with investigative powers, as the committee had no enforcement authorities, Mississippi's Advisory Committee paid particular attention to voting rights, education, and police brutality.

Serving on the committee was life-changing for Schutt. It gave her the impetus to proactively seek ways to act upon the prayer collects that had guided her life, one of which was "make no peace with oppression."[118] At the beginning of her tenure on the committee, Schutt recalled, she was largely uninformed about civil rights issues and the discrimination and abuse Blacks faced. She stated that "I really wasn't conscious of the real damaging effect on all of us brought about by discrimination and segregation."[119] She went from being characterized as a moderate to being labeled as an "extreme liberal," and reflected that "I understand now what is meant by human rights and what is meant by equal opportunity and fair and equal administration of justice for all and I understand the importance of securing these rights for all our citizens."[120] Serving in this capacity helped raise Schutt's awareness about the issues facing Blacks with respect to access and opportunity, as well as the need for improved race relations and the role whites needed to take in addressing segregation.

The opportunity for her to engage in this type of work arose nearly two years later. At UCW's Ninth National Assembly, held in Miami Beach, Florida, in October 1961, the organization created a program titled "Assignment Race" "for the purpose of mobilizing and training women to work toward improved race relations."[121] UCW members were asked to fill out commitment cards on which they were to "write down [their] personal intent in carrying out the national goals for justice in a multi-racial society."[122] This task had the intended effect on Schutt. She explained that in undertaking UCW's official programs to address race relations, she took personal responsibility not only for reporting but also for working to create social change in her community and among her peers. As then national president Louise Wallace indicated, this obligation was something that each member had to fulfill individually, "not something they could watch or receive as a report from the national office."[123] One of Schutt's first actions was to attend a Fellowship of the Concerned meeting in Atlanta. Her plan was to invite Harvey to attend the meeting with her, as she had been informed that Harvey was someone she needed to know. Shortly after returning from Florida, Schutt attended an interracial Methodist Conference at the invitation of John Yungblut at the Methodist assembly ground on the Mississippi Gulf Coast. She approached the registration desk and found herself standing next to a "lovely lady" who in a welcoming and amicable manner introduced herself and who turned out to be none other than Clarie Collins Harvey.[124] This introduction turned into a working relationship on ecumenical and civil rights issues as well as a long-lasting friendship. Unable to attend the meeting herself, Harvey recommended that Schutt contact Womanpower member M. G. Haughton.

During the FOC meeting Schutt and Haughton conversed with other women who had organized integrated groups of women in their respective hometowns. When they returned to Jackson, Schutt and Haughton organized a bimonthly interracial prayer fellowship. Haughton offered Pearl Street AME Church as a location for some of its meetings, and at other times they gathered in people's homes.[125]

In addition to providing an opportunity for interracial communion, the Prayer Fellowship also connected more Black women with United Church Women, setting the stage for the eventual integration of the organization at the state level. Despite the national policy of integration and the adoption of Assignment Race, the Mississippi chapter, like many in the Deep South, did not permit Black members.[126] Through the Prayer Fellowship, Womanpower members and other Black women in Jackson collaborated with local UCW members on events like World Community Day and World Day of Prayer. WU was an important bridge between these two groups of women who, although working for the same goals, were separated by the state's segregation laws, their organizations' policies, and/or personal biases. These relationships laid the foundation for collaboration between local Black and white women on projects such as Wednesdays in Mississippi (WIMS), the interracial and interfaith program sponsored by the National Council of Negro Women in 1964 that brought northern women to Mississippi to facilitate inter- and intraracial communication.

Like the Chain of Friendship, the Prayer Fellowship spread beyond Jackson with supporters throughout the country in places like Berea, Kentucky; Baltimore; New York; Cleveland; Aguadilla, Puerto Rico; and beyond, even to Johannesburg, South Africa.[127] There was a solid contingent of supporters from Tougaloo College, including Ruth Beittel (white), wife of the president; librarian L. Zenobia Coleman (Black); Jeannette King, (white) wife of the chaplain; and Ruth Owens (Black), assistant director of public relations.[128]

Efforts to create an Advisory Committee to the U.S. Commission on Civil Rights in Mississippi had drawn the ire of the Citizens' Council—feelings that were directed toward committee members, including Schutt. Schutt's activities with Womanpower and the Prayer Fellowship, which sometimes met in her home, further heightened her visibility. Characteristic of wu members, Schutt had the full support of her husband, who "was very firm about saying our home was our home and we had who we wanted to have in our home."[129] Though she continued to work with the committee unofficially, she eventually resigned as chair of the Advisory Committee because of the economic pressures her activities caused for her husband, who worked for a company owned by members of the Citizens' Council.[130] Notwithstanding this change in activity, Schutt did not limit her support of Womanpower, the civil rights movement, or interracial ecumenical activities. Unwilling to falter in the face of intimidation, such as a cross being burned on her yard one December, she displayed the same strength of character so representative of wu's activist membership.[131]

The Prayer Fellowship was fundamental in facilitating interracial cooperation. On the most basic level, it provided an opportunity for Black and white women, many of whom otherwise would never have interacted as peers, to break down the socially constructed barriers that separated them and get to know one another. It humanized them for each other as friendships developed and they shared the typical goings-on in their lives. And, as friendships developed, so did trust, which led to collaborations on civil rights issues. Harvey expressed this sentiment in a letter to the fellowship group, stating, "Perhaps the most important thing to share is the fact that our Prayer Fellowship grows stronger, deeper, wider and is a source of enlightenment and strength."[132] The Fellowship also provided an opportunity for visitors outside the state to participate in an integrated meeting and witness women's ability to break through the segregation that dominated the state. wu Friends Honey Knopp, Jean Fairfax, and several participants in Wednesdays in Mississippi shared in this experience. Elizabeth Haselden, who attended the Fellowship as a participant in WIMS, echoed Harvey's sentiment:

> Perhaps one of the most meaningful experiences to me personally was attending the Prayer Fellowship at the Pearl Street AME Church with Jane Schutt on Wednesday afternoon. Here I met mostly Negro women, among them Mrs. Evers, and in the quiet atmosphere of the occasion the Negro women talked about their real thoughts and their experiences and we entered into each other's experiences in a most unusual way. This was true communication. That it happened in Jackson, Mississippi, and has been happening for two years (in this group and in other groups of other types too) gives great hope for the re-building of real community, this time built on justice.[133]

The Fellowship was one of the few safe spaces where such a dialogue could occur, and it was essential for mobilizing moderate white women of this age group to participate in challenging segregation. It built the human relations of friendship and trust among women who would not have otherwise interacted in such a manner and created a foundation for equality in the state chapter of UCW, which moved them closer to accomplishing the larger goals of the civil rights movement.

Through its varied projects, Womanpower stayed true to its goal of sustaining the movement in Mississippi by providing both creative leadership and essential support work. At the same time, it offered a model of Black womanhood for the youth its members nurtured, mentored, and brought into the movement. Verna Polk (Curtis), a Womanpower youth member and a 1962 graduate of Jackson State College, recalled that WU members emphasized that women should get involved in the movement through their churches, sororities, and student organizations to improve their communities, the state, and the nation.[134] Womanpower nurtured social and political involvement among all women—their elders, peers, and youth—with the hopes of transforming American society. With its broad-based agenda, the group offered a variety of ways for people to support Womanpower and the movement.

CHAPTER FOUR

"We Who Believe in Freedom"
Interracial Cooperation and Peace Activism

> If the next hundred years are going to be like the last, we don't care whether there is peace or not.
> —A Black woman's remarks at the First Annual Conference of Women Strike for Peace, 1962

> That until the philosophy which holds one race superior and another inferior is finally and permanently discredited and abandoned; That until there are no longer first-class and second-class citizens of any nation; That until the color of a man's skin is of no more significance than the color of his eyes; That until the basic human rights are equally guaranteed to all without regard to race; That until that day, the dream of lasting peace and world citizenship and the rule of international morality will remain but a fleeting illusion, to be pursued but never attained.
> —Haile Selassie, speech delivered to the United Nations

On March 31, 1962, Clarie Collins Harvey boarded a Delta flight traveling from Jackson, Mississippi, to New York. The following day, bags packed with steadfastness and determination, she flew via Swissair to Geneva, Switzerland, to attend the 17-Nation Disarmament Conference. As one of a hundred women, fifty of whom were from North America, Harvey traveled to the conference as a member of the first international delegation of Women Strike for Peace (WSP).

When Harvey boarded the plane in Jackson, she knew she was embarking upon a special mission. The U.S. delegation, joined by women from Canada and European nations including France, Norway, Sweden, Switzerland, the USSR, and West Germany, addressed the 17-Nation Disarmament Conference in hopes of "dramatiz[ing] to the conference the concern of women everywhere for peace and to underscore their own belief that it is vital to all humanity that the first steps toward disarmament be taken now." Their plans also included "demonstrat[ing] to the statesmen of all nations the growing concern of women around the world for the future of the human race."[1] They hoped to interrupt the negotiations and interject both humanity and urgency into the male-dominated proceedings.

The decision to lobby at the conference was a direct response to President John F. Kennedy having ignored WSP's request for women's representation in the official negotiations. Despite being shunned by the commander-in-chief, WSPers reflected on the unprecedented success they had experienced in the previous four months of existence of the organization and were confident in their ability to have an impact on the nuclear race. They departed for Geneva without any confirmed appointments, ready to challenge those whom they considered to be the patriarchal, militaristic leaders of nations threatening human existence. Upon arrival, the women were disappointed with an initially cool reception from American and Soviet ambassadors, as well as the lack of communication between the two nations. But the WSP delegation found encouragement in how they inspired representatives of some of the underdeveloped nations who were similarly in a position of little influence at the conference. By the end of the conference, they were able to secure meetings with representatives from each of the participating nations, including several meetings with U.S. Ambassador Arthur Dean and Soviet Ambassador Valerian Zorin who co-chaired the conference.[2] From these meetings, the women learned that the primary impediments to disarmament were the tense relations and distrust between the United States and the USSR. Shocked at their discovery, they soon witnessed how this distrust manifested itself in their interactions with Soviet women. Each harbored skepticism of the other and bent over backward to ensure that her comments were not misinterpreted.[3] The group of women worked diligently to overcome these suspicions. By the end of the conference the WSPers had put their own distrust in check by working collaboratively with Soviet women, and they expected the leaders of their respective nations to do the same.

During one particular meeting with Ambassador Dean, the chairwoman of the Independent Political Forum in Rochester, New York, Mary Grooms, suggested that the United States close down one of the many bases that surrounded the Soviet Union to help diminish the mistrust between the two nations. In an attempt to dodge the question, Dean responded that the number of U.S. bases was perhaps not the real reason for Russian distrust and suggested that Grooms ask the Russians, themselves, about the issue. Grooms did just that. The following day, she asked Soviet diplomat Semyon Tsarapkin about his nation's suspicions, to which he replied that the existence of U.S. military bases in more than thirty countries around the USSR was a legitimate reason to distrust the United States. In the course of their conversation, Tsarapkin stated that, if the United States closed even one base, that would alleviate tension and "give us faith" that it was genuine in the disarmament discussions. Olga Chetchetkina, one of the Soviet female delegates, who stood with WSP in presenting a formal statement to the conference, confirmed this sentiment.[4] Grooms and the other American women went back to Ambassador Dean with the proposal that the United States disarm one of its military bases and transform it into a "center for cultural exchange."[5] Dean, again deferring comment, replied that they should ask the president. This suggestion provided the impetus for their first strategic activity once they returned stateside.

Toward the end of the conference, the women staged a "silent, illegal, two-mile march of women from the center of the city to the Palais des Nations," hoping to interject a sense of urgency and vigor into the proceedings while at the same time channeling the frustrations they had from their "lack of impact."[6] Despite warnings that protesters would be arrested, the WSP delegates marched and were prepared to spend the day in silent vigil at the gate. As Harvey recalled, "two by two, in silence, a hundred women walked through the streets of the Old Swiss city up to the wide, curving boulevard to the former League of Nations, now housing a part of the United Nations."[7] In a surprising turn of events, and "an unprecedented breach of United Nations regulations," the women, who were joined by women from Europe, Russia, and Switzerland, were invited inside to meet privately with Ambassadors Dean and Zorin. WSPers took this opportunity to humanize their disarmament efforts and discuss their concerns for their children's lives. The women also presented their petitions and chided their hosts to keep the survival of future generations as their primary concern, not national security.[8] Of their efforts in Geneva, Harvey wrote, "We are in Geneva to create a climate in which the Geneva Disarmament Conference might break its deadlock. We have said loud and clear for all the world to hear that women and mothers everywhere want and need peace."[9]

WSP used this trip to mobilize support among women internationally. On the way home from the conference, WSP delegates attended a mass meeting of members of the British peace movement in London at which they were well received.[10] Harvey commented, "as a member of a minority group in America, I was proud that the Nigerian delegation's resolution stressed the moral responsibility of the nuclear powers for the other people of the world."[11] This comment speaks to two key aspects that influenced Harvey's activism with WSP. First, her participation and perspective were shaped by her ideology as a Black woman. Second, she believed in unity among humankind and the responsibility of every individual to bring this into fruition. The women returned to the United States with new alliances and insights, ready to confront the American government.

After returning from Geneva, the WSP delegates requested a meeting with President Kennedy to discuss one of their solutions toward easing tensions — the dismantling of one base. Although they were denied a meeting with the president even after a "week-long, 'round-the-clock vigil before the entrance to the grounds," their ideas were brought to his attention.[12] In a press conference in April, a reporter asked President Kennedy for his thoughts on the proposal. A flabbergasted Kennedy, when pressed by the reporter about the information, which was new to him, commented that Ambassador Dean would look into it. For WSPers, this was a phenomenal success as it demonstrated the power of the "voiceless" to participate in foreign policy decisions by bringing the issues of Geneva to "international public attention."[13] This was the type of role that WSP had envisioned for itself. At the same time, they were happy to have "made the negotiations pause" regardless of how brief, reminding them of the "human, moral purpose" underlying their efforts — concern for the preservation of the human race.[14]

Upon returning home to Jackson, Harvey gave presentations about her trip, the first of which was sponsored by Delta Sigma Theta on May 6 at Pratt Memorial Church.[15] Harvey understood the unique opportunity to give witness to this international women's movement and wanted to connect it with the local civil rights work she was doing. She desired to get others involved who were not in a position to make the journey. Not new to peace activism, as it was her work with the Peace Division of the Methodist Church's General Board of Social Concerns that brought her to the attention of Women Strike for Peace, this pilgrimage heightened her visibility and strengthened Womanpower Unlimited's peace work, both locally and nationally.[16] Harvey had long since made the connection that fighting against injustice meant fighting not only *against* inequality but also *for* peace. It was likely the focus on women's empowerment that drew her to Women Strike for Peace.

Harvey's first trip abroad in June 1939 to attend the Christian Youth Conference in Amsterdam, Holland, prompted her adoption of pacifism.[17] Becoming a pacifist was a logical step given Harvey's background in the Methodist Church, which heavily informed her ideas about peace. Her father was a national leader in the Methodist Church and Harvey followed in his footsteps, serving on both local and national levels. At seven years old, she went to the 1924 General Conference with her father, who attended as a lay delegate and began introducing her to service to the church and the responsibility of carrying out the church's mission.[18] Harvey's service included being a youth member of the General Board of Education during 1940–44 and membership on the Board of Social and Economic Relations during 1952–60. The Methodist Church advocated a progressive stance on issues of peace in a broad sense, which is evidenced by its social creed. With regard to the principles of "Peace and World Order," the creed dictates: "It is not enough to declare the evil of war: We must actively and constantly create the conditions of peace and the organization for peace. These tasks include the promotion of understanding, reconciliation and good will; the relief of suffering, the lifting of living standards around the world; concern for the freedom and welfare of dependent and subject peoples; the removal of racial tensions; the taking of all available steps toward disarmament; the giving of encouragement and support to patient negotiating by our leaders."[19] Harvey's understanding of peace, and subsequently what she infused into Womanpower Unlimited, was the idea of everyone's individual responsibility to work for peace, in the sense of disarmament, and with respect to actively transforming human relationships.

Prior to the creation of either Womanpower Unlimited or Women Strike for Peace, Harvey acted upon her pacifism. This is evident in many of her pre-civil rights activities, including her signing of the Peace Information Center's "Partial List of Prominent Americans Endorsing the World Peace Appeal" in 1950, and in her numerous presentations.[20] For example, in a lecture given at Anderson Chapel in Jackson in 1959, Harvey stated, "It is no longer possible to survive the use of force in the world. We must find a way to ensure the elimination of force as an instrument of policy & to learn how to get along in a world where one can't use force."[21] When Harvey founded Womanpower Unlimited, she brought to the organization a clear understanding of the correlation between militaristic force and racial oppression on both local and global levels. She was aware of the simultaneous effort that needed to take place internationally and locally to achieve peace with respect to war and human relations in general and was primarily responsible for guiding WU's peace initiatives in these areas.

Part of Womanpower's uniqueness lay with the prominent position peace activities held on its agenda. Members were able to bring a practical, humanistic approach to their activism by engaging in broad-based activities of social justice that extended well beyond their local communities. Consistent with their goals of exercising their "right to coordinate our activities with and to be a part of peace movements," Womanpower Unlimited placed a high priority on promoting and supporting peace efforts.[22] In justifying their involvement in such endeavors, Harvey maintained that "we can't just be concerned about Jackson and its problems and America and its problems. If we are going to have peace and brotherhood and real understanding of peoples, then we must have it on an international scale also."[23] The emergence of WSP afforded them the opportunity to do this. Womanpower members viewed collaboration with WSP as a way to engage with the peace movement internationally and to support women's empowerment and participation in the public sphere.

Harvey was the only member to actively participate in disarmament-focused peace activities with WSP. Other members engaged in local and national activities that focused on the human relations aspect of peace, and the organization collectively supported WSP's work as evidenced by their financial contributions to the organization.[24] Examining WU's and Harvey's peace activism illuminates the key role Black women activists played in linking these social movements. WU was a conduit that raised the awareness of both communities of activists to their mutual concerns. Reflective of the intersectionality of Black women's identity that grounded their activism, WU embodied this focus in its infancy and worked to ensure others did the same.

WSP Beginnings

Just five and a half months after Womanpower began its civil rights work, Dagmar Wilson, Jeanne Bagby, Folly Fodor, Eleanor Garst, and Margaret Russell gathered in Wilson's Washington, D.C., home to discuss how women could halt the arms race.[25] Under the banner of "End the Arms Race not the Human Race," their initial proposal was for women to hold a "one-day peace strike" to draw attention to the issue and their efforts to halt the progression of the Cold War toward what they perceived as an impending "nuclear catastrophe."[26]

The organizers of this initial march, and most Women Strike for Peace members, were similar to Womanpower Unlimited organizers. They were women of social prominence who had experience working with sex-integrated (read: male-dominated) organizations. For the WSP founders, peace activism was not a novel endeavor, as all were members of the Washington, D.C., chapter of the Committee for a Sane Nuclear Policy (SANE), a group organized in 1957 by Lawrence Scott, who attended the first WSP meeting and proposed the march.[27] Although the group of "liberal political, intellectual, and religious leaders" who founded SANE was responding to radiation contamination, Wilson believed that the organization's efforts did not reflect the urgency necessitated to address the issue of "the contamination of milk by radioactive isotopes."[28] At the same time, the women in SANE experienced marginalization by the men, not unlike that described by Harvey in her explanation of why women's organizations were necessary for cultivating women's activism. Yet, this core group of women embraced the limitations placed upon American women and purposely organized themselves as "a proper middle-class women's group." Promoting traditional ideas of womanhood, Amy Swerdlow, historian and former WSPer, asserted that she and her fellow activists "wore their status of middle-class wifehood and motherhood proudly, while asserting their responsibility for nurturance, moral guardianship, and life preservation."[29] Motherhood imagery notwithstanding, they were subversively defying these traditional ideas with their public efforts to influence foreign policy. Under the direction of National Coordinator Dagmar Wilson, Women Strike for Peace developed into a collective of women throughout the United States (and abroad) who were concerned about the Cold War arms race and nuclear proliferation.[30] Hoping to achieve "general and complete disarmament under effective international control," WSP called for the banning of atomic weapons testing and increased spending for and more productive use of the UN to achieve this state of peace.[31] Similar to Womanpower Unlimited, WSPers structured their organization around activism rather than around memberships or dues, encouraging participation by anyone willing to contribute energy, ideas, or other resources.

The similarities between the two organizations are striking. First, both grew out of initiatives that began as a response to immediate concerns: Womanpower Unlimited, collecting items to be delivered to the incarcerated Freedom Riders; and Women Strike for Peace, a one-day strike to protest nuclear arms. The WSP's demonstration on November 1, 1961, was a strike from their responsibilities as mothers, wives, and professionals to exert pressure on elected officials to engage in disarmament and end the arms race.[32] The impetus, like that of WU, was the arrest of an activist engaged in peaceful protest—eighty-one-year-old peace activist Bertrand Russell in London that September.[33] On the appointed day, approximately 50,000 women in over 60 cities throughout the country held meetings and sent delegations to public officials.[34] The overwhelming response enjoyed by both groups in such a short period demonstrated the seriousness of the issues as well as women's desire to engage in efforts to advance the cause.

Both organizations worked to remain flexible and to avoid the bureaucratic hierarchies that plagued male-dominated organizations, thereby limiting women's voices. Organizers purposefully designed both groups to avoid such exclusionary practices. Specifically, Swerdlow commented that "there was an implicit understanding that the most exciting ingredient in WSP, and a constant source of energy and empowerment, was the community of women working together, receiving and giving the kind of support and respect they had not experienced in male-led organizations for social change."[35] Additionally, the founders conceptualized their organizations as movements with no "formal requirements for membership."[36] Like Womanpower Unlimited, Women Strike for Peace offered women a safe space where women's ideas, talents, and organizing skills were valued and developed.

Despite their similarities with respect to development and organization, there are a few points of divergence. One glaring difference between the two groups was WSP's disconnect from earlier generations of women activists. Many WSPers noted that they had no role models, unaware of the previous generation's activists such as the Women's Peace Party, the Women's International League for Peace and Freedom (WILPF), suffragists, or first-wave feminists.[37] This was typical and not surprising, since they presented themselves as apolitical (a stance that irked Bella Abzug, future congresswoman and founder of WSP's national legislative caucus), but not true for all WSPers. Kay Hardman, for example, a member of the Los Angeles chapter of Women Strike for Peace (LA WSP), "identified WSP with its radical foremothers in the antislavery movement," which might explain that chapter's early efforts to support civil rights issues.[38] Womanpower members, on the other hand, were grounded in a legacy of Black women's activism. They were aware of the Black women's organizing tradition that had been sustained by their mothers and grandmothers and recognized their responsibility to continue those efforts. Bernice Johnson Reagon, student activist from Albany, Georgia, and a member of the SNCC Freedom

Singers, captured this sentiment when she wrote, "I am in fact doing the same thing that my mother did and that my sisters did. The sands have shifted, but the motion I carry is from them. If we understand that we are talking about a struggle that is hundreds of years old, then we must acknowledge a continuance: that to be Black women is to move forward the struggle for the kind of space in this society that will make sense for our people."[39] It is this foundation upon which Womanpower members and other Black women during the 1960s stood in their pursuit of social justice.

Furthermore, the two organizations had different ideas about peace. WSP employed a rather narrow definition of peace that focused on the absence of war and directed its activities at disarmament, ending the Cold War, and draft resistance. A far more expansive definition of peace guided Womanpower. For many Blacks, particularly those living in the South, life was a war zone, so peace meant freedom from domestic terrorism and racial oppression—equally, if not more so, relevant to their day-to-day lives. Womanpower's peace activism reflected mainstream, war-focused peace ideologies, a philosophy that promoted equality and understanding among peoples of difference races, and a commitment to international issues of justice with respect to colonialism and racial oppression globally.

Perhaps the most dramatic difference between WU and WSP was that, during the early years of the organization's existence, with the exception of a few local chapters, WSP did not become directly involved in civil rights activism.[40] WSP had a rather homogeneous membership of white middle-class, middle-aged women, largely oblivious to the need for either racial or socioeconomic diversity. Swerdlow argued that WSP "was nonexclusionary in that it refused to bar any woman, regardless of her past political affiliations, from membership."[41] However, efforts of inclusion with respect to race and class appear to have been rarely considered. Because of racism and segregation, and even though many Womanpower members were themselves middle class, they were not isolated from working-class and poor Blacks, were familiar with the economic hardships African Americans faced, and embraced this type of diversity in its membership. Womanpower embraced diversity by reaching out to white women as well as women of different faiths.

On the first day of the first WSP national conference held in Ann Arbor, Michigan, in June 1962, civil rights and Black women activists became issues of contention. Four Black women from Detroit were in conflict with the Detroit chapter of WSP, which had prevented the women from participating in a WSP rally with placards reading "Desegregation Not Disintegration."[42] As Chinese American leftist activist and feminist Grace Lee Boggs recalled in her autobiography, "WSP leaders hesitated to raise civil rights issues for fear of alienating their white middle-class constituency . . . [but] a few members, including Frances Herring, Eunice Dean Armstrong, and Kathleen Gough, welcomed our initiative."[43] In fact, a week before the conference, Eunice Armstrong penned a letter to Belle Schulz (Dagmar Wilson's volunteer secretary), emphasizing the need to have Black women present "at all WSP meetings" and questioning the fact that two Black women from Detroit, Delores Wilson and Gwendolyn Mallett, who had created an organization called the "Independent Negro Committee to Ban the Bomb and End Racism," as well as Boggs, had their registration fees returned with the explanation that there was no space for them.[44] Swerdlow recalled that WSP had a contentious relationship with civil rights activists and some of its Black (as well as a few of its white) members.[45]

The official WSP policy, which was adopted at the second national conference in Champaign-Urbana the following year, was not a policy statement in fact but more of a vague statement that read in part: "As women dedicated to bringing about a world where every child may live and grow in peace and dignity, we identify ourselves with the heroic effort of Negro citizens to achieve this goal."[46] Despite the natural connections between the peace and civil rights movements, many WSPers endorsed Wilson's position that WSP remain a single-issue movement. In response to WSP's lukewarm support of the civil rights movement, the LA WSP issued its own statement: "We feel that the time has come for all women to stand up and be counted on this matter of grave concern. We feel that the time has come for us to match the thought with the deed. We call upon all women working for peace to dedicate themselves to the struggle of the Negro people for freedom."[47] This chapter adopted a progressiveness that the national organization did not accept until the mid- to late 1960s.

Harvey's recognition of how issues of poverty and inequality manifested themselves in larger international forums, just as they did in her home state of Mississippi, solidified her conception of the interdependence of domestic and international human rights struggles. She cited this experience as most salient in raising her consciousness to the abiding need for international peace and the cooperation of all peoples in struggles for human rights.[48] Black women's efforts tended to pursue a multifocal strategy. This is not to say that white women were unable to pursue a similar course of action. WU's multidimensional approach was not lost on all WSPers. For example, in a letter to Harvey written after reading Womanpower's self-published *Womanpower and the Jackson Movement*, Eunice Armstrong, whose support of Black women's inclusion in the movement began during the organization's infancy, recounted that her husband "said that wsp could learn a lot from your methods and your organization" and that she would "take it in to our NY Central Coordinating Committee meeting tomorrow to show how much better we could be doing than we are."[49] There were individual women and entire chapters of wsp that worked toward greater cooperation between the two movements, efforts that came to fruition in the latter part of the decade.

Despite wsp's general eschewing of civil rights activism, wu maintained a working relationship with the organization for a few reasons. Peace activism was a key aspect of wu's agenda, yet, given its primary focus on civil rights activism in the state, giving the same attention to peace would have been unmanageable. It was more effective to work with a national organization whose goals they supported. There was no chapter of wsp in Mississippi; therefore, the collaborations with wu were an excellent opportunity to raise awareness among Jacksonians.

Harvey, and wu in general, worked toward women's empowerment and likely viewed wsp as an additional avenue through which this could be accomplished. Harvey witnessed the impact wsp had on the national and international consciences and wanted to both support and guarantee that Black women were represented in these voices. wu did important work toward raising the consciousness of activists in both movements. Black women, such as Harvey and Coretta Scott King, were necessary in wsp's developing awareness and its evolution to eventually supporting civil rights. wu was a movement designed to foster relationships among women of different faiths, races, and backgrounds, and maintaining a working relationship with wsp facilitated this goal. wsp was a way to educate more women about Womanpower and the civil rights struggle in Mississippi. Harvey used the wsp publications to disseminate information about the group and to reach a larger audience, expanding Womanpower's Chain of Friendship.

The World without the Bomb, Accra

Womanpower participated in three additional international conferences with Women Strike for Peace and also collaborated with the group on local initiatives. Prompted by the progressive LA wsp, Women Strike for Peace declared that it should try to send representatives to all international conferences.[50] One of the first invitations WSP received after the Geneva trip was to attend the World without the Bomb Conference in Accra, Ghana, on June 21–28, 1962. The impetus for the conference came from President Kwame Nkrumah in July of the previous year. He proposed to parliament that a portion of the defense budget be earmarked to sponsor an "international disarmament conference." Subsequently Nkrumah convened a Preparatory Committee that met in Ghana in October and December 1961 to develop the focus of such a conference the following year.[51] Nkrumah's pursuit of world peace was an integral component of his diplomatic strategy, which rested on the belief that "without [world peace] our newly-won freedom would be insecure, and our development retarded."[52] In discussing Ghana's foreign policy, former High Commissioner to the Court of St. James and Cabinet Minister Kwesi Armah explains, "from its first day of independence, Ghana was concerned with world peace as a priority for its own development and for humanity's survival of the nuclear age. . . . Thus, the basic aims of Ghanaian foreign policy under the First Republic were: (1) African independence, and (2) the maintenance of world peace through positive neutrality and non-alignment."[53] Nkrumah wanted to make certain that no African nation was under foreign rule and that Africa was not used for nuclear testing.[54]

The conference proposed to address various aspects of disarmament such as effective inspections and "the transformation of the existing military nuclear material to peaceful uses." Moreover, it provided "an examination of the fundamental problems of hunger, disease, ignorance and servitude and concrete suggestions as to their solutions in the World Without the Bomb by liberating all these resources now misused by the armament race."[55] From its inception, the conference connected nuclear disarmament to colonialism and oppression.

Conference planners hoped those nations that previously had no voice in the nuclear arms race would develop innovative solutions to disarmament, with the ultimate goal of securing the abolition of nuclear weapons and ending the Cold War.[56] With this understanding, invitations were directed to individuals, observers, and "experts chosen both from the leading nuclear powers, and from organizations working for the lessening of world tensions."[57] Excluded from the list of invitees were government officials. As indicated in the booklet disseminated by the Preparatory Committee, organizers "intended that the majority of those attending the Assembly should come from Africa, Asia and Latin America. These Continents contain the vast majority of mankind but the collective voice of the leading citizens from many of the States of these areas has as yet not had adequate expression."[58] Invitations were also extended to representatives of international peace organizations. As a representative of both Womanpower Unlimited and Women Strike for Peace, Harvey attended this conference with less than one month's notice and only weeks after attending the WSP national conference. She again packed her bags with determination and went.

WSP requested space first for two observers, and then for four. It sent a delegation of two Black women, Clarie Collins Harvey (Jackson, Miss.) and Selma Sparks (New York City), and two white women, Francis Herring (Berkeley, Calif.) and Nancy Mamis (Bennington, Vt.). The representatives, who attended the conference on behalf of WSP, seemed to reflect the organizers' respect for racial balance, but in reality it revealed another incident of WSP's shortcomings with respect to diversity. The initial delegation proposed by WSP members consisted of four white women.[59] Eunice Armstrong and Harvey raised opposition to sending an all-white delegation to the newly independent African nation. In a letter to Mary Clarke, Armstrong wrote, "I would much prefer to try to raise funds to Accra or to contribute what little I could personally if WSP were sending one negro and one white observer rather than two white observers."[60] Yet some members, including founding member Eleanor Garst, saw no problem with the initial decision. Most WSPers were oblivious to the similarity in struggles between African Americans and those in the African nations fighting for independence from colonial powers or that there might be a sense of kinship among the two. In fact, the location was the precise reason that Sparks opted to attend because she "was also greatly involved in the Black struggle. . . . That's why, of course, I went to this particular conference because of where it was being held."[61] Sparks was a thirty-one-year old native of Philadelphia, who grew up in New York, and had become both a journalist and secretary of the National Negro Labor Council. Although she had participated in one WSP demonstration prior to the trip to Accra, she directed the majority of her activism toward Black and labor rights and did not work with WSP after the Ghana trip.[62] There was seemingly no thought of what the perception of WSP might be if they did not include Black women. Such blindness speaks directly to the organization's homogeneous orientation and myopic focus in contrast to Womanpower's broad-based platform.

Ultimately, Harvey, Sparks, Herring, and Mamis joined 126 individuals representing over 40 countries in Accra for the weeklong conference.[63] In his opening plenary address, Nkrumah argued that what was necessary to ensure disarmament was an international code of morality that could overcome the "attitude of mind" about war as an acceptable political policy and as economically expedient. He was confident that the time had arrived to eradicate this destruction-oriented ideology. He likened the struggle for world peace to the abolitionist struggle, arguing that abolitionists had to resist individuals who believed that their nation's progress, socially and economically, was dependent upon the continuance of slavery, yet the abolitionists were able to prevail through "courage and perseverance." He assured the attendees that they too could "stir the conscience of the world [and] teach a new doctrine of hope. It is because war has thus ceased to be an essential instrument of policy that moral opposition to it has a real possibility of success, particularly if it is organized and developed on the basis of hard practical argument, and upon the teaching of a new international morality."[64] Stirring the conscience of their community became WU's primary course of action.

Nkrumah spoke at length about the need to respect all of humanity. He believed that armaments held no place in such a world with this "new public morality, which will teach that what is wrong in private life is equally wrong in international relations. . . . Not only the defence of small nations," he argued, "but the defence of the greatest powers on earth, ultimately depends not on weapons of mutual mass destruction, but upon the collective conscience of mankind. If by coming here you can do something to arouse that conscience, then your journey will not have been in vain."[65] These ideas resonated with Harvey as she expressed similar ideas about her own peace work. In her recollections of the Geneva conference Harvey stated, "Ours was a people to people mission. We moved as a spiritual and moral force into the high courts of Disarmament proceedings."[66] She echoed this sentiment in her account of the Accra trip, saying, "the greatest obstructions to peace are in the areas of the moral and spiritual. They can best be removed by the use of spiritual and moral laws and methods, rather than intellectual, for they are not primarily intellectual problems."[67] Underscoring the ecumenical spirit that inspired her activism in general, Harvey focused on the common humanity and "soul force" that existed among all peoples as a fundamental directive in promoting change.

After the plenary session, attendees participated in committee groups addressing one of the five issues that were generated by the preliminary committee: (1) the reduction of international tensions, (2) the disarmament process, (3) the transformation of existing military nuclear materials to peaceful uses,

(4) economic problems involved in or arising from disarmament, and (5) disarmament and the fundamental problems of hunger, disease, ignorance and servitude. Committee five, while dealing with alleviating problems stemming from poverty experienced in underdeveloped nations, addressed using funds freed through disarmament to prevent the development of neocolonialism.[68] Not surprisingly, Harvey chose the latter committee.[69] Harvey understood the relationship between racial oppression and militaristic aggression. Additionally, these were the same issues plaguing Blacks in her home state of Mississippi, giving her firsthand evidence of the fact that poverty and powerlessness domestically are connected to poverty and powerlessness internationally.

At the end of the week, participants had drafted seventy-five pages of "findings, recommendations and proposals," which were to be sent to the UN Disarmament Conference at Geneva and to the heads of governments of the United States and the USSR.[70] Participants decided to continue the Accra Assembly as a conference and to establish a permanent council "with a secretariat at Accra and liaison with the United Nations."[71]

Accounts of the Accra conference indicate that WSPers were unanimous in their positive views of the event. Harvey's recollections offer praise about the conference similar to fellow WSPers. Hers stand apart from theirs because of her interpretation of the conference and the personal impact the trip had on her. The fact that the conference was held in the recently independent African nation was not lost on Harvey. In a piece for a WSP publication, she wrote: "The Accra Assembly was held on the red clay soil of Africa in the midst of teeming millions of warm, friendly black people. . . . Everywhere I experienced 'Negritude'. . . . This is something far richer and deeper than riveters erecting steel skyscrapers or designers of machinery bent over their drawing boards. This is a way of life that will enrich and hasten our search for world peace. Surprising to me, I felt my identity complete with my unknown African background and heritage. It was like coming home for the first time and forever."[72] The possibility of this type of connection was perhaps what led to Harvey's and Armstrong's criticism of WSP in not including any Black women in the initial group of observers. It is indicative of Harvey's groundedness within her multiple identities—as a woman, a person of African descent, and a world citizen—and an example of the variety of identities that informed her understanding of self with respect to her activism. Without question, Harvey was an internationalist. The foundation for her political activism was firmly rooted in her identity with and commitment to the Black community. She saw something inherently valuable about the culture and humanity that she witnessed among the people of West Africa and felt connected to it.

Chief Justice Annie R. Jiagge, Ghana's first woman magistrate, reciprocated Harvey's connection to the people and the place, commenting to Harvey, "Your American whites are so childish. They lean over backwards in being nice to us here & then go back home & do not wish you to sit beside them. How do they think we feel when they are nice to the Mother and kick the child."[73] Just as Harvey felt a connection to the motherland, she was delighted to be embraced by Ghanaians. The sentiment of connectedness, feeling and being perceived as being the "children of Mother Africa," was, Harvey believed, partly a result of the "stand they were taking in the Civil Rights struggle."[74]

Harvey's account addressed the needs of the newly independent nation— "Developing Africa has four basic needs: Freedom from fear, better health, education and life for women. A world without the bomb can turn its thinking and finances to the solution of these problems."[75] Harvey's activism was always multifocused. She weaved together activist efforts directed at what she perceived as intertwined oppressions facing Blacks, women, and impoverished people throughout the world.

Selma Sparks's recollections were comparable and influenced by her other activism as well as her connection to Africa as a Black person. In her report of the conference, she wrote, "It is realized over here that as long as there is colonialism or imperialism of any kind in any part of the world there can be no true peace. Ideologies can co-exist but imperialism and peace cannot live in the same universe. . . . Any peace conference taking place in Africa would automatically be rooted in reality and part of this reality is that any thing which tends to keep a whole continent in subjugation to any other part of the world plays an important role in a discussion on peace."[76] Her conclusions underscore the comprehensive definition of peace that guided her own and other Black women's activism as well as the connections between disarmament and the dismantling of colonial rule.

Not surprisingly, as a labor activist, Sparks offered a class analysis of the peace movement, stating, "Most of the people in the world are workers and if they can be shown that in a world without war or threat of war there will not only be more bread and butter for all but meat and potatoes too, they might move towards exerting the kind of pressure on the governments which will force them to create the proper atmosphere for such a world. . . . In moving to save us all it must first be recognized that inherent in the struggle for peace is the necessity for freedom of all peoples without which there can be no peace and therefore no world."[77] Sparks's comments echo those of the Black woman at the first annual conference that opened this chapter. As Black women became involved in peace activism, they believed freedom and equality were preconditions to peace and that the struggle to achieve peace would not be successful if other forms of oppression remained. Sparks's and Harvey's peace activism was not divested from their other areas of focus, likely because of the intersectionality they experienced as Black women. Not being able to, and not wanting to, separate their race from their gender they brought all of those identities to bear on their activism. Mamis's and Herring's accounts, on the other hand, offered no such analysis about Ghana, colonialism, or freedom in connection to achieving peace.[78] They focused solely on the logistics of the conference and issues related to disarmament. The connections made between peace and other forms of activism, both at the World without the Bomb Conference and by Black women like Harvey, Sparks, and members of the Independent Negro Committee to Ban the Bomb and End Racism, shed light upon why WSP needed to devote greater attention and effort to supporting civil rights. This policy change eventually occurred in the latter part of the decade when WSP began reaching out to women of color and poor women.[79]

Women for Peace Vatican Pilgrimage

The following spring, Harvey journeyed again with Women Strike for Peace as a part of the Vatican Peace Pilgrimage that took place April 20–May 4, 1963. Harvey announced the trip at WU's March 14 officers' meeting. The $402 cost of the trip and the two-week commitment made it prohibitive to members, and Harvey was again the sole Womanpower delegate.[80] Approximately sixty women from eighteen countries comprised this pilgrimage organized by Virginia Naeve and Alice Pollard.[81] The trip was designed to demonstrate support for Pope John XXIII's April 11 "Peace on Earth" encyclical as well as "for his contributions as a humanitarian and champion of peace. . . . It would represent further a plea and a prayer: an appeal to Pope John in his role as great spiritual leader to call once more upon the world's rulers to withdraw from the nuclear arms race."[82] On the return trip, the women flew to Geneva to meet with representatives from the World Council of Churches (WCC) and with the UN Disarmament Commission and delegations.[83]

In response to their having little success with political leaders, WSP decided that pursuing a moral route might prove most effective. The initial proposal was based on four purposes:

1. To stress the moral issues involved in a continuing arms race which puts mankind's survival in jeopardy.
2. To show that many women from different countries and various political and religious beliefs agree with and strongly support Pope John's repeated urgings for peace.
3. To make an impact on public opinion at several levels: religious, feminine and political.
4. To enlist, and reach, more women, to cut across national barriers, in our deadline struggle for peaceful solutions to international conflicts.[84]

WSPers asserted and inserted their voice in an attempt to offer an alternative paradigm—feminine and motherly—from which to generate solutions to the masculinist and militaristic stance that created the problems of the nuclear race. In so doing, they proclaimed their positions as housewives and mothers and characterized their activism as the responsible act of women protecting their children.[85] Although Harvey was not a biological mother, like many Black women activists she embraced othermothering as integral to community survival. What set them apart from most WSPers was that they did not believe that motherhood was necessary to justify or legitimize their participation in the public political sphere.

While in Rome, women from various European nations joined the thirty American women. They were part of the group of 10,000 in attendance at the Pope's April 25 address to those who had made the pilgrimage in support of his encyclical.[86] He addressed his audience by saying, "Thank you for having come to us. In our turn we say to you: in returning to your homes, to your countries, be everywhere ambassadors of peace. Peace with God in the Sanctuary of your conscience, peace in the family, peace in your work, peace with all men inasmuch as it depends on you."[87] Echoing the ecumenical sentiment that undergirded Harvey's activism, this message inspired WSP to take a more active approach with regard to civil rights.

Upon returning home, WSPers sent a telegram to President Kennedy regarding the treatment of Blacks in Alabama:

> On our return flight we were shocked to see on the front page of the International New York Times a picture of a police dog attacking a human being in the United States of America.
>
> In our search for world peace we cannot remain silent about this appalling event in Alabama which is a disgrace for our country and is liable to provoke dire consequences.

We beg of you Mr. President to take immediate and resolute action to end this violence in the south which casts such a stigma on the name of our wonderful country.[88]

They addressed the president with the same urgency that they had previously used to discuss disarmament, expanding their own consciousness about what peace entailed and how it should be achieved. Their international work was important because it allowed them to participate in international debates, and it also helped them understand the peace work that needed to be done domestically in their own communities. Ironically, traveling abroad helped them embrace an expansive definition of peace that had a more local impact on their activism. Through Womanpower Unlimited, Harvey was able to connect some white women whom she had met on these trips, such as Honey Knopp and Virginia Naeve, to tangible ways to support civil rights activism in Mississippi and in their own communities.

On April 30, thirty members of the Peace Pilgrimage delegation traveled to Geneva and held an all-night vigil in the rain outside the gates of the Palais des Nations "to express their thanks to U Thant and the non-aligned nations for their attempts to break the test ban deadlock."[89] Additionally, they passed a resolution requesting that heads of states reject nuclear armaments and instead use those monies to aid developing nations address issues such as starvation, disease, and subjugation.[90] The delegation met with the World Council of Churches and presented a statement expressing its thanks for the declarations by the WCC concerning the Cuban missile crisis and urging them to continue efforts for peace through advocating disarmament.[91] WSPers also met with representatives from the United States and USSR disarmament delegations and delegations from the United Kingdom, Sweden, Canada, and Poland. On the return trip, they met with women from peace groups during stopovers in Munich, Frankfurt, and Paris.[92]

Harvey used this trip to increase support for civil rights activity in Mississippi. She reported on the pilgrimage at an event sponsored by the Independent Political Forum in Rochester upon her return. According to the press release, Harvey's "participation in such international peace conferences . . . brings a more realistic, and more favorable, picture of the Negro in America to people of other countries than the view many have presently. Also, it enables her to bring back to Mississippi and Louisiana international views often lacking in the Deep South."[93] Donations from the lecture were to support Womanpower's voter registration drive. This was the perfect opportunity for Harvey to connect the civil rights and peace movements and inform those outside of the South about how they could work toward peace domestically.

As a follow-up to the Vatican Pilgrimage, WSP planned a Mother's Day Lobby in Washington, D.C., to advocate for a test ban treaty with hopes of influencing the Geneva negotiations. Coretta Scott King, who was unable to attend, sent her support via telegram, stating, "Peace among nations and peace in Birmingham, Alabama, cannot be separated. As we seek to achieve peace within our nation we are also concerned about world peace for we cannot ultimately benefit from the fruits of our labors until we secure both from within and from without."[94] A Black woman, again, highlighted the need to connect the two struggles and to work simultaneously on both issues. This was not the first time that King advocated this position to and on behalf of WSP. A member of the WILPF, King's peace activism, like Harvey's, predated WSP and was a natural way for her to connect with the emerging wave of women's peace activism. Women rallied at Union Station and met with senators and members of the House of Representatives. WSP maintained pressure on Congress during stalled negotiations with Russia. Two weeks after this rally, "thirty-three senators introduced a resolution declaring it to be the sense of the Senate that the United States undertake unilateral efforts to secure a test ban."[95] In recognition of the role WSP played in the development of the Test Ban Treaty, U Thant received three WSP representatives before leaving for Moscow to witness the signing of the Treaty Banning Nuclear Weapons Tests in the Atmosphere, in Outer Space and Underwater (Test Ban Treaty) in August. Despite the fact that the treaty did not ban underground testing, WSPers were ecstatic and held celebrations across the country. The Test Ban Treaty was a solid victory not only because it limited nuclear testing but also because it garnered greater media attention for WSP. WSPers also took pride in the fact that their efforts were the impetus behind President Kennedy's endorsement for women to become more involved in "foreign policy debate," which helped legitimize their activism.[96]

The Hague

The final WSP international peace effort involving Womanpower Unlimited was the cosponsorship of a Tougaloo College student, Dora Wilson, to the Multinational Peace Rally and Demonstration in the Netherlands, May 12–14, 1964. This meeting, which coincided with NATO's Ministerial Council's meeting in The Hague, was organized in opposition to "a NATO plan for a multilateral nuclear fleet (MLF)" equipped with Polaris missiles in cooperation with West Germany.[97] In January 1964 WSPers Ruth Meyers and Amy Swerdlow began coordinating efforts with women in attendance at the Inaugural Congress of the International Confederation for Peace and Disarmament in Sweden, Copenhagen, the Netherlands, Geneva, and London. WSP invited women from all the NATO countries to participate in a "women's counterforce"—the NATO Women's Peace Force—which arranged a conference and protest march.

Womanpower's support was an expression of its desire to nurture educational initiatives among local youth and to encourage the need for involvement in peace issues from all segments of the population. Student/youth activists were integral to the civil rights movement, nationally and locally, and Womanpower wanted to develop the leadership potential among this segment of the population. They thought it expedient to support the efforts of someone who could connect Womanpower's work to her peers and hopefully to the larger Tougaloo community. Harvey, who likely did not attend because of her preparations for both Freedom Summer and Wednesdays in Mississippi, selected Dora Wilson to represent WU and WSP in The Hague. Wilson, a native of Leland in the Mississippi Delta, was an eighteen-year-old sophomore majoring in music. Her parents, Lucille (Dunlap) and Walter Grey Wilson, were both teachers in the Leland school system, and her father later became principal of the district's Breisch High School. Dora grew up in a middle-class family and was the daughter of college graduates. Her mother had graduated from Jackson State and her father from Tennessee State, where he also received his master's degree in education administration. Dora was always expected to attend college.[98]

Like Harvey, Wilson's childhood was both typical and unique for a Black person growing up in the South. Being middle class afforded her exceptional opportunities for Black Mississippians, such as being the only family in her neighborhood to own a television set and extensive traveling, including attending the World Series in New York one year. Class privilege did not prevent her from experiencing the oppression and discrimination that defined the South with separate schools and the rampant segregation of businesses owned by racist whites. Equally typical was the extended family and close-knit community that loved and nurtured young Dora.[99] Upon graduation at age sixteen, Wilson enrolled at Tougaloo College with intentions of becoming a history or English major. Although she had taken piano lessons from about the age of six, music was the furthest discipline from her mind. In her parents' eyes, Dora was too young to attend her college choice (Fisk University in Tennessee) so she was bound for an in-state school and, most certainly, a historically Black college or university with a great reputation.

During her tenure at Tougaloo, Wilson was not on the front lines of civil rights protest like some of her peers. She was active in student government, but she did not believe that college was something that could be delayed and did not want to forestall or jeopardize her academic career. Wilson was, however, drawn to Harvey's appeal to students to become involved in peace activism and potentially make a difference in peoples' lives on a global scale. She recalled that, at the time, "I [was] very young and I [didn't] know much, but the sense of what this [was] about I think affected me very deeply and that I was going to be given this opportunity." She also believed that Harvey "was trying to instill that we have a place in this world. You grew up Black, segregated, privileged but still within a confined world and that there's a great deal available and you need to see it, know it."[100] Harvey was a world citizen and wanted to provide the opportunities to which she had access to others. Wilson was the only student as well as the only person from Mississippi. She was one of four Black women in the forty-one-member American delegation.[101] Harvey asked Virginia Naeve, a WSP member from Vermont whom she had befriended on the Geneva trip, to "look out for her." Naeve later gave a praise report to Harvey that Wilson was perhaps "the most important person to have gone. . . . You couldn't have made a better choice."[102] Wilson departed from Jackson on May 9 to meet up with the other representatives of WSP in New York.

Congressional representatives and lobbyists warned WSPers against challenging NATO, yet they pressed on with full force.[103] Swerdlow, Clarke, Garst, and Gordon arrived first to make preparations and publicize the event. On May 10, Ava Pauling from the United States and Katherine MacPherson from Canada were prohibited from entering the country. The WSP preparatory committee soon learned that the same fate awaited the U.S. delegation preparing to depart from New York the following day. After a day of negotiations the American delegation secured admission to the Netherlands by "sign[ing] a statement pledging to obey all police rules."[104] Of particular importance to the local law enforcement was that demonstrators did not "sit-down" and refuse to move, thereby causing a physical confrontation between the women and police. The women consented, signing a statement to that effect, and Dora Wilson boarded KLM flight 642 to The Hague with the American delegation.

On Wednesday, May 13, well over 1,300 women marched silently in protest outside the Princess Juliana Kazerna, the military barracks where the council met, and they delivered a statement of protest concerning the MLF to the meeting. "Meanwhile," reported WSP, "a delegation of one woman from each of the 14 NATO countries (except Turkey) headed by Dagmar Wilson, presented their appeal to the NATO ministers to achieve security by countering the dangers of m.l.f. and to seek negotiated solutions."[105] At their hotel, 141 women participated in the conference with sessions led by representatives from each country. Between sessions women met with their respective NATO ministers. At the American Embassy, Mary Clarke, Ava Pauling, Delores Wilson, and Dora Wilson attempted to see Ambassador Rice. Dora presented petitions signed by 300 of her co-eds.[106]

The participants drafted a "Peace Pledge," vowing to continue their work toward securing a comprehensive test ban treaty, and established networks to maintain communication with women from the various nations as well as to plan future events in opposition to the MLF. After the demonstration and conference, American WSPers met with peace groups and leaders in France, Germany, and England.[107] The protest of the MLF continued throughout the year and into 1965, concluding with the Pentagon's decision not to deploy the MLF.[108]

When Dora Wilson returned, she shared her experiences with her peers at Tougaloo, giving a couple speeches on her trip at the weekly chapel service. Her continued peace work was limited and she returned to focus on her studies, graduating from Tougaloo in 1966.[109] She cited the Hague trip and her brief involvement with Womanpower and peace activism as integral to her developing consciousness of world affairs and her place within them.

Through all of these international conferences and demonstrations, WSPers and WU members presented themselves as world citizens and declared their right to have a voice in world affairs concerning the Cold War, the nuclear arms race, and peace. They demanded inclusion and asserted their legitimacy as female participants and as Black women specifically. For Womanpower, these initiatives enhanced their consciousness-raising efforts within the Jackson community.

Local Activities

Although participation in international activities was not new to Harvey, affiliation with Women Strike for Peace did provide Womanpower additional opportunities for discussing issues of war and peace within the greater Jackson community. While other members of Womanpower were unable to attend these peace conferences, through Harvey they became equipped with the knowledge to better educate others and intelligently interpret conflicts, such as the Vietnam War. Moreover, this knowledge nurtured their humanistic approach to civil rights activism in seeking broad-based measures of justice.

Committed to disarmament efforts, Womanpower did not believe that peace depended solely upon disarmament and the "absence of war." Members advocated an all-encompassing ideology of peace that included creating a "beloved community." This ideology was guided by the principle that "communication begets understanding; Understanding begets love for one's brother; love for one another begets peace."[110] In an effort to promote such understanding, Womanpower developed ways to spread knowledge and generate activism within the Jackson community.

Concerning issues of international peace, Womanpower members responded locally by fasting for world peace, "reading and study[ing] in depth on peace issues; getting petitions signed; writing letters, articles; speaking, sharing an international peace fest, etc."[111] They reprinted WSP announcements in their newsletters and incorporated peace issues into their civil rights forums. To celebrate their first anniversary, Womanpower held a "Mothers for Peace and Freedom" meeting on May 13, 1962, highlighted with addresses by Coretta Scott King (SCLC), Lula Peterson Farmer, James Farmer's wife (CORE), Ruby Keeler Shuttlesworth, the Reverend Fred Shuttlesworth's wife (SCLC), and Diane Nash Bevel (SNCC), who was pregnant at the time. Nash recalled that Womanpower was visionary in this respect because "in 1962 that was very early for many people in the movement to have gotten involved in the peace struggle because we were so involved in trying to desegregate it took a little time for people to make that connection."[112] With representatives from three of the major civil rights organizations, this celebration, reportedly attended by 700 people, emphasized the role of women in attaining peace and justice at home and abroad, particularly as (other)mothers concerned for the state of the world for the future generations.[113] Not unlike the posture taken by WSP, WU focused on the role mothers needed to play in ensuring peace. For Womanpower members, embracing motherhood did not mean accepting its traditional limitations. Instead, they designed a program around women who were active figures in the civil rights movement, perhaps to demonstrate the role that women must play in all levels of social and political advancement. The women on the program echoed this sentiment, and Nash stated, "We will not be free until we forget our excuses—when we women decide to stand up, the Negro race will be on its feet instead of its knees."[114] Womanpower promoted an activist mothering that placed women squarely on the front lines of activism and leadership, and Nash was the perfect embodiment. Only days before the rally, the twenty-three-year-old served ten days in the Jackson county jail for contempt of court for defying segregation laws by sitting in the front row of the courtroom.[115]

On November 1, 1963, in observation of World Community Day, an ecumenical celebration organized by Church Women United and celebrated on the first Friday in November, Womanpower held a celebration at the Farish Street Baptist Church to inform the public of their involvement in the Rome, Geneva, and Ghana Peace Conferences. They hoped to share the knowledge they had gained about international relations and the role that individuals could play in working to achieve world peace. At this event, Womanpower solicited donations for children in "church institutions and in areas of acute human need," as Harvey had done after her trip to Accra.[116]

In the spring of 1964, Womanpower signed on as an honorary sponsor of the Hiroshima-Nagasaki World Peace Study Mission to the United States that took place April 25–June 7, 1964. As part of a world pilgrimage, "a group of Hiroshima and Nagasaki A-bomb survivors . . . present[ed] their experiences of the atomic bomb and its aftermath and to exchange ideas and information with others in an effort to help the world find ways to abolish war."[117] Once again, Womanpower worked to raise the consciousness of Jackson's citizens so that they better understood the implications of war and thereby engaged in peace activism and became active in the international affairs of the day.

In an effort to achieve peace through an understanding of numerous and diverse peoples, Womanpower provided opportunities for edification on race relations for both its members as well as the community at large. Womanpower held a series of "Workshops on Race" for the community during January and February 1964. These interracial workshops were designed "to inform, to stimulate right action, to create an intelligent awareness of the basic truths behind what is happening to all Americans in the present crisis."[118] Tougaloo's business manager George Owens led the first workshop on "Races of Mankind," and Reverend Charles A. Jones of Campbell College facilitated the second workshop on "The Bible, the Church and Race." These workshops addressed the social construction of race and the unchristian way in which race has been used to divide human beings via public policy such as segregation. The final workshop was a panel that included Ann Hewitt, a local white activist and friend of Womanpower, M. H. Hulett, and Reverend T. B. Brown (Mount Helm Baptist Church) who discussed Silver's *Mississippi: The Closed Society*. This series culminated with the cosponsorship of Race Relations Day with the Terrell Literary Club on February 9, 1964.[119] Womanpower previously cosponsored this event in 1962.

Womanpower sent representatives to New Orleans in February 1964 to attend a weeklong leadership conference led by Rachel DuBois. Such opportunities better prepared Womanpower members to create interracial groups to pursue improved race relations as both a civil rights and a peace issue. Upon returning from this conference designed to train participants in using conversation to bridge differences among people of different backgrounds and to generate a sense of humanity and community, members organized "interracial groups to help build a better line of communication across racial barriers."[120] In June and July 1964, Pearl Draine attended the Twenty-First Annual Race Relations Institute at Fisk University in Nashville, Tennessee, as a representative of Womanpower. Participation in the Institute, which worked to "establish better relations between peoples regardless of race, color, creed or religion," allowed Draine to interact with people from across the nation as well as four foreign countries.[121] Learning of the differences and similarities of people from around the world afforded Draine firsthand knowledge of true diversity, similar to the experiences Harvey obtained on her peace pilgrimages. It also prepared her to disseminate these ideas in her own community through such avenues as the Workshops on Race.

Womanpower Unlimited espoused the belief that issues of international peace were as central to their lives as issues of domestic civil rights. They thought it futile to fight for justice solely in one's own community, particularly if the world at large would not provide a forum for furthering the attainment of equality and the pursuit of understanding among different races. The struggles for domestic and international human rights were interdependent in that success was not complete unless it was achieved in both areas. Womanpower worked to facilitate understanding among the races and thereby worked toward peace on all levels.

Just as they had done with respect to the civil rights movement, Womanpower positioned itself as a movement to fill the gaps in the peace movement and encourage a more comprehensive agenda. In so doing, WU brought to the forefront the need for involvement on a broader scale, a position that WSP embraced as the sixties advanced. Womanpower Unlimited demonstrated great vision by connecting these movements locally, nationally, and internationally in its infancy, demonstrating a core concept of Black feminist ideology—that theory and practice are inseparable and that the role of Black women in the political sphere is not simply fair, but vital and transformative.

CHAPTER FIVE

"Welcome, Ladies, to Magnolialand"
Womanpower and Wednesdays Women

They appeared to know in advance that we were up to no good.
—Alice Ryerson, Team 2, 1964

When I left Jackson, I knew I had been to another world.
—Gladys Zales, Team 1, 1965

The mess belongs to us, as citizens, to clean up, to set right in the eyes of the world. And Baby! If you weren't committed before you went, you will be afterward.
—Jane McIlvaine McClary, Team 5, 1965

The summer of 1964 was indeed a long, hot one in Mississippi, not just for Freedom Summer activists but also for many journeying to the Magnolia State in support of the civil rights movement. On July 14, 1964, an interracial group composed of eight Black and white women from Boston and New York were greeted by sweltering heat as they stepped off their plane at Jackson International Airport. Having spent the previous weeks getting acquainted, they were now to implement their plans. Upon their arrival, they would act as strangers and go their separate ways, with their Mississippi guides adhering to the dictates of southern segregation—the Black women would go with Doris Wilson and the white women with Susan Goodwillie and Diane Vivell. This was the beginning of their three-day, two-night journey into Mississippi to help crack open the "closed society." Charged with opening communication between Blacks and whites, these women were part of a larger cadre of women participating in the Wednesdays in Mississippi project (WIMS). Most had been socially and politically active in a variety of causes prior to the sixties. The onset of the civil rights movement provided an opportunity for them to work for racial equality through interracial cooperation. During the summer of 1964, Womanpower members, local white women, and women from outside the state asserted their influence to further the local and national civil rights agendas through the Wednesdays in Mississippi program.

WIMS was designed to bridge the gap between Black and white communities and expand civil rights activism through consciousness raising (and later in direct action). Womanpower had been working toward interracial cooperation; however, the reality of forming such alliances was an arduous task, particularly in the South. Indeed, except for a few white women such as Jane Schutt, Ann Hewitt, Ruth Beittel, and Jeannette King, interracial cooperation was virtually nonexistent in Jackson, Mississippi.[1] When successful, such alliances expanded civil rights activism beyond the Black community and raised awareness that this was an American problem, not just a "Negro" problem. Understanding the nature of racial oppression and the needs of the Black freedom struggle was integral to the conception, development, and implementation of this interracial project. Womanpower members who participated in WIMS understood their involvement as a part of their continued responsibility of activism aimed at maintaining the momentum of the movement and raising awareness about the oppression of Black people. In return, WIMS provided Womanpower a much broader avenue through which to accomplish the goals of its Chain of Friendship. In fact, WIMS embodied many of the ideas in Womanpower's Friends appeal, including encouraging local whites to work in support of movement goals and influencing the government to pass legislation that would create equal opportunities for Blacks. Through WIMS, Womanpower anticipated being able to expand its friendship base by having women from across the country make a personal connection with Mississippi and its residents. They hoped these relationships would motivate them to use their social and political clout to influence their peers inside and outside the state to change Mississippi.

That the projects' teams were composed primarily of white members belies the fact that WIMS is rooted in Black women's community activism and is representative of Black women's social and political organizing traditions. Two of the essential forces behind the development of WIMS were Clarie Collins Harvey, who proposed the program because she understood what was necessary to reach the women within this closed society; and, collectively, the National Council of Negro Women (NCNW; the Council), whose philosophy was premised on race uplift and which took primary responsibility for organizing and coordinating the project.[2] WIMS demonstrates Black women's acumen for political organizing in that they understood the necessity of women's contributions for the success of the civil rights movement and the necessary connection between local and national civil rights agendas.

For Womanpower, participation in the program exemplified members' commitment to women's empowerment for effecting change. This working relationship with the NCNW also laid the foundation for WU's future dissolution into the Council. Although guided primarily by the Council's ideas of how the project should be carried out, many of the day-to-day activities in Mississippi were a result of Womanpower's efforts. Its members served as a bridge by connecting local individuals and organizations to national ones.

The Council is a nonprofit organization that was created in 1935 by Mary McLeod Bethune. Developed during the Roosevelt administration, Bethune envisioned the NCNW as a means by which Black women could be recognized and incorporated into the activities of Roosevelt's new agencies. Through the NCNW, Bethune created an expansive agenda that incorporated alliances across races and social movements in progressive organizations such as the NAACP, the National Urban League, the Commission on Interracial Cooperation, the Southern Conference for Human Welfare, and the Southern Conference Educational Fund, to name a few.[3] The National Council of Negro Women addressed civil rights issues from its inception, while focusing primarily on representing Black women. With the emergence of the civil rights movement, the organization took an active role, shifting its mission slightly from the philosophy that working for the Black woman was working for the race to the belief that working for racial uplift was inherently working for Black women.[4]

Under the leadership of Dorothy Height, who assumed the presidency in 1958, the Council was instrumental in forming an interracial coalition of women's organizations that generated cooperative activism between northern and southern Black and white women. Height, in particular, was guided by her interpretation that "the basic concept of the NCNW, [is] to use your collective power, but never for yourself, but for others."[5] She continued Bethune's emphasis for the NCNW that "women were the key to change" and that interracial cooperation was a necessary aspect of Black women's activism.[6] Thus, Womanpower and the NCNW, while working from different positions—locally versus nationally—embraced a similar philosophy about Black women and race uplift.

The Council's Southern Travels

The Council's direct involvement in the southern civil rights movement began in the fall of 1963, at the request of James Forman, executive secretary of SNCC, and Prathia Hall, a SNCC staff member.[7] Forman and Hall were seeking the Council's assistance in addressing the police brutality experienced by young civil rights workers engaged in voter registration efforts in Selma, Alabama. At their request, Height traveled to Selma in October 1963, along with former Freedom Rider Shirley Smith, who was then executive director of the National Women's Committee for Civil Rights; Pauline "Polly" Cowan, also a white woman, who represented both the NCNW as a board member and volunteer and the New York Citizens Committee for Children; and Dr. Dorothy Ferebee, a Black woman who served as the director of health services at Howard University Medical School and succeeded Bethune as president of the NCNW. Their goal was to meet with civil rights activists, their parents, and concerned white women.[8] Height selected these women to accompany her because they comprised an interracial group and because she had worked with them on civil rights issues.[9]

Aware of the dangers of Black and white women traveling together in the South (with the exception of Black women working as maids for white women), they had initially decided to separate upon their arrival in Selma and to visit the white and Black communities separately. Unexpectedly, Height's and Ferebee's hostess, local activist Amelia Boynton, had to pick up James Forman and Dick Gregory from the airport, leaving no more seating room in her car. Height and Ferebee, then, had to ride in Cowan's rental car, traveling together to attend a meeting with local Black activists.

During their stay in Selma, the Council delegation received firsthand accounts of the difficulty of voter registration—the harassment potential registrants and activists experienced as well as the fear and ignorance that impeded registration efforts. Activists described the physical abuse they suffered, including their confinement in a makeshift incarceration facility. At the conclusion of this meeting, members of the delegation were asked to speak at a "Freedom to Vote" rally that evening to encourage voter registration efforts.[10] Their inclusion on the program was an effort to connect local efforts with the national civil rights agenda. The Council represented the external support, but, if not for the activities of local people, there would have been no movement. Thus, it was important for the Selma residents to understand the national context for which their activities were an essential contribution.

While in Selma, Cowan and Smith attempted to make inroads into the white community. They met with two female residents sympathetic to the student activists with whom they had a mutual friend. Although it was a difficult meeting, they persuaded the women to meet with Dorothy Tilly from the Fellowship of the Concerned. Prior to Tilly's arrival, the local newspaper published an account of Height's activities in Selma that cited Cowan's and Smith's participation in the Freedom Vote rally. Feeling betrayed by Cowan's and Smith's participation and "collaboration" with the protesters for a "communist inspired voter drive," the Selma women refused to meet with Tilly. While upset about the abuse of the youth, they were not in any way supporters of the protest itself or "outside agitators."[11] Consequently, the possibility of working with local white women in Selma was severed. The NCNW learned that to enlist the support of southern white women, they would have to be mindful of and sensitive to the customs of southern whites. Specifically, they had to understand the social position of white women who might have been sympathetic to the civil rights struggle but were bound by white supremacy and limited by social customs (and their husbands) concerning with whom they could associate. Even those women who were ready to deny such customs did not have the will or desire in an equally patriarchal society to ignore their husbands' limitations on their activities. Furthermore, as members of the middle class, these women feared being ostracized by their peers. Such societal limitations persisted during the WIMS program and were often articulated by southern white women. As detailed in a WIMS report, "fear of their husbands—or of reprisals to their husbands—was a constant theme among the white southern women. 'My husband told me he would divorce me if I got involved with civil rights,' said a young wife at an inter-faith meeting."[12] This valuable lesson was integral to the structuring of WIMS.

After returning to Washington, D.C., Height made a report on the Selma experience to the national board of the Young Women's Christian Association (YWCA), which disseminated the information to the National Council of Jewish Women (NCJW), the National Council of Catholic Women (NCCW), and the United Church Women (UCW). The leaders of these organizations, who were interested in solidifying the bridge between local and national civil rights agendas by using the clout/power of their national organizations to elicit change on the local level, decided to direct their energies toward the South.

The collaborative effort began in March 1964 with an interracial, three-day meeting in Atlanta, Georgia, to address ways in which women's groups could assist women and youth being arrested in the South because of their civil rights activism. Each organization invited local leaders from the seven southern cities (Jackson, Miss.; Danville, Va.; Albany and Atlanta, Ga.; Montgomery and Selma, Ala.; and Charleston, S.C.) that were deemed the most problematic and where at least one of the sponsoring organizations was firmly established. Organized as the "Inter-organizational Women's Committee"—a purposefully ambiguous name, chosen to avoid attracting attention—approximately seventy-five middle-class women of different races and religious backgrounds met at the Americana Hotel to discuss local southern conditions and strategize for action. Conveners asked the representatives to visit their local jails and courts prior to the meeting to enable them to provide eyewitness accounts. They also instructed these representatives to pay particular attention to possible human rights violations in areas such as the supervision of prisoners, medical and health services, sanitation, and legal rights.[13] The Mississippi delegation included Womanpower members Clarie Collins Harvey, Thelma Sanders (NCNW), and Jane Schutt (UCW). Also in attendance from Mississippi were Ann Ashmore (UCW), Lillian Burnstein (NCJW), Dorothy M. Cote (NCCW), Beatrice Gotthelf (NCJW), Arene Nussbaum (NCJW), Edina Rodrigue (NCCW), and Mrs. Walter C. Williams (YWCA).[14] Harvey was an obvious choice to attend the Atlanta meeting, as she and Height were well acquainted. Height had met Martin Harvey while she was a student at NYU. She met Clarie in 1939, during the World Conference of Youth trip to Amsterdam, and explained, "Our lives touched all through the years in so many different ways."[15] For example, in 1960, Harvey attended the Golden Anniversary White House Conference on Children and Youth at Height's request, as a representative of the NACW.[16] Height was well aware of Harvey's ecumenical and civil rights activism and knew that she was invaluable to mobilizing Jackson.

During this three-day gathering, participants reported on the conditions in their respective communities and heard firsthand accounts from youth activists Joyce Barnett, Joann Christian, Gwen Gilliam, and Gwen Robinson. After discussing the particulars of jail conditions and the treatment of prisoners, the women turned their attention to the role of women and consciousness raising. They divided into small groups, by city locale, to discuss local problems, possible solutions, and ways that the national organizations might assist the women in implementing them. Then they reconvened to report their results to the entire body.[17]

The large group discussion exercise led to an awareness of the similarity of conditions and problems across the South. One concern that stood out among virtually every group was the lack of communication between Blacks and whites and the need for consciousness raising among whites. According to the Mississippi delegation, Mississippians' closed minds that resisted "soul change" were the real culprits of the closed society. Various groups proposed the idea of inviting representatives from national organizations into their local communities to study and document the situation.[18]

Harvey articulated this idea of national/local communication most clearly, reasoning that national organizations could provide both inspiration and information to generate activism and supply additional forces to work with the local activists. She stated, "we want you to know that we need to be part of a national organization, because you can operate like a long-handled spoon and you can stir us up, just like you have brought us together."[19] Harvey's own activism within the state as well as her work with white women led her to conclude that interracial cooperation on the local level required a force greater than the individual women who were living in these polarized communities. She believed that challenging the rules of segregation in the Deep South would be most effective if initiated by a larger structure with a base outside the South. The Atlanta meeting, itself, demonstrated the potential for the success of this strategy. Harvey proposed that "northern women could visit us regularly during the [upcoming Freedom] summer, to act as a quieting influence by going into areas that are racially tense, to try to build bridges of communication between our Black and white communities—to be a ministry of presence among us— it would be of tremendous help to us."[20] This open invitation was for local Black and white Mississippi women to participate in a national movement as well as for women from outside of the state to lend their assistance with the civil rights agenda, locally and nationally. Harvey felt that these women could engage in consciousness raising to assist in creating an environment conducive to change. She believed that, by identifying with the movement and observing demonstrations or hearings without actively participating, northern visitors could provide a ministry for sympathetic local whites and Black activists with whom they interacted. Harvey made the connection between the local and the national, recognizing that the movements on both levels were contingent upon each other and that women were playing a central role in both arenas.

Harvey believed that Freedom Summer was the perfect opportunity for such a project, further underscoring another one of her strengths—her ability to read the evolving movement. The previous year, a few of Harvey's fellow Women Strike for Peace activists—Alice Hamburg, Hazel Grossman, Sarah Humes, Betty Winter, and Mrs. Aaron Chapman—proposed a pilgrimage to Mississippi of the sort WSP had done in Geneva, Accra, and Rome, pledging to fight discrimination in the South. Going against the grain of WSP, these women argued that:

Support by Women Strike for Peace for the civil rights movement in the South is of crucial importance. . . . Without an active, deep concern for civil rights in our own communities, we cannot expect to succeed in the difficult task of achieving enough broad support for peace and disarmament. Without such a concern on our part, Negro women might well question whether we are sincerely interested in peace with people abroad, when we are indifferent to the fate of millions of our own citizens, who face chronic unemployment, discrimination and violence in Birmingham, Jackson, and alas, in our own hometowns.[21]

Harvey wholeheartedly agreed with this philosophy, but she did not believe the time was right for such an undertaking of outright, bold, and direct action on the part of white women. She replied to Hamburg:

Our greatest needs here at the moment are for leadership skills in the white and Negro communities. We seek a sizeable group of white women who will work behind the scenes, individually and through organized groups, to create a climate that will help social change come as painlessly as possible. We have few bridges to the white community. A major contribution that persons like yourself can make is to stimulate activity within the white and Jewish communities. I am not sure that a pilgrimage to Mississippi is the best way to [fulfill] this need. It may widen the barriers rather than build the needed bridges.[22]

Her response demonstrates the value women placed on their contribution, regardless of whether they were behind the scenes or in the spotlight. It is also an indication of Harvey being in tune with the evolution of the movement in Jackson. A short six months later, Harvey believed that the proverbial time had arrived. COFO's plans to bring in hundreds of activists from outside the state for the Mississippi Summer Project meant specific projects for which women could provide material support and opportunities for women to implement their own ways to advance the movement. WIMS was also a means of expanding the emotional support that WU had been providing to the youth activists through encouragement from across the country. COFO intended to work mostly with college students during the summer, and Harvey believed that this was an opportunity for older women to inspire activism among their generation.

The Emergence of Wednesdays Women

Clarie Collins Harvey offered the idea and Polly Cowan designed the means to execute it. Cowan proposed enlisting the support of the "Cadillac crowd"—women of social and economic prominence—to carry out Harvey's proposal. These women were expected to bring material and emotional support for the activists working in the state (similar to what Womanpower had done for the Freedom Riders) while observing the local situation. They were supposed to encourage dialogue among their peers in an effort to increase and prompt (in the case of most white women) their involvement in civil rights. Although the women had Harvey's invitation, they were trying to open communication with white women and knew it was prudent to gain the support of local white women before committing to such a program. In May 1964, Polly Cowan and Shirley Smith (who had made the Selma trip the previous October) traveled to Jackson to meet with the Black and white women who had attended the Atlanta meeting in March, as well as other prominent members of the key women's organizations, to garner support for the idea of northern women coming to Jackson that summer. The trip included meetings with Barbara Barnes, director of the Central Mississippi YWCA; Dorothy Cote of the National Council of Catholic Women; and Lillie Bell Jones, director of the ("Negro") Branch of the YWCA in Jackson. Although Jones and local Black women were supportive, Barnes and Cote were apprehensive about the project. Despite the apprehension felt by some of the white women, no one suggested that the efforts be abandoned. After securing the approval of local women, Cowan and Height proceeded with formulating their plans to send northern women to Mississippi in July and August 1964 to coincide with Freedom Summer.[23]

Further discussions between Cowan and Height resulted in the creation of the "Wednesdays in Mississippi" project. They designed a program for which Cowan served as director and the NCNW assumed sponsorship, with participation from all of the organizations present at the Atlanta meeting as well as the League of Women Voters and the American Association of University Women.

Womanpower Unlimited, as a local organization, was part of what Height called the "nucleus" of their endeavor.[24] Serving as one of the "anchors" in Mississippi, WU hosted dinners and provided necessary contacts and resources. Wednesdays in Mississippi women were, inherently, more subversive and not expected to become Freedom Summer activists like the college students being recruited from across the country to teach at the Freedom Schools, staff the community centers, and engage in community organizing and door-to-door canvassing for the Mississippi Freedom Democratic Party. They offered their insights, support, and encouragement through dialogue with the activists and Mississippi residents.

Cowan and Height structured WIMS so that northern Black and white women flew to Jackson on Tuesday, spent Wednesday visiting Freedom Summer projects in different cities, returned to Jackson Wednesday night for rallies or meetings and dinner with local women, and departed Thursday morning. These short trips to Mississippi, which accommodated the women's schedules and ideally prevented them from being a burden on the local people, occurred over seven weeks during the summer. Aside from visiting various projects, the women were charged with facilitating "understanding and reconciliation" by opening lines of communication between Black and white women. Wednesdays Women were to adhere to the customs of racial segregation in Mississippi and work within their respective communities to generate communication, to promote understanding and activism, and to act as observers, not demonstrators. WIMS proceeded with its quiet assault on the barriers to equality.

In addition to the teams and coordinators, the project included a local staff in Mississippi and a national staff in New York. With this framework in place, the NCNW hired an interracial staff to coordinate the project in Mississippi. The New York staff, which consisted of secretary Deborah Loft (white) and volunteers Shirley Smith (white) and Francine Stein (white), were responsible for coordinating teams, disseminating the information to team members that prepared them for their trips, and coordinating the gathering of supplies to take for Freedom Summer. The southern-based staff for the summer of 1964 included two paid members, Doris Wilson (Black) and Susan Goodwillie (white), and one volunteer, Diane Vivell (white), all of whom attended the COFO training in Oxford. Susan Goodwillie, a native of New York City, attended Stanford University, where she studied French and the humanities. While at Stanford, Allard Lowenstein introduced her to the struggle of Black Americans, raising her awareness of social justice issues. Upon Goodwillie's graduation in 1963, she accepted a position with the NCNW as director of special projects, becoming the organization's first white employee. This introduced her directly to civil rights activism for both women and Blacks. Vivell, a native of Los Angeles, who started law school there in the fall of 1964, was Goodwillie's roommate at Stanford and signed on as a volunteer.

Doris Wilson, who was much older than Vivell and Goodwillie, exemplifies the type of woman recruited for the project. Born in Pittsburgh in 1920, Wilson was the daughter of a mill worker and a stay-at-home mom. While her parents were not wealthy, they were "privileged" and enjoyed comforts unavailable to most members of the Black community.[25] She attributed her humanist philosophy and ideas of social responsibility to family, the close-knit community in which she was raised, and the Episcopal Church. Although her parents were not involved in any civil rights organizations, they kept her and her two brothers politically informed. They were aware of the social circumstances affecting Black people and the reality of living in a segregated society. Moreover, her close community of Caribbean immigrants (her father was a native of Barbados who was sent to obtain an education in the United States to avoid British colonialism) demonstrated the reality of social responsibility as they shared food during the Depression and rallied to her family's aid at her father's death. The church taught her the ecumenical spirit demonstrated by her work with the YWCA.

By the time Height asked her to join the WIMS staff, Wilson, who had earned a bachelor's degree from Tuskegee and master's degrees from Union Theological Seminary and Case Western Reserve, had worked for the YWCA for twelve years and had interacted with Height previously at their hometown Y in Pittsburgh.[26] Of her experiences with the Y, Wilson commented that "the YWCA, in the area I worked in years ago, was very active in bringing women together. I worked in the national student-wide YWCA where we had interracial conferences in a segregated community. The struggle was to try to fight [for a] facility. So Dorothy asked me I think because she knew I knew how to function."[27] Wilson was the same age as many of the Wednesdays Women and typified Height's profile of women who had skills to contribute to the cause. Her age and her previous experience in working with women's organizations, coupled with the segregation she endured in both Pittsburgh and Alabama, provided her with insights that were beneficial in the development of the program and prepared her for the work in Mississippi. Wilson recognized the depth of racism the women faced when she stated that "one has to understand that it wasn't just segregation of racists but dehumanization of people that was the backdrop for what was going on in Mississippi. . . . The dehumanization created a problem for Black and white people because nobody could do anything."[28] Her awareness of and sensitivity to the position of activists and Mississippians, both Black and white, shaped her desire to go and why she was recruited. Wilson's work with WIMS was limited to one summer because she had accepted a position with the Chicago Metropolitan YWCA to begin in September 1964. During the summer of 1964, her local coordination efforts laid the groundwork for the success that resulted in the project's continuation.

The Mississippi staff was primarily responsible for arranging stays for participants in Wednesdays in Mississippi, which included coordinating housing, travel within the state, dinners, meetings with local women, and attendance at rallies and/or mass meetings. While local women worked with the program, Wilson, Goodwillie, and Vivell were the only full-time staff in Mississippi and bore the brunt of the responsibilities. Their arduous task of coordinating such activities for "outsiders" in that environment, especially being "outsiders" themselves, was complicated by the fact that they were subjected to segregated housing and limited places to meet. Wilson, like the other Black women who traveled to Mississippi, found housing in the Black community with the assistance of Womanpower member Jessie Mosley. Ann Hewitt rented an apartment for Goodwillie and Vivell next-door to her own in the Magnolia Towers because local white women were either unwilling or unable to open their homes to them.[29] In addition to securing housing, and like Womanpower did with the Freedom Houses, Hewitt provided linens and dishes for the apartment.[30]

Ann Hewitt was a native of Illinois, whose great-grandfather was sent to Meridian, Mississippi, as a Presbyterian missionary in 1865. Her grandfather returned to live in Mississippi after Ann's mother married. Ann and her mother, who divorced when Ann was around seven years old, later followed him to Mississippi. Hewitt's mother, Helene Alford, was active in ecumenical affairs and interracial cooperation, chairing the Negro Women's Conference of the Presbyterian Church in the 1930s.[31] It is not surprising that Hewitt continued in her mother's activist tradition and became involved with WIMS. The social custom of racial segregation in Mississippi that prevented the Jackson WIMS staff from meeting in each other's places of residence or finding public space to meet proved difficult. They eventually had brief, clandestine meetings in a back office of the local Black YWCA, under the directorship of Womanpower member Lillie Bell Jones, who offered her full support to both the Freedom Summer volunteers and the WIMS program.

The core projects involved two summers of visits to Mississippi by northern women, meeting with local women to foster dialogue, generate activism, and support local projects. While Womanpower Unlimited was key to connecting Wednesdays Women with local Blacks and some whites, white women relied upon contacts through national organizations, such as the League of Women Voters and the National Council of Catholic Women, as well as those who had attended the Inter-Organizational meeting in Atlanta to connect with local white women. The women were dedicated to developing both inter- and intra-racial communication among southern women as well as between northern and southern women. In a project report, Cowan stated, "as the project progressed . . . we realized that this process of working with the southern women in order to open their eyes, their hearts and their minds, would also cause the northern women to re-examine and re-evaluate themselves in the northern world."[32] The planners anticipated a ripple effect in which northern participants returned to their communities with enhanced ideas of how to engage in the struggle for civil and human rights, especially after witnessing and/or experiencing firsthand the effects of America's racial injustice. In essence, WIMS was similar to WU's Chain of Friendship, designed to bring everyone into the struggle for freedom and justice and generate support for all civil rights organizations working in the state.

The northern women targeted to participate in this endeavor were "busy, active women who were leaders in community affairs, or in local and national organizations, or professional women, or a combination of the three . . . they were women who could observe intelligently, assess what they saw out of an experience . . . and then be able to bring back their stories to communities and organizations that would listen to them."[33] These women were respected community leaders who could lend legitimacy to movement participation and encourage others to become activists or supporters of the Black freedom struggle. During July and August 1964, of the forty-eight women (about one-third of whom were Black) who sojourned to Mississippi, forty were college graduates (fifteen of whom had advanced degrees); twenty-nine were employed in occupations ranging from public school teachers and college professors to attorneys. Many had organizational affiliations, including the American Civil Liberties Union, the National Urban League, the Girl Scouts, and Black Greek letter organizations. For example, Flossie Dedmond was an associate professor of English at Coppin State College, Ilza Williams was the assistant principal at Clara Barton School in New York, Mary Kyle was a reporter for the *Twin City Observer*, and Marjorie Dammann was the president of Jewish Family Services of New York. And some had specific connections to the state, like Alice Ryerson (Boston, Team 2), whose daughter Susan was volunteering in a Freedom School in Moss Point; Jean Davis (Chicago, Team 6), whose daughter Linda was volunteering in a Freedom School in Ruleville; Henrietta Moore (Chicago, Team 6), whose son Phillip W. Moore III was a Freedom Summer volunteer; and Mary Cushing Niles (Washington, Team 3), mother-in-law of Staughton Lynd, coordinator of the Freedom Schools. The forty-eight women traveled in seven interracial teams to Mississippi, two from New York (to Hattiesburg) and one each from Boston (to Canton), Washington, D.C. (to Meridian), Minneapolis/Saint Paul (to Vicksburg), Chicago (to Canton), and New Jersey (to Hattiesburg). Womanpower Unlimited established contacts for Wednesdays Women, particularly the Black participants. Local women, often wu members or their associates, housed the Black Wednesdays Women. During the course of the summer, Geneva Blalock (wu), Doris Green, Clarie Collins Harvey (wu), Ruby Stutts Lyells, Marie Miller, Daisy Reddix (wu), Esther Sampson (wu), Thelma Sanders (wu), Ruth Shirley, and Aurelia Young (wu) welcomed Black Wednesdays Women into their homes. Additionally, they helped coordinate meetings, provided transportation, hosted dinners, and offered their insights about the movement. Initially, no local white women were willing to host the white Wednesdays Women who stayed at the Sun-n-Sand hotel in Jackson.[34]

Participants in wims documented their experience in Mississippi through both a written report and an oral debriefing. wims staff provided guidelines for the reports that included general observations, an assessment of Freedom Summer projects, and the implementation of the 1964 Civil Rights Act. Additionally, the women were asked to consider their own purposefulness and what they learned that could be useful in their respective organizations or communities.[35] This was a professional undertaking commensurate with the lifestyles and experiences of the women chosen to participate. An indicator of the participants' affluence and/or connections is that they were responsible for covering their own expenses "either personally or through organizational or foundation support."[36]

Once accepted and committed to participating, women received a "kit of background materials" to study in preparation for their southern sojourn. The wims staff compiled a booklet of necessary information for the team members, which included statistics on educational and economic disparities to demonstrate the impact of racial segregation and discrimination within the state. The booklet also provided information on local civil rights activism, such as the purpose and activities of various civil rights groups as well as detailed information about the Freedom Summer projects. This brief overview of the condition of Blacks in Mississippi served to educate the "outsiders" to the reality of the closed society and also to warn them about the level of poverty and subjugation they would soon witness. This information was essential to the Wednesdays Women's preparation, although in most instances it was not enough to fully prepare them for the segregation and harassment they experienced. Another orientation component was education on how to handle the press. Initially, there was no publicity because the goal was to keep a low profile and keep their visits out of the press altogether until the final trip was completed. WIMS employed this strategy to avoid limiting the participation of southern women or the ability of the Mississippi staff to make contact.

NCNW staff briefed the Wednesdays Women on appropriate behavior in Mississippi in light of the violence and harassment to which Blacks in general, and civil rights activists specifically, were subjected. Attempts were made to teach these northerners how to fit into southern society and be effective without drawing too much attention to themselves by violating the status quo. Socialization, such as the wearing of white gloves, was a minimal adjustment in comparison to the segregation the women faced as they neared the Mason-Dixon Line and entered the Magnolia State. They were entering a state in which segregation was law, and they were instructed to comply with both de jure and de facto segregation to prevent drawing attention to themselves. Though the idea was offensive to some (Ruth Batson, a Black team member from Boston, considered abandoning the trip for having to comply with such practices), the women adhered to this code of conduct to ensure their success and, most important, their safety. Many Wednesdays Women recounted similar memories of the shock of their segregation experience. Although the women knew what to expect as they entered the Deep South, the discomfort and fear that accompanied segregation and the need to ignore one's companions for their own protection was not something the women fully comprehended until they had to personally experience it. A report from a Minneapolis team member reveals a similar feeling upon realizing the gravity of the situation upon which they had embarked. As she described:

In Chicago we all had a cocktail together as we waited for the Jackson plane. . . . When we boarded the plane in Chicago, our two Negro companions told us they would sit together for the rest of the trip. . . . We visited across the aisle until our first stop, St. Louis, and then there was a gradual tapering off of any communication as the plane continued to Memphis. At Memphis we two white women got out of the plane for a bit; our Negro companions remained in their seats, with no explanation. When we re-boarded, they did not speak to us at all, and I could see that this was to be the pattern from then on. Any gaiety that had existed up to that point disappeared, and I could feel the grave seriousness that surrounded our trip. I became almost frightened by what lay ahead.[37]

No booklet could prepare the women for what they witnessed and endured. Mississippi was not, in fact, the Hospitality State.

"Welcome, Ladies, to Magnolialand"

Despite differences in personality and temperament, as well as organizational and professional backgrounds, women who participated in WIMS had similar assessments and outcomes.[38] A 1964 team member, Ruth Batson, was a self-described "racial agitator."[39] A native of Boston, Batson was born on August 3, 1921. Prompted by concerns for equitable educational opportunities for her daughters, Batson became involved in improving public school education for Blacks in the 1950s. Batson's efforts in Boston taught her firsthand about segregation and the resistance to change. She recognized that Boston was a racially divided city in which people experienced the same type of mistreatment that women described in the South. Additionally, she had experience with inter-racial cooperation through her work with the Parent's Federation and as a commissioner for the Massachusetts Committee Against Discrimination (MCAD). In these respects, Batson was the prototypical Wednesdays Woman.

The Boston team, which included eight women from Massachusetts and New York, departed for Mississippi on Tuesday, July 14, 1964. Upon their arrival on the same Jackson flight, the women adhered to Jim Crow segregation by separating without acknowledging one other. Batson was taken to the home of her hostess, Doris Green, a "music director in the Miss[issippi] public school system."[40] During their first day in Mississippi, Batson and the other Black team members, Beryl Morris and Ilza Williams, dined at Steven's Kitchen, a

Black-owned restaurant well known for its support of civil rights activists and activities, largely through the provision of free meals and meeting space. After dinner, they attended an NAACP mass meeting, along with white team member Sister Catherine John and Ruth Hughes, a national board member of the YWCA who accompanied, but was not officially a member of, the team. At this meeting, Batson witnessed the closed discussions among southern Blacks about the civil rights struggle. Ministers "both encourage[d] and scold[ed] the group" for their efforts, as others relayed the importance of participating in civil rights activities such as the upcoming school integration and the boycott at local stores.[41] Subsequent teams saw the success of this effort as they observed a fair amount of closed stores in the downtown area due to lack of business. Doris Wilson introduced the team members, who received a warm welcome and words of gratitude for the inspiration they provided and their willingness to come to Mississippi. The local activists' perseverance in their struggle and increasing involvement to ensure that the southern struggle was successful inspired WIMS members.

The remaining team members, Geraldine "Gerry" Kohlenberg, Alice Ryerson, Laya Wiesner, and Pearl Willen, dined in Wiesner's hotel room before their evening activities with local women. Willen spent the evening at the home of Lillian Burnstein, whom she had met at the Atlanta meeting as both were representing the NCJW, with twelve guests. Willen's interactions with the local women were positive as they expressed a moral obligation to integration.[42] Kohlenberg, Ryerson, and Wiesner attended a meeting under the guise of the League of Women Voters (LWV) at the home of Mrs. Rawls, state president of the League.[43] The Jackson LWV typically did not meet during the summer but it was a way to get the roughly one dozen women, some of whom were members of Mississippians for Public Education (MPE), to come out and meet the Wednesdays Women. Despite the work MPE did to keep the public schools open after integration began, about half of those in attendance were opposed to COFO's "invasion" of the state with its Summer Project and looked down on the COFO workers whom they perceived as dirty and unkempt because of their "unsavory appearance." These opinions were expressed despite the fact that those making such comments had not actually seen any of the COFO workers. Jane Schutt, who helped arrange the meeting and transported the Wednesdays Women to Mrs. Rawls's home, was the only local woman to defend the civil rights activists and also the only one to have had any contact with the volunteers or contact with Blacks outside of an employer-employee relationship.[44] Over the course of the evening, a few women seemed to quietly express open-mindedness to their visit and the presence of the civil rights workers and were not appalled by the fact that Ryerson's daughter was actually one of the volunteers.[45]

On Wednesday, Batson and the other Black WIMS team members traveled together to Canton, where they met the white members of the team at the COFO office. There, they were introduced to COFO director George Raymond; county registrar for the Mississippi Freedom Democratic Party (MFDP), Wilber Roberson; and one of the party's congressional candidates, Reverend John Cameron. They learned about the MFDP's agenda and the intimidation and repression to which Blacks had been subjected. The exchange was especially meaningful for Roberson and Cameron because Batson was a delegate to the Democratic National Convention. As such, she pledged to assist MFDP efforts to be seated at the convention.[46] This interaction exemplified the necessity of connecting local and national movement activism that Harvey hoped would emerge when she invited northern women to work in the state.

The Boston group visited two Freedom Schools and a community center and were able to observe and talk with the students and volunteers. While noting the dilapidated buildings and the meager and overused supplies, the women discerned the tremendous impact these efforts had on the community. The curriculum included the basics of literacy and math as well as Black history and movement politics. The desire for improvement and education far exceeded the limited resources and the supplies that the Wednesdays Women brought with them. Batson detected maturity, intelligence, and determination in the local people. The children Batson observed showed an eagerness to learn and an intelligence that was not stifled by the lack of educational resources and opportunities. Discussions of white privilege and Black empowerment inspired the students to insightful analyses. At the community center, housed in the basement of a Black church, which was stocked that day with one old typewriter for twelve children and worn musical instruments, children packed the building creating artwork, making music, and using the library.[47]

Before departing Canton, the team visited a Catholic school for Black children, the Holy Child Jesus Mission—a truly immaculate facility filled with unused supplies, the type of things that were desperately needed at the Freedom Schools and community center. At the suggestion of one of the team members, a COFO volunteer who accompanied them to the school asked the nuns' advice about the community center. This question sparked an exchange between the nuns and the summer volunteer that had not occurred before. By the end of their visit, the Mother Superior had acquired the telephone number of the COFO office. The Wednesdays Women left hoping they had served as a bridge for the Summer Project and the nuns, who had an abundance of unused equipment. At the school, the team met local activist Annie Devine, who discussed the history of her involvement in the Canton movement, which appeared to be new information for the nuns as well.[48]

Upon returning to Jackson that evening, the women dined at the home of Lelia Davis. The guest list included local women, Harvey, Ann Hewitt, Schutt (and a white COFO worker she was housing, who was working on the White Folks Project), Mrs. Moore (white), and Jack Pratt and Robert Lunney, two white attorneys volunteering in Mississippi for the month.[49] During their discussion of the disparities they witnessed in Canton, Batson expressed frustration with the white southern women who focused on the COFO workers' clothing. The local women implied that the volunteers' "poor dress" contributed to the resistance they encountered by whites. Similar to the meeting in Selma, Black women realized that their white counterparts were often too removed from the reality of the struggle to fully comprehend it. This was a poignant example of the perception and communication barriers the WIMS women were trying to overcome.[50]

When Batson returned home, she incorporated lessons from her Mississippi experience into her activism. Relieved to be home and safe, outside the Deep South, Batson recalled, "Suddenly I am overwhelmed by this big, big problem. I feel that I work so hard in this fight for freedom, but after Mississippi this effort that I give seems almost negligible. . . . The next morning I arise to face reality in Boston Mass[achusetts] and I go down to the Democratic State Comm[ittee] office to begin an effort to support the fight being waged by the Miss[issippi] FDP."[51] Batson remained persistent in her efforts to achieve racial equality in Boston and became a founder and director of the Metropolitan Council for Educational Opportunity in 1966, a voluntary school desegregation program. Her connection with WIMS continued as a participant in the Washington, D.C., conference that fall and in future endeavors for establishing a WIMS project in Boston.

White team members had experiences similar to those of the Black women. Their trips included a separate meeting with local white women "usually held in the homes of liberal white southern women who invited friends of various shades of opinion."[52] WIMS organizers incorporated a highly effective method of consciousness raising to affect local politics, a strategy later utilized as a cornerstone of Barack Obama's grassroots efforts to mobilize Black and Latino voters during his presidential campaign. One of the Boston team members, Pearl Willen, met with a group of women from the NCJW, of which she was national president.[53] Gerry Kohlenberg, in recounting her meeting with two of the white team members and women from the Jackson League of Women Voters, recalled the diversity of opinions among white women that ranged from empathy and fear to prejudice and resistance.[54] Like Batson, she recognized the vast differences between the activists and local whites, even those considered moderate or liberal by their peers. In her report, Kohlenberg writes, "In talking that evening with Doris Wilson, it seemed to me impossible for us to have met again with the ladies of the night before. I felt I understood and empathized with them and with the dimension of their fears, but after meeting the lives and fears of the people working in Canton, I for one would not have been able to bridge the enormity of the distances between."[55] Kohlenberg left Mississippi with a reaction similar to Batson's, that she felt "permanently involved no longer just on the fringes, about civil rights."[56] She pledged to work locally and through any available means to assist in the Mississippi struggle.

One exception to this deep divide was Jane Schutt. Team members reported, "These [Jackson] women think Mrs. Schutt is far out. One woman who loves her wouldn't dare walk on the street with her. . . . Mrs. Schutt then told them about brutality from her knowledge—[Advisory Committee to the U.S.] Commission on Civil Rights. Also spoke of why kids were living with Negro families and what students were trying to [do]. Talked about her white student who is working with white community."[57] They concluded that "most important was the fact that they talked to each other freely for the first time."[58]

During these trips, there were few integrated meetings with local white women, which disappointed some of the women. Even meetings among white women to discuss and express empathy for the movement were radical for Mississippi in 1964. Finding "white women who had the courage of their convictions who would be willing to work in fellowship and grow together," as Harvey hoped for Womanpower Unlimited, required patience.[59] While they were women of a particular type—active, intelligent, and connected—they brought different talents, perspectives, and interpretations of their experiences in Mississippi. At the end of the summer, the forty-eight women who ventured to Mississippi met approximately three hundred southern women, about half of whom were white, representing a range of religious as well as political beliefs.[60] During the fall of 1964, WIMS women were debriefed; submitted reports; wrote articles for newspapers and organizational newsletters; raised money and sent supplies to the Mississippi projects; and assessed their accomplishments to determine future plans. Reports reveal that Wednesdays Women's experiences in Mississippi had an overall, positive influence. They learned more intimately about the southern struggle and realized that it was not separate from the efforts in which they were engaged in their northern communities. Visiting Mississippi had given them new insight into racial injustice and brought them face-to-face with their own responsibility to contribute to justice and equality. Participation engendered in many of the women a long-term responsibility to achieving social justice in Mississippi. Justine Randers-Pehrson described experiencing a "realignment of my own loyalties. Mississippi is somehow 'my state' now—not the hated disgusting miasmic white state, but the staunch Negro community that could enrich all America if only its forces could flow."[61] This type of insight reflects what Black women envisioned as a result of interracial cooperation—the awakening of white women's consciousness about the existence of racial oppression and the responsibility that every American has to work toward its eradication.

From the participants' perspective, their impact on the Jackson community was equally beneficial. They received thanks, encouragement, and support from local women of both races. Wednesdays Women accomplished one of their specific goals of opening lines of communication. In the final report, compiled by Polly Cowan, she wrote, "We found that our presence opened conversations between women of the south who have never before gathered to discuss openly their attitudes toward their problems. Many women who have felt completely alone in their thought discovered through our efforts that other women were likeminded and that it would be possible for them to work together."[62] The women combined may have only spent a couple of weeks in Mississippi, but the impact of their efforts was far-reaching. In opening the lines of communication, especially intraracially between northern and southern women, WIMS women helped lay the foundation upon which Mississippi women could actualize their potential in affecting change. Batson believed that "for this effort on the part of Negroes and a few white people to challenge the crippling political structure of Miss[issippi] will in my opinion have far reaching implications and could be a determining factor in bringing about a real change."[63]

By the arrival of the last two teams, some white team members were able to stay in the homes of local white women such as Miriam Ezelle and Katie Harrell Hearn, another indicator of progress.[64] Although some local white women had begun to realize the Wednesdays Women's positive effect and were willing to more openly work with and support them, women such as Ezelle and Hearn were rare in their willingness to host. Ezelle, a member of United Church Women and recently widowed, had been active behind the scenes and used her hosting of Jean Davis (Chicago, Team 6) as her way to come out to her friends.[65] Schutt's involvement in the project may also have been an influencing factor for Ezelle, as three years earlier when Schutt joined the Civil Rights Commission Ezelle wrote her to express "praise for [her] acceptance of a place on the Advisory Committee. I think it was a most courageous and Christian act and I do pray God's guidance for each one of you that you will not be 'used' but that you will be led in helping to create a climate of understanding and goodwill."[66] Hearn, a member of MPE, had been subjected to intimidation when her husband's gas station was boycotted as a result of his chairing the Mississippi Council on Human Relations. That same week, the Hearns hosted Davis's sister-in-law, Miriam.[67] Such a gesture underscores the fact that they paved the way for greater communication among local women, as more were beginning to identify with the movement from learning of this local community of like-minded women, who were willing to engage in movement activism.

This consciousness raising was not limited to the WIMS participants or the Mississippi women. Their activism had a ripple effect in the North, as the Wednesdays Women took on the responsibility of conveying their experiences and knowledge to local organizations in their respective communities and the national organizations to which they belonged. This was instrumental not only in generating more support to sustain the WIMS project but also in galvanizing support for civil rights activism in Mississippi and nationally. For example, Gerry Kohlenberg reported serving on a panel for an NAACP rally in New Bedford in August 1964 and receiving an invitation to speak to the Boston University Wives' Guild.[68] Sister Catherine John, who traveled with the Boston team, reported several speaking engagements about her trip, including Newton College of the Sacred Heart, Maryknoll Sisters Motherhouse in New York, and the College of St. Catherine en route to her home in California, in addition to speaking at her own Sisters of the Immaculate Heart and penning an article for publication. Her students at Immaculate Heart had donated a mimeograph machine and raised funds to send more supplies to the COFO office in Canton.[69]

Dr. Geraldine Woods, president of Delta Sigma Theta Sorority, Inc. and a member of the Washington/Baltimore team, reported, "Due to my enrichment,

I can certainly guide the Social Action Committee [established during her administration] of Chapters of Delta Sigma Theta (DST) in helping financially and materially in the state, in particular, and with the same problems facing other states in the South generally."[70] One way Woods fulfilled this mission was via her work with "Delta Teen Lift," a program begun under her predecessor Jeanne Noble's tenure but "fully developed during Geraldine Wood's administration."[71] The program provided disadvantaged southern youth opportunities to visit cities in the Midwest and on the West Coast to expand their horizons and benefit from the mentorship of women in the organization. Womanpower worked with DST in sponsoring thirty Mississippi youth to participate in this program in the summer of 1965.[72] These activities did not always produce immediate or quantifiable results, but they were necessary groundwork for the movement as such endeavors disseminated information to persons who might have otherwise been un- or misinformed about the civil rights movement and also increased support for movement activities. For the youth specifically, opportunities like the Teen Lift program broadened the experiences and consciousness of the next generation of American citizens.

In respect to the Freedom Summer projects, the women could boast of results that were more tangible. Aside from the emotional support they provided to civil rights workers and community members, once women returned home they increased their efforts to support "their" Mississippi communities' COFO projects with material items. This was important to the women who, because of the brevity of their visits, could not get involved with Womanpower's support work during the summer. Peggy Roach personally provided bolts of cloth for the sewing class in Meridian. After witnessing the inadequate library and limited teaching materials, such as a French class with no books, the women knew what to send to each community. In case women forgot, the WIMS staff compiled a reminder list of "Materials needed by COFO" for fall and winter programming, with items ranging from books, clothing, and household items to automobiles and building supplies.[73] Flaxie Pinkett, a member of Team 3 from Washington, D.C., arranged for her DST sorors to provide clothing for the children integrating the Jackson Public Schools in the fall of 1964.[74] Florynce Kennedy, a prominent New York attorney known for her feminist and Black Nationalist activism, hosted a "Mississippi for Halloween Costume Party" to raise money for the Mississippi Committee for Human Rights, which she sent to her summer hostess, Thelma Sanders.[75] Through WIMS's efforts, material support came in the way of smaller items such as books, literacy kits, and art supplies as well as larger items such as musical instruments and mimeographing and stenciling equipment. The book donations were so large that they morphed into a project requiring its own coordinators. WIMS raised money to meet long-range funding needs of civil rights projects, even while it worked to raise money to cover the more than $2,000 deficit that remained from its own summer operating expenses. Sustained communication between northern and southern women, as well as among the southern women themselves, was a result of the WIMS project. Jean Davis, for instance, began correspondence with her hostess Miriam Ezelle after her return home.[76] Although much work remained, the continued communication and material and emotional support were evidence that they were accomplishing their goals.

In November 1964, Thelma Sanders attended the Council's two-day WIMS conference in Washington, D.C., to discuss how to use the experience of the Wednesdays Women and in which direction the project should proceed. Conference workshops focused on issues such as "protection in Mississippi, unemployment, health, education, and the effective use of the federal government as it prepared to make the changes within the state necessary to comply with the law."[77] In these sessions, participants learned what roles the federal government could legally play and how citizens' groups such as WIMS could be effective in ensuring the implementation of civil rights legislation. These were interactive sessions for which participants were given preparatory worksheets, prompting them with questions for each problem area. In respect to future plans, WIMS developed a trifocal approach: monitoring Mississippi government, business, and industry to ensure compliance with civil rights legislation; organizing a material distribution program; and continuing visits to Mississippi.

"We Return Fighting"

As preparation for the 1965 visits began, WIMS organizers were more confident about their contribution to the movement, in general, and in Mississippi, in particular. Additionally, WIMS had become a "full-time, year-round organization" and had been serving as a liaison for federal agencies and local organizations and activists.[78] With this experience, the staff aimed to create an agenda with a more specific focus than the trips of the previous summer. The structure and recruitment process remained the same. For participants, WIMS coordinators sought women with "professional or personal skills" to assist with the desegregation of the state in compliance with Title VI of the 1964 Civil Rights

Act, which "prohibit[ed] discrimination on the basis of race, color, or national origin in programs and activities that receive federal [funding]."[79] The team configuration and duration of the trips remained primarily the same—a Tuesday arrival and Thursday departure, with a few women extending their trips to accommodate their participation in particular projects. The daily schedule was less structured to allow women the adequate and/or flexible time to participate in various projects.

Interestingly, WIMS's transformation was similar to that of Womanpower Unlimited, which had evolved from a supportive and partially underground movement to one focused on leadership development and direct action. Once anonymity was no longer a concern, WIMS's strategy changed from working solely as observers and engendering communication to include engaging in direct action, reflecting both the shift in movement activism in Mississippi as well as the desire to have a more immediate impact. As WIMS was fully public and organizers no longer perceived press coverage as a possible impediment, they held orientation sessions with local leaders, such as the director of the Mississippi Human Relations Council, Kenneth Dean, upon their arrival. The forty-seven women of the 1965 trips had backgrounds similar to their predecessors—one-third of the women were Black, forty-four had attended college (thirty-one graduated), fourteen had advanced degrees, and thirty-seven were employed. The women who comprised the seven 1965 teams hailed from New York, Philadelphia (two teams), New Jersey, Chicago, D.C./Virginia, and Boston, visiting Greenville, Greenwood, Lexington, Edwards, Oxford, Mount Beulah, and Philadelphia. Like the previous year, the 1965 groundwork included a spring visit by Polly Cowan and Hope Ackerman to Mississippi—meeting again with Barbara Barnes and Lillie Bell Jones from the YWCA, Clarie Harvey, Patricia "Patt" Derian, and many others—to ensure that their presence was still welcome.[80] From this visit, Cowan learned that "the Negro women unanimously favored our return to Mississippi. . . . The feeling among the white women was mixed, but from all indications more wish us to come back than not."[81] WIMS organizers were reassured of local support and moved forward with their planning.

Womanpower members served as hostesses again. Geneva Blalock, who was out of town for the summer, rented her house to local staff member Oceola Walden.[82] This summer, they were able to secure housing for all white participants with local women such as Carol Bergmark, Elaine Crystal, Eleanor Fontaine, Joan Geiger, Mrs. Myers Hollowell, Polly Murphy Keller, and Danelle

Vockroth. The local white women who served as hostesses were similar to their northern counterparts—affluent women who were either active and influential in their own right or had husbands who were. Many were not native Mississippians, having moved there with their husbands in the forties and fifties. They tended to be active in their churches and children's schools. For example, Bergmark was the first president of Spann Elementary's PTA, and Hollowell was the director of religious education for St. Andrew's Episcopal Church. Politically they were involved with the League of Women Voters and Mississippians for Public Education, of which Geiger and Crystal were cofounders. A few women could attribute their activism to their being single. Vockroth was pursuing a divorce and Hollowell, like Miriam Ezelle, who hosted the previous summer, was recently widowed. Collectively they were a group of outspoken and active women who were willing to challenge the status quo and privileges race had afforded them.

In addressing compliance with the Civil Rights Act, WIMS sought and was invited to assist with various projects in Mississippi during the summer of 1965, thus the concern for recruiting women who were qualified to fill these particular roles. In this capacity, they were able to work much more closely with Womanpower members in their civil rights activities with school integration, the Medgar Evers Neighborhood Guild, and Head Start.

One of their chief projects was the new Head Start program, which sought sociologists, psychologists, and early childhood education specialists. During the spring of 1965, WIMS provided classroom materials and books. A week before the schools opened, WIMS sent a special team of four art teachers from the PROJECT, INC. art center in Cambridge, Massachusetts—Rita Delisi, director, along with Mary Austin, Laura Avery, and Myrna Higgins—to train Head Start teachers in arts education for children. Additionally, a white nursery school teacher from Iowa spent three weeks working with the Lexington Head Start program.[83] Special skills with the Head Start programs were not limited to classroom teaching. The New Jersey team met with parents' groups to discuss techniques for supplementing their children's education at home. Wednesdays Women visited Head Start programs in Jackson, Mount Beulah, and Lexington and spent considerable time with Jackson Head Start director and Womanpower member Esther Sampson, who took a leave of absence from her job with the State Department of Public Welfare to direct the program.[84] Some team members met with Pearl Draine, who directed the Blair Street Church Head Start program and also served as assistant director of the Child Development

Group of Mississippi (CDGM), a statewide Head Start program organized in 1965 with funding by the Office of Economic Opportunity (OEO).[85] In addition, Draine and Harvey facilitated interactions with Ted and Carol Seaver, who were planning the opening of the Medgar Evers Neighborhood Guild.

Other projects included a Speakers Program, which afforded team members the opportunity to address an integrated meeting in Jackson on their areas of expertise and served as a means of generating interracial communication and social interaction. This program was proposed by one of the "Mississippi advisers" as a means of facilitating interracial communication in an informal and thought-provoking setting.[86] Esther Cooke (New Jersey) spoke to a crowd of about 175 people at Blair Street Methodist Church about parents' role in ensuring the success of Head Start. Josie Habison and Lorna Scheide, also members of the New Jersey team, addressed a Head Start parents' meeting on the topic of Family Life. Each member of the Philadelphia team spoke at the Unitarian Church, under the leadership of Reverend Donald Thompson, about interracial projects they were working on in their home communities. Mildred Pitt (Washington, D.C.) spoke to a group at the Unitarian Church during her team's visit as well.

The University of Mississippi's "Special Training Institute on Problems of School Desegregation" for rural teachers and administrators, funded by the Department of Health, Education and Welfare, requested WIMS's "woman-power." The Institute enrolled 120 participants (112 white and 8 Black) in two month-long sessions and enlisted 11 WIMS women to serve as speakers, including Dorothy Height, Oceola Walden, Hannah Levin (New Jersey), Molly Harrower (New York), and Marjorie Penney (Philadelphia).[87] Dr. Roscoe A. Boyer, the institute director, stated that "it was through your effort to marshal the forces of WIMS that the program succeeded."[88] As institute speakers, WIMS women dispelled stereotypes about Black teachers and discussed topics such as how to recognize and handle students' mental and emotional stress that would likely accompany desegregation.

The final team, from Boston, focused their direct action efforts on integrated teams engaging in door-to-door canvassing for school desegregation in Jackson. Following the efforts of Womanpower and other local women both during that year and the previous one, these integrated teams connected the local and national civil rights agendas and filled a need for canvassers. They encouraged local Black families to send their children to integrated schools.[89]

The WIMS participants and staff were equally happy with the outcome of their efforts in Mississippi in 1965. From facilitating interracial dialogue to integrated lunches at the Sun-n-Sand Hotel with Wednesdays Women and local women (including Ann Hewitt's wheelchair-bound mother), WIMS helped usher in a new state of race relations.[90] Fear prevented many local women from participating, and many schools and businesses lacked compliance with the Civil Rights Act. Still, some accomplishments were evident. Mississippi could not be opened overnight, and none of the Wednesdays Women were so naïve as to think that their presence, alone, would elicit immediate change. Harvey commented to this effect in a meeting with Mildred Pitt (Washington, D.C., 1965), stating "that we should expect long rather than short range results. . . . Our mere presence often gave the people with whom we met the assurances that someone cares."[91] Drawing on Womanpower's work with the Freedom Riders, the Jackson Nonviolent Movement, and the Freedom Summer volunteers, Harvey had no doubt about the role emotional support played in sustaining activism. Overall, their strategy of facilitating interracial cooperation and opening communication, combined with direct action, was valuable for the movement, locally and nationally.

From the southern, white perspective, Ann Hewitt, also a YWCA board member, concluded,

> I think it was good for Jackson, for Mississippi, and for everyone with whom the women made contact. . . . Elizabeth Haseldon [sic] [Chicago, 1965] being in Jackson to speak to the Interfaith night meeting, and again the following day to the UCW ladies, was absolutely unbeatable. Again, if this is all that was won, it was grand. . . . The visit that Polly Keller (wife of the rector of St. Andrew's Episcopal Church) made with Faith Griefen and Frances Tillson [Boston, 1965] to Mt. Beulah. As Polly Keller said, it gave her a reason for going and she wouldn't have gone without it. . . .
>
> In assessing the ultimate worth of WIMS to the Jackson community, no one will ever know all of the ramifications. For instance, those who *think* they were the powers of decision about Head Start, have no idea how much of their information, facts, etc. were given to them through friends of WIMS; or that the only reason that I was involved in Head Start from the beginning was Polly Cowan took me to Washington for her initial conference with Dudley Morris; or that preceding even that trip was Dorothy Height's being in on the very opening of the Head Start idea when Mrs. Johnson had the original group to Washington.[92]

Women who participated in WIMS from all sides regarded the work as beneficial to furthering civil rights efforts, locally and nationally.

The NCNW held the second WIMS conference in November 1965 during their annual convention. The sessions included reports from each team regarding their activities and accomplishments in Mississippi—a different approach from the 1964 conference, since the teams had specific projects with which to work. Again, discussions centered on the future of the Wednesdays in Mississippi project, particularly the summer visits. Finally, with the assistance of government officials, workshops were conducted on "pre-school education, problems of school desegregation . . . and the use of WIMS techniques in other parts of the country."[93]

While the consensus was that WIMS should continue, opinions varied regarding in what capacity. Some proposed that they continue in Mississippi. Others recommended working in other southern states to avoid saturating Mississippi with their work, while others suggested that they work in northern urban areas. WIMS decided to implement all the proposals. Northern WIMS projects included a "Conversation Caravan" in Patterson, New Jersey, which evolved into the Women's Council for Community Service with a focus on housing.[94] Ruth Batson pursued establishing a similar project in the Boston/Cambridge area with a focus on housing and education.[95]

Simultaneously, Wednesdays in Mississippi became "Workshops in Mississippi" with a focus on economic and community development. In developing a method for continuing activities in Mississippi, the NCNW wanted to ensure effectiveness by working within its capacity and by utilizing the Council's existing organizational networks in the state. Again they were evolving into having a more focused and direct impact upon women's lives. A "training-in-action" program designed to empower local women to navigate governmental agencies to acquire the necessary resources for improving their lives and communities replaced team visits. Womanpower member Jessie Mosley, along with Fannie Lou Hamer and Unita Blackwell, was as instrumental in developing this new phase as was Clarie Collins Harvey to the initial project.[96] NCNW-WIMS designed workshops targeting low-income rural women to bridge the gap between government agencies and the individuals intended to benefit from their services.[97]

In November 1966, Jessie Mosley convened women from across the state for an NCNW-WIMS meeting in Jackson to develop an agenda for Workshops in Mississippi. The first workshop was scheduled for the upcoming January in Oxford with Mosley and Annie Devine of Canton chairing the Steering Committee, underscoring the centrality of Black women's voices in organizing and structuring the project.[98] This new project sought to bring about the type of agency that Ella Baker and SNCC advocated in empowering oppressed people to become full participants in the structures of society that heretofore excluded them. They actualized Baker's philosophy of "participatory democracy" by following an agenda set by the local women and validating the knowledge and wisdom that emerged from their lived experiences.[99] In sessions chaired by Ruth Batson, the participants developed a programmatic focus on issues pertaining to housing, childcare, community centers, food assistance, and single teen mothers. Working with the Department of Agriculture, NCNW-WIMS selected Sunflower County as the location for the pilot program. With funding provided by the OEO, they scheduled the first workshop for June 1967, with a focus on "health, social security, welfare, food stamps and jobs."[100] Sunflower County resident and iconic civil rights activist Fannie Lou Hamer was the local coordinator, and she convened an interracial group of women of which two-thirds were Black.[101] NCNW received an OEO Annual Rural Service Award for the successful contribution of the WIMS program to the "War on Poverty." The NCNW continued these efforts of economic empowerment for poor rural women though collaboration with HUD to increase home ownership among poor Black women via a project known as Turnkey III. The Council also assisted with the creation of the Fannie Lou Hamer Daycare and the establishment of Pig Banks, a program to help lessen hunger in rural Mississippi by supplying poor families with a pregnant sow, which they returned after the litter was delivered. When two sows in that litter became pregnant they were given to the bank to help another needy family.

Individual Wednesdays Women maintained a high level of activism, some of which was influenced by their experiences with WIMS, including ongoing contact with their Mississippi associates. Ruth Batson, for example, collected $200 in December 1965 in response to a request from Ruleville to purchase Black dolls for local children.[102] Edith Savage (New Jersey, 1964) served as a hostess for Fannie Lou Hamer when she attended the Democratic National Convention in the fall of 1964.[103] Shirley Lipsey (Philadelphia, 1965) attributed her appointment to the Mayor's Committee–Neighborhood Development Committee to her WIMS participation.[104] Buddy Mayer (Chicago, 1965) maintained correspondence with Aurelia Young, Womanpower member, WIMS "angel," and Jackson State College professor, and collaborated on art projects in Jackson.[105] WIMS made many additional resources available to Mississippi and sparked a level of awareness and creativity among northern women that resulted in increased efforts to improve their communities as well. Ilza Williams commented that "we're a ripple, and this is good. At no place and no time in our history has anything ever started without a ripple. And we have involved hundreds of other people."[106] WIMS helped fulfill one of Womanpower's goals of expanding its Chain of Friendship by fostering activism among those outside the state that both supported the southern movement and initiated activism within their own communities.

While it is difficult to fully assess the accomplishments of the Wednesdays in Mississippi project because not all of its results are quantifiable, WIMS can boast tangible results. Its success is evident in the request from Mississippians to continue its activities in 1965 and also in the fact that the New York office developed into a year-round operation. Moreover, the women provided essential resources and support to sustain civil rights initiatives in Mississippi, made inroads toward bridging the communication gap among and between Black and white women, empowered local women to improve their lives and communities, and created institutions that lasted far beyond the "civil rights" years. The members of the "Cadillac crowd" engendered participation among their northern and southern peers, thereby creating a more visible network of white women who were sympathetic to the struggle for civil rights. Trude Lash (New York, 1964) acknowledged the legitimacy they were able to bring to middle-class women, stating, "For the white women the realization that we were obviously middle-aged women with some standing in the community whose children were at the same colleges as their own created an uncomfortable challenge to firmly held prejudices. In this respect, we were probably more effective than the COFO workers."[107] Similar to how Harvey, Sanders, Logan, Mosley, and other prominent Black women in Jackson were able to bring legitimacy to the movement locally and engender activism among their peers, Wednesdays Women were able to, in a small way, evoke support from white women in Mississippi and in their own communities.

This sense of accomplishment was not limited to WIMS women. From the southern perspective, Patt Derian wrote: "After two summers of vigorous activity [WIMS] has established a pattern and method of operation that should not be allowed to disappear. . . . A catalogue of Wednesday achievements probably cannot be compiled, simply because they did too much and the things that they did have yet to end. If you looked back over the last two years and marked every forward step in Jackson community relations, you would find that a Wednesday lady had somehow been involved."[108] Florence Gooch, one of the white Jacksonians who supported wims early on by hosting meetings with the white visitors and her friends, concluded that wims was necessary ground-work. She wrote that "while social integration will not be acceptable here for a long, long time, at least the visits of intelligent, dedicated women of both races can be part of the bridge that will have to be built by all of us together."[109] These comments speak to the utility of interracial cooperation and to women's effectiveness in bridging grassroots activism with the national movement and engendering activism among hesitant populations.

As Harvey mentioned, the effects were not always immediately evident. For example, Gladys Zales (New York, 1965) recounted that, when she met with a group of local white women, she encountered a "'Yankee Go Home' approach. And one woman proclaimed 'you should be working in Harlem instead of down here.'"[110] Six months later those women had changed their minds. Zales reported to Cowan that in January 1966, "The V. P. of her organization just came back from giving a speech in Jackson and said that a group of them came up to her after the speech, asked her to take a message back to Mrs. Zales that they were wrong, she was right, and they had been doing a great deal to com-pensate since she left and they wanted her (Mrs. Zales) to return to Jackson."[111] Indeed, wims's long-term effects were worth the wait.

Upon returning home, Wednesdays Women gave lectures and interviews about what they witnessed—the efforts and successes of local people and the sncc and cofo workers, despite the dearth of resources; the police harass-ment; the fear and apathy that existed among both Blacks and whites—and in-fused their insights into their local activism. In so doing, they helped counter-act the media suppression that existed in Mississippi as well as the national and local dissemination of misinformation about Mississippi's "Negro problem." In reflecting on how wims contributed to the movement, Josie Johnson (Minne-apolis, 1964) commented that "our eye-witness to the acts that were going on then helped create the urgency of the effort that people were making to try and end that horrible abuse. . . . We created an on-going constant reminder of what was occurring and what needed to be done."[112] wims provided an eyewitness to both "on the ground" and behind-the-scenes activities and created a national network of women who were concerned about and willing to work on behalf of the cause of human rights.

Assessing wims nearly forty years later, Doris Wilson commented: "The project shows the possibilities of what women can do if they are committed. . . .

I've worked with women all my life, both students and women in the YWCA. We have a capacity if we use it, not to put men down, but to enable men to do better because what's good for men is good for women."[113] Wilson's assessment exemplifies the spirit of the Black women activists in both Womanpower and the NCNW that helped guide the formation of WIMS.

Many Black women regarded their civil rights work as their responsibility to continuing a legacy of Black women's activism. Johnson argued:

> It's important for me and other Black women to demonstrate what all of the Black women throughout history have done from Harriet Tubman and Sojourner Truth on forward; that we have been persistent because we care so much about our children. Because unless we nurture, love, protect, guard our children, we will lose our community. . . . Every phase of what we do as a people in our struggle seems to be a layer added to what others before us did. My opportunity contributed to the belief that you carry on in the tradition of your ancestors. That was my approach— to add my layer to the struggle and the history that is W. E. B. DuBois and Dorothy Height.[114]

Women such as Johnson embraced activist mothering in recognizing their responsibility to the larger Black community and understood that their social position afforded them the opportunity to engage in the Black freedom struggle in a unique way.

The Womanpower/WIMS legacy continued into the twenty-first century. In 2001, the Children's Defense Fund's (CDF) program Wednesdays in Washington and at Home was an important part of a broad-based strategy to raise awareness about children's needs and generate support for passage of the No Child Left Behind Act. CDF President Marian Wright Edelman designed the program with the tactics of Wednesdays in Mississippi in mind, mobilizing at the grassroots level to effect change nationally on behalf of the ignored, neglected, and voiceless members of society.[115] The program's name perpetuated WIMS's mandate that, once the Wednesdays Women returned home, they continued their activism in their own communities.

WIMS underscores interracial cooperation as one of the many strategies embraced by Black activists locally and nationally in their efforts to attain civil rights. Analyzing interracial cooperation in this manner complicates our understanding of WIMS as more significant than merely Black and white women's joint efforts at advancing the civil rights movement under the guise of a traditionally feminine modus operandi. Instead, it allows us to examine WIMS as a decidedly political strategy articulated and embraced by Black women involved in the Black freedom struggle. And for Womanpower Unlimited, WIMS demonstrates the key role members played in providing a bridge for a national organization to the Jackson civil rights movement.

CHAPTER SIX

"When There Was a Need"
Ministering to the People

I'm not a great philosopher, idealist, and I don't like to spend a
whole lot of time talking. I'm more of an action person.
—Clarie Collins Harvey

Whatever glory belongs to the race for a development unprecedented in history for the given length of time, a full share belongs
to the womanhood of the race.
—Mary McLeod Bethune

On July 29, 2012, the Charles W. Capp, Jr. Archives and Museum Building at
Delta State University in Cleveland, Mississippi, hosted a fiftieth-anniversary
celebration of The Box Project.[1] Donna Goldman, who began directing the
project in 2011, commenced the ceremony with a history of the project's origins
during the civil rights movement and a tribute to its founder, Virginia Naeve.
Overall approximately two dozen persons turned out to celebrate this project
that has, over the past fifty years, given thousands of poor people (the majority
of whom were Mississippians) the material resources and emotional support
to survive.[2] Since its inception, The Box Project has given hope in humanity
to people who exist on the fringes of American society by providing families
in need with the resources to attain self-sufficiency. The Box Project pairs up
poor families or individuals with families or groups that commit to sending
a box a month to their recipient families. In addition to providing material
items, sister families are expected to get to know each other through regular
correspondence, developing a friendship and source of emotional support. Key
to the project's creation was Womanpower Unlimited.

As Womanpower sought to bring about societal transformation via enrichment initiatives to ensure community survival and success, antipoverty
initiatives were an integral component of its civil rights agenda. The women

understood that the injustices against which they were fighting were responsible for the conditions being addressed through The Box Project. This insight also fueled their efforts to provide opportunities for Black youth, whose limited experiences and stifled potential resulted from segregation. One of WU's major activities was an Interracial Vacations Camping Project, conducted in collaboration with the American Ethical Union. This program provided kids with a few weeks of fresh air, swimming, hiking, bonfires with s'mores, and camaraderie in an environment free of prejudice at interracial, intergenerational, interfaith camps on the East Coast. Womanpower undertook measures to help families acquire basic necessities and to provide experiences for children that hopefully led to better life chances than those of their parents. Through The Box Project and Interracial Vacations Camping Project, Womanpower provided Black Mississippians with resources and opportunities that they otherwise could not have accessed.

Projects such as these kept the movement focused on the day-to-day needs of Blacks who were not immediately benefiting from the larger battles being waged for systemic change. Just as *Brown v. Board of Education* did not result in immediate educational improvements for the majority of Blacks in Mississippi, registering to vote certainly did not translate to sharecroppers being able to earn a living wage and adequately provide for their families. Womanpower's participation in the development of these programs demonstrates the holistic and unique approach they took to achieving peace and freedom. Although poverty was tied to segregation and disenfranchisement, the women understood that, on a more basic level, people needed to survive. Until the movement's goals were realized, meeting one's immediate day-to-day needs remained a priority for many Black Mississippians. For Womanpower, attaining civil rights and securing basic resources and opportunities for educational and cultural development via the Box and Camp projects were attempts to move people closer to achieving an "abundant life."

The Box Project

The April 1962 Women Strike for Peace trip to Geneva set in motion more than a burgeoning movement of American women for world peace. On this trip, Virginia Naeve of Jamaica, Vermont, met Clarie Collins Harvey and Coretta Scott King. It was the beginning of not just collaborative work on peace, civil rights, and antipoverty initiatives but also lifelong friendships. Naeve discovered that she shared a pacifist philosophy with the only two Black women in the American delegation as she expressed to them her genuine concern over human rights, both abroad and domestically. They discussed the connections between the oppression of Black Americans and issues of peace among human-kind, and they all believed that war and segregation were parts of the same whole. Further, upon learning about Harvey's and King's civil rights activism, Naeve sought to assist in the Black freedom struggle at home as part of her efforts for peace and justice.[3] She agreed with the position her Black WSP colleagues shared—that peace was more than the absence of war. Naeve explained that "for enduring peace we have to consider human rights and civil rights. We can not in truth speak of freedom for the world's peoples and hold down a minority within our own borders."[4] She understood that part of the oppression Blacks experienced was the abject poverty to which they were subjected. Naeve grappled with the question of how she, in supporting peace and freedom, could effect change for her fellow Americans, especially while living in an almost exclusively white area. Despite her wishes, she had limited possibilities for helping those in need because of her family's own lower economic status, yet she worked to realize this shared vision.

Virginia Naeve was born on December 17, 1921, in Chamberlain, South Dakota. Many of her formative years were spent in Oklahoma, which afforded her the opportunity to interact with Blacks and Native Americans. These early interactions with people of color distinguished Naeve from many of her neighbors in Vermont and influenced her desire to help. Her southern upbringing gave her insight into the conditions of poverty and racism that permeated Mississippi and the impact of the civil rights movement. She explained: "Having spent my childhood in the South, I knew that the link between the Negro and the white in the South was severed when the first Negroes went out into the streets for their rights. It became nearly impossible for Southern Negroes fighting for their rights and white Southerners wishing to help them to get together. In many instances where a white person tries, he is ostracized by the white community and subjected to such severe economic and physical reprisals that he desists or is driven out."[5] Understanding the level of regional, racial strife made her aware that material and emotional assistance from northerners was crucial to sustaining the Black freedom struggle. She believed that whites needed to demonstrate their solidarity with Blacks fighting for equality, and she knew of the difficulties southern whites faced in attempting to do so. Northern whites, then, needed to take on this responsibility.

Like Harvey, Naeve found a life partner who shared her commitment to her philosophical and political views. In 1946 Virginia met Lowell Naeve, a native of Iowa, who was a conscientious objector during World War II and served four-and-a-half years in prison for his draft refusal. The two moved from New York City to Vermont in 1948 to "join friends in the country, raise their children in a quieter place and create a different lifestyle."[6] Both of the Naeves were artists and teachers, at one point sharing a teaching position at the Woodstock Country School in Vermont; and Lowell, an activist in his own right, was in full support of his wife's activism.[7]

After continued communication with Harvey and King in 1962, Naeve conceived of sending boxes of clothing that her family had outgrown to needy families in Mississippi and Georgia (hence, the "Box Project"). In addition, Naeve was interested in making a human connection with the people she was attempting to help. Sending clothing (or food and money) was important as was creating a bond that bridged the two separate worlds of white and Black, North and South. This was of special concern to Naeve since she lived in an isolated, rural area of Vermont, seventeen miles from the nearest Black person.[8] This singular gesture of compassion evolved into a program serving thousands of individuals in numerous states.

The Box Project was more than just a few women fulfilling their Christian duty to help the less fortunate. In fact, unlike Harvey, who was deeply ensconced in the Methodist tradition, Naeve had grown up in the church but was a nonbeliever as an adult. Naeve "didn't think the churches for the most part lived up to their Christian ideals of brotherhood of man, etc."[9] Instead, for these women, this undertaking was a step toward achieving the goals of the civil rights and peace movements and also improving greater humanity by helping one family at a time try to overcome the oppressions that thwarted their lives. The Box Project was designed in contrast to the "bank deposit" charity mentality of giving a donation and continuing on with one's life, "without really touching the heart of the problem."[10] Providing a deeper human connection was one of the women's strategies to create a society where people were no longer denied lives of basic human decency because of the segregation and discrimination that developed from racism. In choosing to help the most dispossessed and disenfranchised, The Box Project was a politically driven demonstration of compassion for one's fellow woman. The focus on sharecroppers, the poorest of Black southerners, also subverted the continued separation of Blacks and whites that had been instrumental in maintaining Jim Crow segregation, one of the mores of American, especially southern, society. For many Blacks, whose lives had been characterized by exploitation at the hands of whites, The Box Project introduced them to whites who treated them like human beings.

Naeve enlisted Harvey's and King's assistance in securing names of possible families to which she could send clothing. Her first sister family consisted of sharecroppers in Georgia.[11] Shortly after Naeve began sending boxes to this family, after saving for the postage, a neighbor inquired about adopting a family as well, which Naeve arranged through Harvey and King. She soon discovered that there were many people in a position similar to hers—northern whites living in rural areas with a desire to help alleviate the poverty Blacks faced in the South as a result of racial injustice. Despite the high levels of poverty, the process was not as quick as one might assume; it took some time to generate the names of families who were willing to offer themselves as recipients of these good white folk. As Naeve recalled, "it took a whole year before the wheels and gears got oiled sufficiently down there to produce families in any number, and for the families to accept that we really wanted to help them."[12] When the project finally launched, Naeve and two friends, Myrtle Lane (also of Vermont) and Mary Knight, who had recently relocated to Canada to spare her son from being drafted, formed the first northern-based volunteer staff of the Southern or Mississippi Box Project in June 1963.

Myrtle Daisy Quigley was born in Philadelphia in 1919. Her parents' poverty meant that they moved around a lot in search of work, eventually ending up in Long Island, where Myrtle married and had two sons. In 1961 Myrtle moved to Montpelier, Vermont. As a single parent, having divorced while her children were young and being fond of neither her maiden nor her married name, Myrtle simply changed her last name to "Lane."[13] She worked as a secretarial office manager for a small financial consulting firm while pursuing her activist work and setting an example for her children of how to advocate for peace, justice, and equality. Lane's social activism led to her involvement in Women Strike for Peace, The Box Project, and, later, Vermont in Mississippi, and she served as a newsletter editor for all of these groups. As a single working mother, Lane was quite different from many of her motherly contemporaries in Women Strike for Peace but right at home with the outspoken, publicly active, and independent women in Womanpower Unlimited and those who undertook The Box Project.

Working primarily out of Naeve's home, the storage location for donated items, this group of New England volunteers coordinated the pairing of families, fundraising, publicity, and keeping files. Lane "furnished all the mimeographed material needed for appeals and [reports]," and Mary Knight donated $5 of stamps each month to make the mailings possible.[14] Together, they took primary responsibility for sorting and packaging the donations they received.

The Box Project focused on Mississippi during its inception.[15] The relationship with Harvey and Womanpower Unlimited, which provided intimate knowledge about the needs of Black Mississippians, was important in this regard. Similar to what Harvey and Womanpower would do for Wednesdays in Mississippi, they welcomed the project and provided information, contacts, resources, and womanpower to facilitate the development and success of the endeavor. Harvey sent Naeve reading materials in addition to a subscription to a local Black newspaper.[16] This collaboration was an easy one for Womanpower because collecting and distributing clothing to families in need was part of its agenda. Rosie Redmond, chair of the clothes committee, began working in this capacity with Womanpower when it was founded in 1961. Through Womanpower, Redmond continued with and expanded upon the work she had begun in 1941 to aid needy families in her community by providing clothes for school-aged children, assistance for the elderly, supplies for hospitals, and furniture and food for some families.[17] With the groundwork laid by Redmond and the structure and outreach of Womanpower Unlimited, association with The Box Project allowed Womanpower to significantly increase the numbers of people it helped.

Womanpower Unlimited's Clothing Center in Jackson worked with Naeve and The Box Project to coordinate the needs of particular families with the types of resources they were able to generate, generally pairing families according to clothing size. As Naeve's son Brandon recalled, she "would try to get somebody with a nine-year-old boy and send the clothes down to a six-year-old boy in the South. She was hoping that it would not fit, but be a little loose because clothes would have to last a long time."[18] While the donors were being matched with sister families, Naeve encouraged people to send clothing donations to Womanpower in Jackson for distribution through its existing network.

In addition to clothing, Naeve solicited food, miscellaneous household items, and money for the families. For many, food was the highest priority, especially for those living in rural areas. Despite the high cost of postage, sending boxes of food was deemed the best course of action for several reasons. First, inaccessible or insufficient welfare was commonplace for Blacks in Mississippi, so many families needed food above all else. Second, there was concern that if families were sent cash, they might be forced to use that to pay off prior debts and be unable to purchase food. Sending a one dollar bill when possible was encouraged and deemed a bearable loss if it did not reach its intended recipient. Naeve recalled how, at one point, packages were not being delivered to recipients because postmasters were sometimes stealing the contents or merely holding the packages for spite.[19] In one such instance, a Black postal employee contacted The Box Project to inform staff about nondelivery of packages. The staff in turn contacted the postal authorities in Washington, D.C., to get the packages delivered.[20] Third, they discovered that the supplies were more likely to reach the intended recipients if mailed rather than through sending a truckload of supplies (after securing both a truck and driver) and having to find someone to distribute them, especially given that, on more than one occasion, the supplies never reached the intended recipients but ended up with people who sold them.[21] The program quickly expanded beyond Womanpower members' local communities to minister to the needs of some of the poorest people of the state—residents of the Mississippi Delta. For sharecroppers living in the Delta, scarcity of food was a persistent reality. Some families went days without eating or subsisted on nonnutritive diets such as one composed almost entirely of "neckbones, grits and greens" or "biscuits and greens."[22]

The Delta comprises the northwest part of Mississippi and is home to the state's most fertile soil, which provided the wealth that buoyed individuals like Senator James O. Eastland to political power. The region had a majority Black population, many of whom were subjected to abject poverty resulting from the economic and political exploitation that supported the cotton plantations owned by the region's "Eastlands." Four years into the project, the Delta towns of Cruger and Sidon had more families supported by The Box Project than any other towns in the state.[23] The families being served by the project demonstrate the characteristic poverty of Blacks in the region: many lived on plantations; many had sporadic, if any, work; and nearly all scarcely had the resources for even the most minimal definition of survival. Correspondence from Delta residents offers insight into the living conditions Blacks faced. In a letter requesting assistance from The Box Project, one woman from Sidon wrote: "My husband is not able to work and I can't fine work me and my children could chop cotton in the summer but this year they wont hire no one much if you dont live on someone farm it is hard for you to fine work of that kind I went to another town about ten miles from where I live to look for work I could fine nothin but maid jobs and they will pay from $15 toe 18 dollar a week and it will take hafe of that to go their and come back home every day so if you can help or get me some help please do."[24]

Another individual, who had a helper family, wrote a letter acknowledging receipt of a box, stating: "We receive the box today and was very glad to get the blanket it is very coal here now frost every night. There is no work here much very few people are hireing here. No cotton to pick they picks it with machine. My husband works some time 2 days or 3 days out of a week. The children going to school then we have rent to pay light and groceries bill so we don't have nothing left."[25] The Delta residents faced chronic unemployment and underemployment and were able to get little assistance from the government. Those who could secure "full-time" employment, such as sharecroppers, were often robbed of wages. For example, two sharecropper families participating in the program each netted $0 and $15 for a year's worth of labor.[26]

Reverend Jean Brooks, one of the earliest helpers, recalled that her sister family, the Wheelers—a couple with six children—"lived on a plantation earning $2.00 a day cotton picking. . . . In those early days what we sent seemed so little that it was mortifying to know how much it meant to them."[27] For many of the families the boxes meant everything. For some, they could continue to eat their one meal a day. For others, these boxes meant that they had blankets to protect them from the chills that swept through the shacks that served as their homes. For others, the boxes meant that they could buy medicine for their children. Perhaps what is even more mortifying is that they were able to survive without this assistance.

The Box Project did extensive research on welfare in Mississippi, collecting information from civil rights activists working in the area, such as Charles Horowitz from the Delta Ministry Hinds County Project, representatives from the Department of Agriculture, welfare officials in Vermont, and the Mississippi residents themselves. They learned that Mississippi paid only 26 percent of the need demonstrated by families (compared to the 100 percent Vermont paid) and that, even to secure this meager amount, many families were charged exorbitant amounts for food stamps. A computing table received in a letter from William M. Seabron, Assistant to the Secretary of Agriculture, listed income eligibility requirements for an eight-person household with a monthly income of less than $30, paying $3 for $82 worth of food stamps. Helper families and Box Project staff received numerous letters from people stating they had to pay amounts that far exceeded USDA regulations, such as $32 for $76 worth of food stamps, and some paid as much as $70 for food stamps, which to a family of sharecroppers might as well have been $7,000. One Box Project recipient wrote: "The merchen lend the money for pay for the stamp pay 30 dollar for the stamp and get 70 dollar worth of stamp and he get his 30 dollar out of the 70 dollar that leave 40 dollar worth and we have to traid with the one that buy the stamp, it do not be enough to last the month out for the grocery are so high here, nearly everybody that gettin stamp are buying from this merchen."[28] Newsletters included this type of detailed information about food stamps, so donor families could offer as much support as possible in helping their sister families secure necessary services from the state by informing them of the guidelines and who they could contact to report problems.[29]

The Box Project connected individuals as well as groups to those in need in the Delta. For example, Barbara Richardson of Keene, New Hampshire, contacted Naeve about a family to help. After being paired with a family, she asked Naeve to speak to a group. Naeve recommended McKinley Marcus, a civil rights activist and native of the Delta town of Itta Bena. After his speaking engagement, another resident of Keene initiated a clothing and food drive for Marcus's hometown, raising eight tons of goods, which Marcus delivered during the Christmas holiday.[30]

The epidemic of poverty and the horrible socioeconomic condition of Blacks in Mississippi, the poorest state in the nation, fostered the dedication to this area. And "as the civil rights movement gained momentum, families were referred to The Box Project by civil rights workers in Mississippi. The third world nature of life in Mississippi and the development of field contacts there directed the focus for service into this one area of the country."[31] As the movement developed, it brought greater national media attention to the state, as more people perceived this as a way to support the struggle for civil rights despite being hundreds of miles away.

This was a perfect project for Womanpower because it reflected its organizational style of avoiding bureaucracy. The Box Project connected people to a family and made general suggestions for packages but left the details to the respective families. There was no middlewoman to whom packages had to be sent; they were sent from helpers directly to the recipient families. In many respects, Box Project volunteers acted as facilitators, offering a quick way to make a meaningful connection between Blacks and whites. Womanpower simultaneously fostered interracial communication as it had done with the Prayer Fellowship, making one-to-one connections to deconstruct the misperceptions created by separation, fear, and misinformation. The Box Project, as described by one of its later directors, was "not a substitute for economic development, welfare reform, educational and employment opportunity or improved governmental programs for adequate housing and health care. But it [could] help needy families hold on until significant change comes."[32] Similarly, WU strived to get people involved, build community, and initiate positive change. Its members did not see their endeavors as the end but as a supplemental means to help people survive until a society was created in which every person could access an abundant life.

Relationships that developed between families through letter writing indicated to southern families that there were individuals who cared about them and that they were not alone in their struggle for civil rights and human dignity. Likewise, the helper families witnessed the dramatic impact they could have upon someone's life and better understood the lives and circumstances of Black people from which they were so far removed. In general, it helped to humanize both groups of people in the eyes of the other and allowed them to see the good in members of another race, an exercise for which few opportunities existed in American society at the time.

As The Box Project expanded, Naeve implemented a Christmas appeal for boxes and money to support impoverished families and civil rights projects and solicited assistance from friends to pack and send the donations that she continued to receive. In keeping with Womanpower's objective for the Chain of Friendship, the organization did not seek support solely for its own projects but endeavored to funnel resources to other civil rights organizations working in the state as well and connected Naeve with these groups. The "Report on the [1965] Christmas Appeal" reveals that monetary donations came from places as distant as New York, California, Oregon, and Canada and were used for a variety of activities including a voter education and registration project in Mississippi; donations to the Mississippi Freedom Democratic Party and the Free Southern Theater; and donations to families in Americus, Georgia, and various cities in Mississippi, along with postage to send items they had collected.[33] Some of those Friends to whom the appeal was made requested their own families to adopt. Word-of-mouth, the newsletters, and appeals were the primary means of publicity. After Naeve hosted her first civil rights fair to raise money for the project, to which she invited her and Lowell's artist friends, she added all those who attended to her mailing list. Fellow activists in the peace movement and churches were used as a point of reference. In some instances they were able to secure radio time as one interested person from San Carlos, California, revealed that she obtained Naeve's contact information from an announcement on her local KNEW radio station.[34]

Naeve established an emergency fund and a special s.o.s. was sent out when she was notified of an immediate crisis, such as the needs of the southern civil rights organizations like COFO, the MFDP, or the Delta Ministry; lunch money for children in the Jackson public schools; or the unexpected death of a member of a recipient family.[35] The success of these appeals and the expansion of the project were facilitated by Naeve's and Harvey's connection with WSP as they disseminated information through WSP's clearinghouse and newsletters. As one of the leaders of the Vermont WSP, Naeve made sure that the communiqués on peace included information on the civil rights struggle and what individuals living outside the South could contribute. The Vermont "Peace Concern" newsletter, edited by Myrtle Lane, covered a wide range of current events that included civil rights activities and the happenings of the Labor Department's Women's Bureau.[36]

By 1966, Naeve, still working out of her home, was coordinating close to 200 helper families assisting 1,500 southern Blacks.[37] The waitlist of southern families grew, and many southern families increasingly needed multiple donor families. So Naeve worked to expand the operation, which included matching donor and recipient families, in addition to keeping files, research, writing articles, producing the newsletters and appeals, and recruiting more donors.[38] This work proved to be a major sacrifice for Naeve, whose efforts took away time from her schedule to earn an income for her family, and for Lane, who was a single parent. But just as the response from needy families in Mississippi was great, so too was the desire to help. Assistance came from across the country, even from prisoners incarcerated in the Indiana State Prison in Michigan City, with members of a self-help group called "Convicts Anonymous" adopting one family and another prisoner adopting a family on his own.[39] That prisoners were in a position to help improve the lives of southern Blacks speaks volumes about the destitute conditions of life in the Mississippi Delta.

The Box Project provided civil rights activists material and emotional support akin to what Womanpower had done for the Freedom Riders and Freedom Summer volunteers. Similar to the "thank you" letters Womanpower received from individuals and organizations it had supported, Naeve received letters from both families and civil rights workers. In response to a donation received for the 1965 Christmas Appeal, for example, the MFDP wrote, "Even though we need and must have financial support from people in the north if we are to continue in this struggle, we need, for entirely different reasons, the knowledge that we are not isolated and that there are persons like yourself who share our commitment and concern. It is almost impossible to exaggerate the real, sustaining effect that this knowledge gives to someone who may be in very trying circumstances in the field. For this reason your concern is as appreciated as is your financial contribution."[40] Likewise, correspondence from a Freedom House in Greenville read, "Have just received another of your boxes and a roll of newspapers. Each day seems to be colder than the one before, so all these clothes are being put to good use. In order to get clothing, recipients must first attempt to register at the courthouse. The rationale behind this is that registering to vote is a step toward eventually doing away with the need to take 'handouts.' We've had no complaints yet from the people involved, and about 40 have been down to the courthouse in the last two weeks."[41]

Even though most of the helpers never met the activists or families that received their assistance, they knew they were making a significant contribution to sustaining the movement, in particular, as well as the Black community as a whole. Additionally, these narratives speak to the explicitly political nature of The Box Project—the effort to, in Naeve's words, give "hope to those who are trying so hard for equality," such as the mother of six who represented the MFDP in Washington, D.C., for its Congressional Challenge in January of 1965 and was jailed upon her return. She wrote to Naeve, "We could use everything you sent. I thank you for it and the $1 you sent came in good time. . . . I am out today to get more people to register to vote. You will always hear from me. I will never forget you."[42] The boxes, and the emotional support that accompanied them, provided sustenance and nurtured resistance to racial oppression.

In 1967, illness forced Naeve to decrease her involvement with the project, and she ended her involvement entirely two years later. At this point she had been living in Canada for two years, having moved to spare her oldest son from being drafted, and needed someone to assume coordinating responsibilities for both health and logistical reasons. The Mississippi Box Project had grown to nearly 3,000 recipient families and necessitated the work of more than one individual outside the United States. As a result, a system of approximately twenty volunteer administrators was established to regionally coordinate the program. While there was no paid staff, the Social Action Committee of the Council of Churches of Plainville, Connecticut, sponsored the project in that region under the direction of Patricia Augur. Two other Connecticut volunteers, Janet Johnson of Seymour and Sally DeLeon of Windsor, assumed primary responsibility for the project, keeping the master file and screening and assigning families.[43] As the project continued to expand, assisted in part by national publicity through publications such as *Good Housekeeping*, *Ebony*, and *This Week*, the volunteers knew that a paid staff and additional resources were necessary to sustain the project and accommodate the waitlist of recipient families. Coordinators initially hoped that the project could be relocated to Jackson and become part of the Mississippi Council on Human Relations (MCHR), which had in 1969 sponsored the project's office expenses for six months.[44] This was likely a connection fostered by Womanpower member Jane Schutt, who served as secretary of the MCHR. Unfortunately, that did not materialize. Instead, the name was changed from the Mississippi Box Project to simply The Box Project, and in March 1969 a national office was established at the Plainville, Connecticut, United Methodist Church with Augur as director. The organization was incorporated and Johnson served as the first president.[45] The initial board of directors included one Mississippian, Otis Brown Jr., who was a civil rights activist and native of Indianola and one of the project's first field directors. The organization has had several directors since then and changed locations, eventually moving to Hernando, Mississippi, about fifteen miles south of the Mississippi/Tennessee border, in 2009.

Although her affiliation with The Box Project had ended nineteen years earlier, in June 1988, Naeve traveled to Mississippi to celebrate the project's twenty-fifth anniversary. The celebration, held at Greenwood Lake in the Mississippi Delta, offered a rare opportunity for recipient and helper families to meet and for northerners to see in person the abject poverty that existed in the South. In many respects this visit was quite different from Naeve's first visit to the state in April 1964. During that trip, as she and Harvey traveled to rural areas of Mississippi to visit some of the recipient families, Naeve had to hide in the vehicle chauffeured by Harvey's driver/bodyguard. This time, driving in the car with Blacks posed no threat (although when they stopped in the Delta town of Tchula to visit the project's clothing outlet, the stop was brief as it was getting dark and it *was* Mississippi). Naeve met Rosie Redmond (Holden) on that first trip and saw the chicken coop she had converted into Womanpower's clothing distribution center. In 1988, she had the opportunity to visit again with Holden who still operated a clothing center out of her home as well as WU member Jessie Mosley, who gave her a tour of the recently opened Smith Robertson Museum and Cultural Center she directed. She spent time with Harvey, who hosted a picnic at her home but could not travel to the official celebration in the Delta due to poor health. Perhaps the greatest testament to the changing times since Naeve's initial visit was her meetings with Governor Ray Mabus and Mayor Dale Danks, who gave her a key to the City of Jackson.

As evidenced by Kevin Shirley, the Black deputy mayor, Jackson and Mississippi had made some significant changes since 1964. Conditions outside of Jackson were surprising. Once Naeve arrived in the Delta, it was difficult to believe that they had not somehow traveled back to the 1960s. Twenty-five years after The Box Project had been founded, Blacks were living on plantations and chopping cotton. Just as some sharecroppers avoided civil rights activists canvassing their communities for voter registration in the 1960s for fear of reprisal from the plantation owner, one recipient family asked the camera crew that filmed the celebration not to go to the cotton fields to see the mother, who chopped cotton to support her husband who was unable to work and their fifteen children, because she might lose her job.[46] Additionally, Sara Anderson, one of the first Box Project recipients, was, at more than eighty years old, being assisted by her original helper, Rix Knight, a friend of Naeve's from Quebec. On a positive note, Naeve met Anderson's niece, Mary, who was a member of one of Naeve's sister families. Mary, her husband Lester, and their seven children were living on a plantation in Itta Bena twenty years earlier when they were Naeve's sister family, but after Naeve's illness she had to find them another sister family. They were now living in a home of their own—a brick house with a yard in a housing project in Greenwood. They were, in a sense, a success story—a family that had been helped by The Box Project and was able to hold on long enough to realize an opportunity to do more than just survive. As one recipient stated, "Didn't matter as much what my family sent, what matter is they *care*. Like bein' throwed a rope: You got to hang on!"[47] Mary and her family, and many others, did hold on and arrived at a point where they no longer needed assistance from The Box Project. For many others, the reality of poverty for Blacks in Mississippi was unchanged, and The Box Project was the only lifeline they had.

The Box Project continues to assist underprivileged families across the nation, the majority of which are in the Mississippi Delta. In 2009, the Community Foundation of Northwest Mississippi adopted The Box Project as one of its programs. In 2013, there were fewer than 800 families (donors and recipients combined) affiliated with the project—a drastic decline from the nearly 10,000 families the project had in the early 1990s.[48] Unfortunately, this has less to do with improved conditions, as Mississippi remains the poorest state in the country, and more to do with America's struggling economy that caused many donor families to withdraw from the program. The project's legacy is that it continues to help poor Black families in the South as well as poor individuals throughout the country, including Native Americans and residents of Appalachia. The program provides material needs and information on gaining access to community resources/programs while promoting understanding between different segments of the population. Helper families do not just send boxes to faceless families. They develop a relationship that includes letter writing, exchanging pictures, and getting to know one another on a level beyond donations and "thank yous." Participants are given the chance to see into the life of someone completely different from themselves and hopefully gain a basic understanding of these differences. Womanpower realized the benefits of such a program and provided some of the necessary groundwork for the project's success.

Despite Harvey's and wu's close association with the project, her connection is often overlooked in favor of the better-known Coretta Scott King. For example, in a historical overview of the project in a late-1960s newsletter, Harvey's name is absent, and only King is cited as a resource for Naeve. In a newsletter from April 1978, during the project's fifteenth anniversary, both Harvey's and King's names are left out of the "Brief history."[49] Even the historical presentation given at the recent fiftieth anniversary celebration overlooked Harvey's foundational contributions. Naeve commented on this in her correspondence with Harvey, writing, "Enclosed is [a] writeup just came out since fair. . . . I had to use Coretta King in your place as people do know who she is . . . but *you* were the motivation."[50] Years later, on the eve of the twenty-fifth anniversary gathering in Mississippi, Naeve wrote, "You had a lot to do with it getting off its feet in the beginning. It took me years to get the office to recognise it was *you* rather (more) than Coretta King that helped get me in touch with the right people to get it all started."[51] This lack of recognition is indicative of the invisibility in the historical narrative that Womanpower, and in many cases Black women activists in general, have faced; however, their willingness to do the spadework without recognition is characteristic of Black women activists.

"Summer Magic": Lessons in Diversity and Leadership

In early April 1963, the Alabama Christian Movement for Human Rights and the Southern Christian Leadership Conference launched Project-C (Confrontation) in Birmingham to use sit-ins to challenge discrimination and segregation at white businesses. Birmingham's white power structure, embodied by Commissioner of Public Safety Eugene "Bull" Conner, responded to these demonstrators with massive arrests. Martin Luther King Jr. was among those arrested as part of this campaign in hopes of attracting media attention to the plight of Blacks in the city. During this incarceration he penned his "Letter from Birmingham Jail." As organizers made plans to continue the demonstrations, they decided to use children to dramatize the brutality of Black oppression and inspire others to action. The youth participants in the Children's Crusade, as it was called, were attacked by police dogs, beaten by police officers, and sprayed with fire hoses.[52] The media captured this display of violence for the world to see.

In the wake of, and in response to, this violence, the New York–based American Ethical Union (AEU) created the Commission on Race and Equality "to develop projects which might assist in Southern areas of high racial tension," with a particular focus on the children.[53] Walter Lawton, an AEU leader and previous Birmingham resident, had been watching the unfolding of Project-C with interest. He, along with Robert Stein, visited Birmingham in the latter part of April and, after witnessing firsthand the "absolute segregation [that] was enshrined by local and state law as well as custom," sought a local organization with whom they could partner to bridge the widening divide between the races.[54]

After three failed attempts to convene Black and white leaders for a conference to discuss ways to bridge the expanding chasm between the races in the wake of the recent events, a serendipitous meeting with a member of the Friendship and Action Committee yielded results in the fall of 1963. A group of ten white and ten Black women organized this committee the previous year to open the lines of communication between the races. One of their projects was to bring together Black and white children who were to attend newly integrated Birmingham public schools, one of whom was Carole Roberts, one of the four girls later killed in the bombing of the Sixteenth Street Baptist Church.[55] Like Womanpower Unlimited had done through its Prayer Fellowship, this biracial group had taken the courageous step of trying to connect the women of their respective communities to foster dialogue and social change. This encounter led to the Friendship and Action Committee's cosponsorship with the AEU during the summer of 1964 of an interracial playschool, a program for Birmingham children to attend interracial northern camps, a college prep workshop for Black high school juniors, and a seminar for adults.[56]

The program was successful, with 55 children attending the Playschool, 12 participating in the camping program, 30 attending the college prep workshop, and 150 adults, Black and white, participating in the seminars.[57] As a result, the AEU explored expanding to other southern cities—Tuskegee and Auburn, Alabama, and Jackson, Mississippi—the following summer. Integral to this expansion was securing the support of a local organization, like the Friendship and Action Committee, to take responsibility for local organizing. As the project director explained, the AEU wanted to work in conjunction with local leaders to establish "new institutions whose programs of education, recreation and cultural enrichment demonstrate alternate forms of action in areas hostile to the basic principles of universal democracy."[58] In Mississippi, the AEU obtained the support of Womanpower Unlimited. The interracial camp program was adopted, and Womanpower Unlimited provided the local community leadership. Specifically, the camping program sought to "expose culturally deprived Southern youth to interracial camp experiences in Northeastern States."[59] Womanpower members considered this especially useful for children enrolling in newly desegregated schools.[60] Additionally, many campers spent a day or two in New York with a host family before going to camp, and some were groomed as future leaders at the camps or in their communities.[61]

It is not surprising that Womanpower undertook such a project. In 1963, as Project-C was underway, Womanpower contemplated its future. In addition to providing continued support to civil rights projects, members envisioned themselves making "significant contributions to youth educational, recreational and job opportunities."[62] Womanpower's efforts supporting school integration partially fulfilled this goal. Not satisfied with the piecemeal integration that was implemented, Womanpower sought additional ways to enhance the quality of life for Black children. Womanpower's desire to develop the total child—helping to meet her educational, material, psychological, and cultural needs—was a perfect fit for the programs being proposed by the AEU.

In the fall of 1964, Clarie Collins Harvey hosted an informational session at her home for Jackson leaders to learn about the AEU's projects in Birmingham. Here she met Robert Stein, associate director of the AEU's Southern Projects, and his wife Anita, Race and Equality Commission secretary, who planned and coordinated the camping program. This connection was likely facilitated by Mrs. Ruth and Dr. A. D. Beittel, former Tougaloo College president, whom Robert met during an April 1963 trip to Jackson.[63] The possibilities for both the interracial camping program and an integrated playschool for the following year were discussed. Womanpower was the only organization to respond affirmatively to cosponsoring a program and decided that it could take on the camping project but not a playschool because it was committed to working with Head Start and could not provide leadership to both.[64]

Once committed to the project, WU used its well-established connections through churches, organizations, and neighborhoods to recruit children to attend the camps and to raise funds to supplement the scholarships provided by the AEU. Local churches joined the effort, for example with the Mount Nebo Baptist Church's Women's Department sponsoring a bazaar to raise money. Womanpower hosted concerts, fishfrys, and theatrical productions by the Little Theater to raise money to support this endeavor.[65]

In 1965, in conjunction with the AEU's Commission on Race and Equality, Womanpower began a program that afforded predominately poor Black and some white children from the South the opportunity to spend part of the summer at camps in New York, New Jersey, Vermont, and New Hampshire.[66] These trips to camps like Trumbull Hill and Camp Elliot enabled participants to broaden their experiences in a way unattainable to most of them. It provided them with the chance to interact with and learn from people of other races and exposed them to new educational, religious, and extracurricular activities.

The most common destination for Mississippi youth was Camp Madison-Felicia, which was established in 1956, with the merging of Camp Madison, an all-boys camp originally founded in 1921, and Camp Felicia, an all-girls camp founded in 1898. Madison-Felicia was "an independent, interracial, non-sectarian, non-profit organization associated with the New York Society for Ethical Culture" (NYSEC). Similar to NYSEC's goals of creating and nurturing a beloved community by acting on the ethics of respect for humanity and nature, Camp Madison-Felicia aimed to "build a more fulfilled, a more healthy, and a more productive citizenry."[67] Campers for this co-educational facility ranged in ages 7–12 for girls and 7–13 for boys. The board of directors encouraged attendance by a diverse group of children, which included not only various racial and religious backgrounds but those with mild physical and mental disabilities as well as economically disadvantaged youth. In fact, "preference was given to children referred by professional casework, child care and family agencies."[68] In creating a diverse community, Camp Madison-Felicia incorporated a range of ages for staff members. It employed regular counselors, who had to be at least nineteen years old, and had a Service-Corps of leaders in training who were between sixteen and eighteen years old. A group of Program Aides, age sixty-five and older, served as specialists and "grandparents" and were intended to create a realistic familial setting for campers. This type of diversity, with respect to race, class, religion, age, and ability, was the type of exposure Womanpower hoped Mississippi youth could experience: one that was drastically different from that which the segregated South offered.

Philosophically, Camp Madison-Felicia embraced values similar to Womanpower's. Promotional literature stated that it provided "an opportunity for those from different religions, racial, cultural and socio-economic backgrounds to learn to understand each other and live harmoniously together. . . . To build a more fulfilled, a more healthy, and a more productive citizenry is the aim of the camp."[69] The camp was a microcosm of the society (indeed, a "beloved community") that Womanpower had been working diligently to create. And they were taking immediate steps to create these opportunities in the present, understanding the long-term focus of their goals and the movement's.

Amy Tubbs, who attended Madison-Felicia during the years 1965–68, worked as a counselor in the seventies, and her parents, Shirley and Marvin Fleishaker, also worked there. Tubbs described a typical day, which began with rising early to raise the flag before breakfast. After breakfast and cleaning the cabins, campers participated in activities that included "Arts and Crafts, swimming, nature, ball play on the fields, Music, cooking and sewing with the grand parents." Then they ate lunch and had an hour of rest. This was followed by more activities, dinner, free play, and a planned evening event. Special activities including weekly field trips of hiking and picnics, camping outdoors, "tribal ceremonies in the Indian Circle, an Olympics which lasted 2–3 days," and a host of other memorable events.[70] Former campers Anthony Rose and Chris Butcher recalled days filled with singing and evening bonfires.[71] Steven Powell, who attended the camp in the mid-seventies, remembered that this was when he first learned to bake cookies and, in spite of the domesticated animals at the camp, he was almost sent home for catching a pet of his own—a snake.[72] Academic enrichment opportunities, such as a special program to improve literacy skills, sponsored by the New York City Board of Education, offered campers a well-rounded schedule of activities.

Womanpower created a Camping Committee, initially chaired by Doristine Parker Carey, to handle the camping program. Carey, who sent all five of her children to camps, recalled how the children profited from the experience. In addition to exposing the children to people of various racial and ethnic backgrounds, where everyone was treated equally, and providing them with new social and educational opportunities, Carey believes that the camp experience prepared some students for desegregating the public schools in Jackson. She thinks that the exposure to different races provided them with the understanding and ability to recognize all people as human beings and to better manage the stresses attendant to integration.[73]

Dwight Henry, whose mother, Maddye Lyne Henry, was a Womanpower member, attended camp in New Hampshire as a teenager and confirmed this feeling from the youth perspective. He stated that "prior to going I began to have a hate for white people; things were real bad . . . until I finally went to that camp . . . [where] these people genuinely exuded this warmth and love and they believed it; and so consequently from being there that hatred towards white people just started waning and waning and waning. And I felt better about myself. Truly I felt equal in that environment."[74] Henry's experience at camp prompted him to integrate a bowling alley with his older brother and best friend when he returned from his first summer at camp. Despite leaving the bowling alley with a broken nose in response to his integration efforts, Henry credits his experience with whites at camp with preventing him from returning to a place of hatred. Additionally, he established a long-term relationship with the camp, returning the following summer as a counselor and then again after his service in the Navy. The camp also sponsored him to attend college in England. Overall, Henry believes that the camp was important in helping him deal with the racial antagonism he experienced in Mississippi by providing a "structure that kept [him] away from being mean and nasty."[75] Henry's experience is precisely what the AEU Commission hoped to accomplish in reaching out to the children in these southern communities, "who had borne the brunt of emotional experiences associated with these struggles for change."[76] Equally important, he fulfilled Womanpower's hopes of broadening Black children's lives with experiences that were often unattainable, thereby setting them on a course for lifelong success.

Interacting with whites as peers was a new experience for Linda Marie Redmond Taylor, who attended Madison-Felicia in 1965 as a fifth grader. Her mother, Mariah Redmond, learned about the program from her neighbor and fellow parishioner at Mount Nebo Baptist Church, Pearl Draine. She believes that it might have eased her transition to Hardy Junior High School, which she and her sister integrated a couple of years later.[77]

Camp participants ranged in age from seven years old to high school age. The high school students usually traveled to the campsite unaccompanied, while the younger children were chaperoned by Womanpower members to the state in which the camp was located, or they were chaperoned to Alabama where they traveled with children from Birmingham to the northern states chaperoned by Alabama mothers. Both Doristine Carey and Maddye Lyne Henry, who were cousins, volunteered as chaperones. Host families, usually white, wealthy friends of the AEU, greeted the children upon arrival. They stayed with these families for a few nights before being escorted to the camp where they spent anywhere from two to four weeks at a time. This hosting experience provided them opportunities for sightseeing in New York, with activities like seeing a Broadway show or attending the World's Fair.[78] In recalling the experiences of her youngest son, Larry, who first participated in the camp program at age seven, Carey explained that the first night her son stayed with the host family he had so much fun that they neglected to contact Carey and inform her that Larry had arrived safely. The camp exposed Black students to a world they knew little or nothing about. For some, this exposure broadened their experiences and led to tangible lifelong benefits of pursuing a college education in Connecticut and Rhode Island.[79]

Comments from counselors echo the sentiment of mutual respect and acceptance of the southern campers. Said a counselor in a 1968 report, "Larry Carey is intelligent and aware he really knows what's happening around camp and around him. He's also friendly, cooperative and helpful—humorous—don't have to tell him what to do he[']s already done it. We all recommend him highly."[80] And another, "Bobby Crudup is generally the kind of kid a counselor dreams about—remarkably mature."[81] The staff enjoyed the campers as much as the campers enjoyed being there.

Parents believed the camp provided invaluable experiences for their children. One mother wrote of her daughters that one "seems to have lost her inferior complexes toward other children which she once possessed. She feels like she is equal to any other child regardless of race." Of her other daughter, her "English has improved plus her vocabulary is broader" as a result of the classes provided by the New York City Board of Education. "And she talks about been [sic] able to have seen so many things that she had only read about in books. . . . She has learned to appreciate her family more. . . . I am truly convinced that camp was the cause of all these improvements."[82] These comments address two key aspects of life for Black children at the time—internalized oppression and an inferior education—both brought about by segregation and discrimination. Womanpower tapped into a way to address these negative realities of Black life in a manner appropriate and engaging for children.

The camping program continued throughout the decade and well into the seventies, with Maddye Lyne Henry, Mary Cox, and Carolyn Parker serving as chairs. By the 1970s, the campers came from diverse socioeconomic backgrounds. Additionally, those attending camp in the mid-seventies had integrated the Jackson public schools and were not new to mixed-race settings. Despite shifting somewhat from its initial focus, the interracial camps were valuable and provided new experiences and relationships for Mississippi youth. For example, camper Byron D'Andra Orey, who, with his older brother, attended Madison-Felicia in 1975 and 1976, developed a strong bond with his host family and engaged in activities like tie-dyeing, hiking, and learning about plants that were new to him.[83] Orey came from a middle-class family; his father was a union organizer, and his mother was a social worker. Although family vacations were not atypical for the Oreys, Byron believed this was a unique opportunity.

A classmate of Orey's, Steven Powell, joined him at Madison-Felicia in 1976 and went again in 1977. Powell explained that his parents, who were upper-middle-class, wanted him to have experiences with other people and explore the world.[84] While both had integrated McLeod Elementary School, Powell admitted that camp was the first time he had been around that diverse a group of people. Even Amy Tubbs, who grew up in a "moderately diverse" area in New Rochelle, New York, said that the camps "immersed [her] in a world of diversity."[85] Orey and Powell recalled with fondness the time spent at camp and affirmed that it afforded them an opportunity for educational and cultural enrichment. Powell has pleasant memories of the time he spent before camp with his host family, visiting the Empire State Building and attending a Yankees game. During the few days spent with their host families, the campers established bonds that sometimes resulted in tearful departures and were sustained beyond the summer. For instance, Taylor recalled that, over the years, her host family from Scarsdale sent her boxes of clothes that their daughter had outgrown, and Orey kept in touch with his family via letter writing.[86]

Through the camping program, Womanpower Unlimited demonstrated its ability to engage in creative ways of enhancing Black life and creating a beloved community. This opportunity for enrichment focused on a variety of objectives. They wanted the children

to learn about and develop respect for each other's differing views and ways; to participate with those of other racial and cultural backgrounds than ours; to understand the major issues of our times, challenges to our democracy, and the meaning of citizenship within a democracy; to appreciate good health, physical fitness and the value of working together; to develop interests and goals for leisure time; to develop the ability to think and discuss critically; to gain friendships and associations with others; to discuss and develop one's sense of the values and meanings in life, while respecting differing religious backgrounds, in an open exchange of personal beliefs and to recognize, honor and encourage the essential individuality of each camper.[87]

Womanpower hoped that the children who attended these camps developed the same qualities the organization strove for for all Americans with its civil rights agenda.

The camping initiative was Womanpower's final, major project. Like The Box Project, this educational and cultural program demonstrates Womanpower's dedication to quality of life issues for all members of its local community. This project, too, outlived Womanpower. After the group disbanded, the local NCNW maintained the camping project. Although the Jackson section of the NCNW remains active, the camping program ended in the late 1970s.

Through The Box Project and the Interracial Vacations Camping Project, Womanpower immediately altered the courses of the lives of Black Mississippians. Like the survival programs created by the Black Panther Party in the late 1960s, Womanpower engaged in community outreach to some of the most vulnerable members of the community—the poor and the youth—endeavoring to achieve "abundant life for all."[88] The projects exposed the inequities of American society for which the Black freedom struggle sought redress. Given white resistance to the civil rights movement in general, and "outside agitators" in particular, these projects could not have existed without Womanpower's efforts.

Women's Power Transformed
Joining Forces with the National Council of Negro Women

Keep on moving, keep on insisting, keep on fighting injustice.
—Mary Church Terrell

I am, was, and always will be a catalyst for change.
—Shirley Chisholm

"Ms. Harvey's final remarks, after a brief prayer, were that we would not meet again until a need arises at which time she would call the group together. 'Womanpower for Freedom Task Force'—Women doing whatever they can to meet human needs based on divine power."[1] So read the September 27, 1976, minutes of the Womanpower for Freedom Task Force. Harvey convened the taskforce on September 15 of that year. It met for three weeks to assist the NAACP in fundraising for its defense against a lawsuit filed by white businesses in Port Gibson, Mississippi, which had been boycotted by the organization.[2] Just as they had done during the organization's heyday, Womanpower Unlimited members used their churches, businesses, and community groups to generate funds for civil rights organizations to further the fight for justice and equality.

Eight years earlier Womanpower had officially disbanded with the waning of civil rights activism in the state, bringing to an end its seven years of leadership and support of the civil rights movement.[3] These local women sustained the movement in Mississippi by generating new forms of activism among uninvolved populations, supporting other civil rights organizations, creating alliances between Blacks and whites, and improving the quality of life for members of their community. Furthermore, Womanpower bolstered Black women's social and political activism in the state. They did not compete for resources or seek authority within a given geographic location or among a particular population but sought to engage everyone in the work of universal social justice. Womanpower connected, supported, facilitated, and cooperated with others, serving as a bridge between social movements and activists. John R. Washington, a Freedom Rider who traveled to Jackson from California, emphasized Harvey's role in this capacity when he stated that "[Harvey] was a good bridge because she knew the community and its people and respected them, and she was respected by and trusted by them. . . . [Womanpower] communicated to the people of Jackson their right to engage power in the political arena."[4] This role as a bridge-leader was not an avenue of activism that was limited to Harvey. As businesswomen, Sanders, Logan, and Mosley encouraged others to participate and were perhaps more easily able to acquire untapped resources. Through their efforts they upheld a legacy of Black women's activism that gives them significance beyond their contributions to the civil rights movement.

Womanpower grew out of a desire to assist civil rights workers and the organizations to which they belonged, but it developed into much more than a support group. Many of its members were already involved in the Black freedom struggle through civic groups and civil rights organizations and acted as community leaders. When they came together through Womanpower, they were easily able to develop new and creative strategies to further the movement. They filled voids left by other civil rights organizations, which often resulted from a lack of resources or oversight by groups that focused heavily on direct action or particular projects. Womanpower worked with all civil rights organizations to secure citizenship rights for African Americans, and it also operated independently at times to address issues its members deemed pertinent to Black progress. Through its campaigns for voter registration and school desegregation, Womanpower encouraged Black Mississippians to become not only active citizens claiming their rights as Americans but also activists supporting the civil rights movement in general. Members solicited and obtained support from residents of the rural areas surrounding Jackson, middle-class people who shied away from the movement, and a host of women who simply needed a forum for their engagement.

Clarie Collins Harvey fashioned Womanpower as a supporting movement of the civil rights struggle—ever ready to take action. She did not plan for Womanpower to become a permanent organization. Rather, Harvey intended to create the avenues by which change could occur locally and nationally and she believed that, with such progress, its work would be complete. She was certain the group would accomplish its goals, not anticipating a need for permanency. In a January 1966 newsletter, Harvey explained Womanpower's ending:

For a while longer, we shall continue to assist in providing for the clothing needs of our children in desegregated schools and work with the American Ethical Union of New York City in sending our children to the East for marvelous camping experiences. Unless God sees fit to use us further in this work, we shall "silently fold our tents and fade away." We do not intend to become just another club. Really, we feel that our role has been . . . to prepare the way for all of the great and wonderful things that have come and that are coming. With them on the scene, it would be presumptuous of us to continue in the active role we have carried the past years. And so we gracefully move from the center of the stage to the sideline to await our call.[5]

Harvey crystallized the desire for activism she witnessed among Black women and established Womanpower as a vehicle for mobilizing people and propelling them into action. Her energies focused on Womanpower's productivity rather than longevity and prioritized the immediate needs of the larger movement and the community. Central to its efficacy was the ability to act in accord with the evolving direction of the movement and operate without hesitation to assist and develop strategies to sustain the movement. From an action-oriented ideology based on "woman power," race uplift, and humanism, WU provided emotional and material support that sustained the activism of civil rights workers, thereby maintaining the struggle itself.

After Freedom Summer, Womanpower moved from the center of community and civil rights activism as the movement itself was shifting direction. Many of the veteran civil rights workers, who had been organizing in Mississippi since Womanpower's inception, left the state. New organizations emerged including the Delta Ministry, the Poor People's Corporation, and the Child Development Group of Mississippi. This rapid change in leadership disrupted the movement's momentum. The dissolution of COFO in July 1965, stemming from increased intra- and interorganizational tensions, further exacerbated this disruption and caused a decline in civil rights activism from organizations like SNCC and CORE that had kept Mississippi in the public eye.

Despite the decline of movement activity in Mississippi, signaling to Womanpower that its end was near, members viewed their undertakings as successful. Bringing women to the center of activism, helping Blacks claim their civil liberties, and promoting interracial understanding were all steps toward reaching their broader goals of achieving freedom and peace in American society. Having accomplished these goals and having helped to open the "closed society," Womanpower sought to redirect its energies to a broader platform of Black women's activism. Harvey desired to channel the empowerment and activism wu had generated into other forums that allowed them to maintain their effectiveness. They pursued this through the National Council of Negro Women (ncnw).

Given its status as an established national organization, Harvey believed that participation in the ncnw provided a better means for Womanpower members to achieve goals that extended beyond the civil rights movement in Mississippi. In explaining why Womanpower disbanded, Harvey stated, "the life of a movement, it's just like a task force. And then when you have done that job you move on to something that is permanent and has established roots to it. The National Council of Negro Women was the logical place to go because they have a headquarters, they have a national budget . . . and all the rest of it."[6] The Council embraced interracial cooperation and an international humanist focus that was central to Womanpower's philosophy. Additionally, by the time of Womanpower's dissolution, the ncnw had shed the middle-class orientation that dominated its early years and adopted a grassroots focus that was more in line with the civil rights movement and reflective of Womanpower's agenda. By the mid-1960s, the ncnw was "developing Head Start programs, homes for unwed mothers, pig farms, and victory gardens"—initiatives that attracted a diverse population of Black women.[7] Much of this work was a result of collaborations with leaders in Mississippi such as Fannie Lou Hamer, Unita Blackwell, and Jessie Mosley. Lawrence Guyot surmised that Womanpower recognized the ncnw as a "logical alternative" and a "supervening power that could do more."[8] Formal affiliation with the ncnw was a reasonable step in furthering the activism Womanpower had generated among this group of women.

Harvey explained that, while the ncnw was an effective organization, they had not established a chapter in Jackson because Dorothy Height believed that Womanpower was already doing what the ncnw would do. When civil rights activism began to decline, Womanpower "became a part of the National Council of Negro Women as a committee" because the ncnw had a much broader program.[9] The development and success of Wednesdays in Mississippi had established the effectiveness of a national organization in addressing the problems wu focused on and demonstrated the Council's dedication to the region. Likewise, the success of and the support for the Council's programs in Mississippi revealed the local following a chapter could expect to have.

The Jackson section of the ncnw was organized in 1967, under the leadership of Jessie Mosley, who had coordinated the ncnw-wims project the previous year. With the expansion of the Council's programs in the state, it made sense to establish a base locally. And Mosley was the logical person to do so. Upholding the mission of providing a foundation from which Black women could mobilize to combat racism in America, the Jackson section of the NCNW proposed:

> To recruit, stimulate and train Negro women for more effective participation in community action.
> To develop both independent and cooperative projects for service to the community.
> To work for the enforcement of law, and for administrative and legal action to protect civil rights and to combat poverty.
> To broaden the base of participation by women of widely different backgrounds to achieve these common goals.[10]

With these goals in mind, they undertook a variety of programs including a summer day camp for working mothers and a program for needy girls.[11]

The following year Womanpower Unlimited disbanded and many of its members joined the Council, which adopted two of Womanpower's programs—the clothing project (which continued under the direction of Rosie Redmond Holden) and the camping project. The NCNW maintained the camping project for a few years, then let it lapse. As a result, some of the original Womanpower members created a taskforce to continue the program. Harvey explained that, regrettably, upon joining the NCNW, Womanpower members "didn't find the climate and the acceptance that we expected. So now the ladies who were identified with Womanpower have started the Womanpower Unlimited Camping Fund, so it continues on that one [issue]."[12] Harvey's justification for Womanpower's end is rational, but not all members shared the belief that disbanding was the best course of action. Susie Noel commented that the organization's dissolution was "an awful thing."[13] Noel was likely saddened to see the end of an organization that had cultivated new bonds of sisterhood, valued their contributions and skills as women, and provided them with an avenue for community and civil rights activism. The lukewarm reception by the NCNW and Noel's disappointment speak to the possible loss of autonomy experienced by Womanpower members, who had previously maintained the independence and flexibility to act spontaneously in response to movement and community needs. Not unlike the limitations the national office placed upon local NAACP branches, these women were now responsible to a larger body and perhaps limited by a national agenda, which may or may not have reflected local desires and needs.

By the time Harvey realized that the Council did not provide the type of union she anticipated, she had accepted the presidency of Church Women United and was unable to revive the group.[14] Despite Womanpower's less-than-ideal reception into the National Council of Negro Women, some Womanpower members, such as treasurer Jessie Mosley, had a long and highly active role in the organization. Mosley, the first president of the chapter, became the state convener for the NCNW, a position she held for twenty-five years, with the responsibilities of organizing and overseeing sections in Mississippi. She remained an active member of the organization well into her nineties.[15] Womanpower members Ineva May-Pittman and Lucille Penquite served as the second and third presidents, respectively, of the local NCNW. In addition to initiatives like starting the Fannie Lou Hamer Day Care Center in Ruleville, Mississippi, the NCNW established "Pig Banks," food cooperatives, and a "Day Care and Child Development Center on the site of the former Okolona Junior College."[16] Womanpower Unlimited's affiliation with the National Council of Negro Women brought its status as an independent entity to an end, but its legacy of Black women's activism in Mississippi continued. In 2013 there were eleven sections of the NCNW in Mississippi, and the Jackson section of the NCNW had approximately one hundred members.[17] The organization created an annual award to honor the legacies of both Mosley and Harvey. The Dr. Jessie B. Mosley Award recognizes someone who carries on her legacy of historic preservation and demonstrates "leadership in civic, social or educational areas on the local, state and national levels." The Clarie Collins Harvey Business Award honors an individual who has demonstrated "involvement in reconciliation efforts to promote social harmony" and "commitment to the spiritual, social, and holistic well being of the community."[18] Through these awards, the Council recognizes two women who directly and indirectly led to the establishment of the Jackson section.

During its brief existence, Womanpower contributed in numerous ways to the success of the civil rights movement, to immediately improving the quality of life for many African Americans, and to fostering racial reconciliation. Like many women generations before them, and in other southern cities during the civil rights movement, members of Womanpower Unlimited engaged in community work that was a vital force for social change.

The members of Womanpower Unlimited fostered sisterhood, political activism, and community empowerment through women's participation in the civil rights struggle. Womanpower created a sisterhood that connected women across socioeconomic backgrounds. A. M. E. Logan recalled that Womanpower members were from "all walks of life, we had some of the higher ups and some of the lower downs. Any woman that wanted to participate . . . just whoever, if you were a woman you could join because there wasn't no fee that you had to pay. But we just needed your strength, your support."[19] This sisterhood was the key to building a successful movement. Womanpower avoided the elitism that characterized some of the earlier Black women's organizations and eliminated the schism that sometimes existed between middle- and working-class Blacks. The members built support networks for each other, knowing that the work they were undertaking could not be accomplished through individual effort. They created "safe spaces" for women to organize to fight against injustices and to bond with one another through social and religious fellowship.

This sisterhood, too, is part of the legacy that Womanpower left to future generations. The bond that WU members had was evident to the younger generation. Loretta McGowan, daughter of longtime Womanpower member Maddye Lyne Henry, commented, "they loved one another. . . . It was kind of like a family. This was a group of women who actually cared, not just about the cause, but for each other. . . . It really, really was a sisterhood. I've seen them pray together, I've seen them cry together over something that didn't go like they wanted it to go. Then I've seen them praise together because things went through; they worked."[20] A. M. E. Logan's daughter Shirley Montague similarly remarked that Logan, Harvey, and Sanders "made such a good team. They really did. They worked together. They talked together. It was just amazing how well. . . . They were so much alike in a lot of ways."[21]

Politically, Womanpower encouraged Blacks to become registered and active voters, instituted letter-writing campaigns to support civil rights bills, and worked on political campaigns.[22] All of these aspects gave Womanpower a broad-based, multifaceted agenda. They put their political beliefs into practice on the personal level, too, demonstrating the importance of combining theory with action. For example, while returning home from a buying trip for her boutique in 1962, Thelma Sanders was arrested in Memphis for refusing to comply with the segregated seating at the airport, a case for which she was later acquitted.[23] This incident was recounted in WU's newsletter, citing Sanders's application of nonviolent techniques as key to the successful outcome of the case. In 1965, Clarie Collins Harvey filed a complaint against Jack's Texaco Service Station in McHenry, Mississippi, for refusing to allow her to use the restroom after she purchased gas there.[24] Harvey joined the boycott of Sears in 1968, closing her business account with them and selling the Sears stock held by the Collins Pension Funds portfolio, because the "company has become wealthy from the dollars of poor people and yet the racist practices of [the] local manager prevent recognition of their basic needs for human dignity and job opportunities."[25] Individually the women practiced what they preached and were persistent in challenging racial inequality.

Womanpower members fulfilled their obligation to nurture and empower the community. As historian Stephanie Shaw explained in discussing how Black women created community, they envisioned community as "both a product and a process—a sociopolitical entity that was the product of collective consciousness and a process for producing that consciousness as well."[26] They offered their community members what many Black women activists throughout time have given their family members, biological and fictive alike: the knowledge and support base to engage in the freedom struggle.

Finally, Womanpower Unlimited demonstrates the necessity of Black women's leadership and activism for the success of Black freedom struggles. Although not traditionally acknowledged as such, Black women have always been leaders in Black liberation movements. While often subjected to an existence on the margins of recognized leadership circles, Black women have historically been leaders in their communities as organizers, strategists, and negotiators.

Harvey recognized the power they had as women, as evidenced in the name she chose. Womanpower members' ability to define themselves and the nature of their work is an important aspect of Black women's activism. Womanpower did not accept a marginalized position in the movement but created for itself a definition of woman's power that was predicated on action and the necessity of their leadership. Its members recognized the power and ability of women to be a strong force for change and accepted this responsibility. Harvey encouraged the younger generation to do the same. She continued to promote women's necessary role in the Black liberation struggle, as evidenced in her 1974 commencement address at Grambling College (now Grambling State University). She exclaimed, "The Revolution of Black awareness, Black pride and dignity has real meaning for all Black Americans. . . . A new dilemma for Black women arises from Black men's desire to determine policy and progress of Black people without female participation in decision-making and leadership positions. . . . The struggle for liberation must include male and female, black and white and all persons."[27] Harvey remained persistent in advocating women's importance to the Black liberation struggle.

Without question, wu made a significant contribution to the Mississippi movement. Equally important is the impact Womanpower had on its members. Harvey credits her civil rights activism with her effectiveness as a leader in other forums, such as Church Women United. She recalled her involvement in the civil rights movement "as perhaps the most significant part of what I've done . . . because it was so strong for change—social change, emotional change, all kinds of changes. Changes in the way people felt about themselves as individuals, changes as they felt about the race. Black was beautiful came into being. Changes came with regard to the relationship to your brother and sister in other countries that were of the same color and those that were not."[28] Although Harvey was socially and politically active before Womanpower Unlimited, her experience with the organization was fundamental in her development as a leader. It allowed her to actualize her vision of the strength and possibilities of women's leadership and activism.

Aura Gary stated that Womanpower was so significant because, as was the case for her personally, "it motivated [people] to want to become active. . . . We were fortunate to have women who had the spirituality, economics, and education and charismatic ability to unify women, unify people, and motivate them. You could just see things being accomplished."[29] Womanpower members used their personal resources and abilities to empower the community. For women like Harvey, Logan, Sanders, and Mosley, Womanpower was one phase of their life's work of social and political activism. For others, like Gary, it was an extraordinary beginning.

Womanpower Unlimited had clearly articulated goals that far surpassed the glimpses others have had of their activism. For the Freedom Riders, they were women who provided them with toiletries, food, and a place to stay after their release from Parchman Farm. For the Freedom Summer volunteers, they were the women who fed them for the summer and helped establish the Freedom Houses. For many others they were the women who provided them with clothing or helped send their children to camps. For each of these groups, Womanpower was a great support system, yet many remain unaware of the widespread and systematic nature of their activism.

Examining the history of Womanpower Unlimited exposes us to a legacy of activism in which Black women's leadership has been consistent and valuable. Leadership, support, and love is what these women gave to one another, their families, and their communities. Viewing their legacy as a part of the collective of Black women's activist history values the lives and contributions of these "regular" women to Black history in particular and to American history in general. Womanpower stood, and stands, in opposition to the marginalization and devaluation of Black women's history.

"This Woman's Work"
Activism in the Post–Civil Rights Years

> Negro women, historically, have carried the dual burden of Jim
> Crow and Jane Crow. They have not always carried it graciously
> but they have carried it effectively. . . . Not only have they stood
> shoulder to shoulder with Negro men in every phase of the battle,
> but they have also continued to stand when their men were de-
> stroyed by it.
> —Pauli Murray

> I'm on call 24/7 and it's never too early or too late for me to do
> what needs to be done.
> —Ineva May-Pittman

On February 12, 2011, homegoing services were held for Mrs. A. M. E. Logan
at the Pearl Street AME Church in Jackson, Mississippi. Mayor Harvey Johnson Jr. eulogized Logan for the hundreds who turned out to celebrate the life
and legacy of the "mother of the Jackson civil rights movement." Logan was
ninety-six years old and the last of Womanpower Unlimited's primary organizers to make the transition. In the years preceding her death, she maintained
a commitment to freedom and equality that translated into tireless efforts in
grassroots organizing and community mothering. In fact, on the day she died,
she had made a trip to the food bank to pick up and deliver food to some of her
"elderly" neighbors.[1] Ever the caregiver, Logan maintained the same selflessness
that had led her to open her doors to hundreds of activists during the 1960s.

Logan was the only member of this cohort to witness the election of Barack
Obama as the United States' first Black president. She also had the opportunity
to attend his September 2008 presidential debate held at the University of Mississippi, the same institution where a riot erupted in 1962 after the admission

of its first Black student (and then again in 2012 after Barack Obama's reelection). The significance of this event—an institution once known as a symbol of white supremacy in the closed society of Mississippi opening its doors to Obama during his campaign for the most powerful office in the country—was not lost on Logan.

When asked about having the opportunity to vote for a Black president, she replied, "I never thought I would not live to see it. What do you think we've been fighting for all these years?"[2] And fight she did. A. M. E. Logan remained committed to the NAACP and was a regular fixture at meetings. Former Mississippi Supreme Court Justice and NAACP National Board Member Fred L. Banks Jr. observed that "over the past eight decades, one could hardly attend a meeting having to do with the struggle for equality and justice without noting her presence and hearing her voice."[3] Stephanie Parker-Weaver, a former executive secretary of the Jackson branch of the NAACP and Logan's mentee, believes that her legacy is one of selflessness. Partially through Logan's mentorship she became an outspoken civil rights activist in her own right, reorganizing the Jackson Southern Christian Leadership Conference in 1995, with Logan once again as a charter member.[4] Parker-Weaver remembers her as a woman who "was dedicated to her family, her church and the struggle for first-class citizenship for African Americans."[5]

Logan was the consummate grassroots organizer. She continued the voter registration efforts she engaged in during the civil rights movement—campaigning for worthy candidates and picking up people to take them to vote.[6] She even continued her work as a saleswoman, which had afforded her the economic independence to participate in the movement, and was the "oldest working Avon lady in the country."[7] Logan's was a life well-lived. She loved and was loved by her community. As her daughter Shirley Montague said, "Mother didn't just belong to us; she belonged to the people."[8] She devoted her life to the cause of Black equality.

As they directed their energies toward their individual interests, A. M. E. Logan, Jessie Mosley, Thelma Sanders, and Clarie Collins Harvey shaped local, national, and international politics, guided by the same philosophy that directed their civil rights activism—"creat[ing] the atmosphere, the institutions, and traditions that make freedom and peace possible."[9] The era of Womanpower Unlimited marked neither the beginning nor the end of their work; it was part of a unique moment in history when they combined their knowledge, wisdom, organizing skills, and desire for justice and equality to usher in a new day in Mississippi. After Womanpower disbanded, each of these women continued to impact the state, creating opportunities for the dispossessed—Blacks, the poor, women, and youth.

Jessie Mosley's fight for civil rights was not limited to issues concerning racial minorities but concerned those of gender as well. After the National Council of Negro Women (NCNW) came into the state with its project Wednesdays in Mississippi, Jessie Mosley became intimately involved with the Council's expansion throughout the state with Workshops in Mississippi. Through the NCNW, she continued the legacy of Black women organizing for racial uplift and societal transformation through women's activism and sisterhood.

Mosley lobbied for passage of the Equal Rights Amendment (ERA) during Mississippi legislative sessions and joined the national ranks of the women's movement in 1977, when she was selected as one of thirty-two members of the Coordinating Committee for the Mississippi International Women's Year (IWY) conference.[10] Convened in every state, these conferences responded to the United Nations' declaration of 1975 as the International Women's Year and the period 1976–1985 as the Decade for Women. Delegates were to be elected from each conference to represent their state at the National Conference, which developed resolutions to theoretically "guide the federal government on policy regarding women."[11] At the committee's first meeting, sponsored by Dr. Katherine Rea at the University of Mississippi (who worked with WIMS in organizing the Special Training Institute on Problems of School Desegregation at Ole Miss in 1965), Mosley was elected committee chair for the Mississippi Conference. Although a conservative, antifeminist contingent mobilized and took control of the July conference, electing an all-white delegation to attend the National Conference that November in Houston, Mosley attended as a member of an at-large delegation appointed by the National IWY to offset the elected delegation's lack of diversity.[12] Mosley returned from the conference with renewed vigor, speaking to women's groups and building on the interracial coalition the conference had generated, as she had done with Womanpower Unlimited through its Interracial Prayer Fellowship and WIMS.

That same year Mosley spearheaded efforts to preserve the Smith Robertson School, joined by Dr. Alferdteen Harrison (then professor of History and director of the Margaret Walker Alexander National Research Center at Jackson State University). Mosley's interest in preserving Black history and culture had long been evident through her publication of *The Negro in Mississippi History* (1950) and creation of the Negro in Mississippi Historical Society (1963). The alma mater of famed author Richard Wright, Smith Robertson was the first public school for Blacks in Jackson, located a couple of blocks from Farish Street. The school closed in 1971 following desegregation and was scheduled to be demolished after sitting vacant for six years. Through Mosley's and Harrison's leadership, the efforts of community organizers like Ineva May-Pittman and Doris Smith, and the support of the community, the Smith Robertson Museum and Cultural Center opened in 1984 with Mosley as director. In describing Mosley's activism and efforts with Smith Robertson in particular, longtime friend Cora Norman, with whom Mosley worked on the IWY Coordinating Committee and later the Mississippi Humanities Council, wrote:

> Jessie bolstered people, promoting their sense of personal worth as well as community values. Her spirit was infectious; her diplomacy, extraordinary; her courage, boundless. From her myriad activities and accomplishments, it was difficult to select one specific project to cite for her qualifications as a person of action. Nonetheless, her mobilization of volunteers while spearheading the Mississippi Association for the Preservation of Smith Robertson School in Jackson represented the qualities that made her unique. It was a project of lasting value for itself and of high potential for education and economic gain for the region.[13]

Mosley continued to display the leadership and inspiration that contributed to Womanpower's and the NCNW's success.

For Mosley too, the community mothering that influenced Womanpower's nurturing as resistance maintained a prominent role in her life. She helped organize the first Women, Infants, and Children (WIC) program in Jackson as well as the NCNW's day care center for working mothers. Moreover, she and her husband assisted more than twenty students in attending college at Jackson State University.[14]

Although never one to seek out the spotlight, Mosley received much deserved national recognition for her activism. In 1978 she received the Religious Heritage of America's Award for Outstanding Community Service, for which Harvey had nominated her.[15] And, in 1987, the National Education Association awarded Mosley the Carter G. Woodson Memorial Award for her work preserving and promoting Black history. She remained active in her community through organizations such as the NCNW and served as the director of Smith Robertson until 1991.[16] Jessie Bryant Mosley died on June 6, 2003, at the age of ninety-nine, and her homegoing was punctuated by a community celebration of her life held at her beloved Smith Robertson Museum.

Thelma Sanders became one of the state's most successful businesswomen and maintained a level of philanthropic service that matched her success. She devoted a great deal of time to mentoring and encouraging entrepreneurship among women. Just as she used her business to provide opportunities for Black women to shop and to have gainful employment with dignity and respect, she used her skills and connections to help other women develop their own businesses. In addition to her individual efforts to empower women in business, Sanders organized Jackson's chapter of the National Association of Negro Business and Professional Women's Clubs, Inc. (NANBPWC) in 1968, and by 1973 she went on to establish seven other clubs in Mississippi locations including Meridian, Vicksburg, Hattiesburg, and Gulfport. She also developed her own cosmetics line designed for Black women, Nu U Natural Cosmetics, and distributed it in stores throughout the state.

Sanders's philanthropic work continued outside her business endeavors. In 1967, she chaired the Free School Lunch Program for Underprivileged Children sponsored by the NANBPWC.[17] And for over twenty years, Sanders coordinated the Ebony Fashion Fair, garnering the United Negro College Fund's Distinguished Leadership Award in 1980. She used this campaign to raise funds for and promote the visibility of both Rust College and her alma mater, Tougaloo College, where she served on the board of trustees. Sanders served on the Executive Board of WLBT TV-3 after it lost its broadcast license for violating the Federal Communications Commission's (FCC) fairness doctrine. Lamar Broadcasting operated WLBT from 1953 to 1971, when the FCC ordered that its license be vacated after African Americans and the United Church of Christ alleged that the station did not fairly serve its large Black audience.[18]

Sanders was recognized for her accomplishments in both business and community development. In 1974 she received the NANBPWC's Business Woman of Distinction Award, and in 1979 the local group Women for Progress honored her with its Activist Award.[19] Sanders Boutique remained a thriving business in the Jackson community until Thelma Sanders's death in 1989.

Clarie Collins Harvey made history in May 1971 by becoming the ninth national president and the first Black woman to lead Church Women United, the largest organization of American women with a membership of over 30 million. According to historian Bettye Collier-Thomas, she became "the most influential black woman in America."[20] Her presidency was the result of almost a decade of work with CWU on the national level, beginning with its "Committee of 100," as the local CWU chapter was not integrated when she joined the Committee in the early 1960s. Womanpower member Jane Schutt, who nominated Harvey for the Committee of 100, gave a presidential nomination speech that characterized Harvey as "eminently qualified to lead us at a time in history which requires unique talents and gifts."[21] Harvey brought to CWU spiritual depth—"a deep spiritual commitment for her own life, for the lives of others and for the movement"—coupled with the business skills and acumen to ensure the continued success and progress of CWU.[22]

Harvey continued to break barriers in the ecumenical realm, serving as a consultant for the World Council of Churches Central Committee (Geneva) from 1972 to 1975 and becoming the first woman and first Black person to chair a unit of the World Council of Churches—Unit III, Education and Communication.[23] In 1974, she received Religious Heritage's "America's Churchwoman of the Year" Award, and in 1976 she became the first Black person to receive the Upper Room Citation.[24]

She remained committed to peace activism, attending the Vietnam Peace Talks in Paris with other American Protestant leaders in March 1971 and the Second International Assembly of Christians in Solidarity with the Vietnamese, Laotian, and Cambodian Peoples in 1972. In October 1973, Harvey traveled to the USSR to discuss the role of women and peace with the Soviet Women's Committee. She continued to be guided by the belief that we must all contribute to peace among humankind in our local communities as well as globally.

Locally, Harvey sustained her efforts for improving race relations and opportunities for Blacks through groups such as the Hinds County Community Service Association, which she chaired in 1968, the Farish Street Management Association, Jackson's Progressive Action Committee, and the Jackson Chapter of the National Business League. She continued the service to HBCUs that she began in the 1960s, serving on the Boards of Trustees for Rust College, the Tuskegee Institute, and the Atlanta University Center. Her alma mater, Spelman, honored her with the college's first honorary Doctorate of Humane Letters in 1977. And she blazed yet another trail by becoming the first Black trustee of Millsaps College in 1974, a position she used to advocate for the hiring of Black faculty and administrators.[25]

Emma Augusta Clarie Collins Harvey departed this life in May 1995. Her homegoing services were held on Thursday, June 1, which was befitting, as Thursday was her spiritual day—her day of prayer.[26] Dr. Thelma Adair, a longtime friend and the second Black woman to lead Church Women United, eulogized her, calling Harvey "one of the world's greatest spiritual leaders."[27] Her compassion for people reached far beyond her local community and state, and she dedicated her life to creating peace, justice, and equality throughout the world.

The Black freedom struggle of the 1960s ushered in undeniable changes in American society that transformed the nation and brought it closer to democracy. Although they were not alone, these four remarkable women and their cohorts were what sociologist Delores Aldridge describes as "long distance runners"—life-long advocates of justice and equality, extending the struggle for civil rights beyond the decade of the sixties. These women had the knowledge, skills, ability, and determination to challenge the injustices that defined American society and they did.

In the eyes of some Americans, the election of Barack Obama marked the nation's transition to a postracial society, an era where race is no longer an obstacle to achievement. Now, Americans can more freely laud the movement and the individuals that helped transform the country. Thus, in the "new" Mississippi, state and federal buildings bear the names of civil rights activists: the Jackson–Medgar Wiley Evers International Airport; the downtown branch of the post office also named for Evers; the James Chaney, Andrew Goodman, Michael Schwerner, and Roy K. Moore Federal Building; and the A. H. McCoy Federal Building. This recognition is but a superficial and disingenuous way to honor the legacy of those who risked their livelihoods and their lives for freedom and equality. This present focus on symbolism over substance is significant, especially at a time when affirmative action and many other hard-won civil rights, including the right to vote, face constant challenges, such as outright reversal of victories already won. Reflecting on the state of Mississippi today, former SNCC activist and Mississippi Delta native Euvester Simpson said:

> In spite of the progress we have made in Mississippi, and we have made progress, there is still a great racial divide in the state. As an example, in 2011, history was made in Mississippi when an African American won his party's nomination for the office of governor. He was soundly defeated by the white candidate from the opposing party who said that he wants to be known as the most conservative governor in the country. The jury is still out on what this means for race relations and the hard fought gains made during the civil rights era. It is imperative that we remember the words of Ella Baker when she said in a speech at the Masonic

Temple in Jackson, Mississippi in 1964, "We who believe in freedom cannot rest." We must remain vigilant because there are those who, I believe, would seize any opportunity to turn back the clock.[28]

Honoring the legacy of civil rights activists means more than engraving their names on the sides of buildings. Rather, it means ensuring that we continue the fight for equality and justice for ourselves and our children.

Womanpower Unlimited embodied the uniqueness of Black women's organizing tradition that is informed by their intersectionality and demonstrates their ability to traverse organization lines; to simultaneously lead and support social movements; and to link seemingly disparate organizations and issues. The organization is a testament to the love and leadership Black women have given their families and communities. Even more so, it is a testament to Black women's power to create an oppositional knowledge that allows them to articulate and work toward a humanist and democratic vision for all humankind.

NOTES

Introduction. "Women Are the Humanizers of the Struggle"

1. Womanpower and WU will be used interchangeably for Womanpower Unlimited.

2. Ineva May-Pittman, telephone interview by author, May 13, 2013.

3. First names are used to refer to individuals solely when the subjects are children or when they are discussed in conjunction with relatives who have the same last name, to avoid confusion, and to preserve historical accuracy. The author is aware of the importance of propriety and nomenclature in reference to this generation.

4. Ineva May-Pittman, interview by Steven Classen, Jackson, Mississippi, August 25, 1993; May-Pittman, telephone interview by author, November 27, 2012.

5. Intersectionality refers to Black women's position at the crossroads of various forms of oppression, including racism, sexism, and classism. For an in-depth discussion, see bell hooks, *Feminist Theory*; Collins, *Black Feminist Thought*.

6. Lee, *For Freedom's Sake*; Crosby, *A Little Taste of Freedom*; and Hamlin, *Crossroads at Clarksdale*.

7. Barnett, "Invisible Southern Black Women Leaders in the Civil Rights Movement," 177.

8. Crawford, "Beyond the Human Self," 24.

9. Mary Fair Burks founded the Women's Political Council in 1946 to mobilize middle-class women in Montgomery. Its programs were based on activism in the areas of political action, protest, and education. For sources on the WPC, see Burks, "Trailblazers: Women in the Montgomery Bus Boycott"; Garrow, *The Montgomery Bus Boycott and the Women Who Started It*; and Burns, *Daybreak of Freedom*, 15–16.

10. Burns, *Daybreak of Freedom*, 16; Robnett, *How Long? How Long?*, 64.

11. Greene, *Our Separate Ways*, 43.

12. Ransby, *Ella Baker and the Black Freedom Movement*, 6.

13. Hine, *Hine Sight*, xxii.

14. Cooper, *A Voice from the South*, 124.

15. Ibid., 31.

16. Logan, *We Are Coming*, 18.

17. Reagon, "African Diaspora Women: The Making of Cultural Workers," 87–90.

18. Collins, *Black Feminist Thought*, 192–93.

19. For a discussion of activist mothering see Naples, "Activist Mothering," 441–63; McDonald, "Black Activist Mothering," 773–95; Hamlin, *Crossroads at Clarksdale*, 59–70.

20. Aptheker, "Directions for Scholarship," 207.

21. See Jones, *Labor of Love, Labor of Sorrow*; Gilkes, *If It Wasn't for the Women*; Naples, "Activist Mothering"; Payne, *I've Got the Light of Freedom*, 271, 275–76.

22. Irons, "The Shaping of Activist Recruitment and Participation," 692–709; Hamlin, *Crossroads at Clarksdale*; Morris, "Black Women Activists in Mississippi."

23. For discussion of this type of nurturing resistance see White, *Ar'nt' I a Woman*; Thornton, "'The Means to Put My Children Through'"; and Shaw, *What a Woman Ought to Be and to Do*.

24. Oshinsky, *Worse Than Slavery*, 37.

25. Royster, *Southern Horrors and Other Writings*, 28–29.

26. Oshinsky, *Worse Than Slavery*, 100.

27. Ibid., 102–3; McMillen, *Dark Journey*, 233–45; Payne, *I've Got the Light of Freedom*, 7–14; Allen, *Without Sanctuary*.

28. McMillen, *Dark Journey*, 73.

29. Payne, *I've Got the Light of Freedom*, 16–19; McAdam, *Political Process and the Development of Black Insurgency*, 73–77, 81–82.

30. Thompson, *The History of the Mississippi State Federation of Colored Women's Clubs*, 92.

31. White and Bishop, *Mississippi's Black Women*, 4.

32. Thompson, *The History of the Mississippi State Federation of Colored Women's Clubs*, 92.

33. Ibid., 25–26.

34. Ibid., 20–29.

35. Thompson, *The History of the Mississippi State Federation*, 119; McMillen, *Dark Journey*, 69.

36. Jeffries, *Bloody Lowndes*, 8. Jeffries uses freedom rights to describe the civil and human rights that Blacks have historically been denied.

37. Dittmer, *Local People*, 29.

38. Ibid., 25, 32.

39. Dittmer, "The Politics of the Mississippi Movement," 68.

40. Payne, *I've Got the Light of Freedom*, 24–66.

41. Ibid., 35; Dittmer, *Local People*, 46–51.

42. Silver, *Mississippi: The Closed Society*, 6.

43. The Student Non-violent Coordinating Committee was created in April 1960 at Shaw University under the guidance of Ella Baker, an SCLC founder and veteran activist, to give the students autonomy in their choices. It served to coordinate the students throughout the various southern cities who were engaged in civil rights activism. SNCC was fashioned as a "loosely structured coordinating committee" to incorporate Baker's ideas of "participatory democracy." Lawrence Guyot, interview by author, Washington, D.C., March 30, 2002.

44. Gilkes defines womanist insurgence as using autonomous women's organizations in a patriarchal society to lead men. Gilkes, *If It Wasn't for the Women*, 30–33.

45. White, "Mining the Forgotten," 237; Gilkes, *If It Wasn't for the Women*, 8; Hine, *Hine Sight*, xxvi.

46. Ineva May-Pittman, telephone interview by author, May 13, 2013.

Chapter 1. "It Was Just Women Who Dared to Dream"

1. Clarie Collins Harvey, interview by John Jones and John Dittmer, April 21, 1981, Oral Histories Collection, MDAH.

2. Clarie Collins Harvey, interview by Deborah Denard, July 2, 1976, Oral History Collection, MWANRC.

3. Harvey, "Freedom Riders Please Go Away," CCHP, Box 19, Folder 8.

4. Clarie Collins Harvey, interview by Deborah Denard, July 2, 1976, MWANRC.

5. Parchman Farm was a "penal plantation" erected around 1904 in the Yazoo Delta under the initiative of Governor James K. Vardaman to house the large population of convicts that had been created by the convict leasing system, which was abolished in December 1894. Parchman, a self-sufficient farm fueled by profit that produced cotton for the state's economy, was operated by forced Black labor that was subjected to "overseers" and whippings. Parchman came to represent a new form of servile labor in Mississippi and developed a notorious reputation within the state and across the country. For a detailed discussion, see Oshinsky, *Worse Than Slavery*.

6. Womanpower, *Womanpower and the Jackson Movement*, 7.

7. Clarie Collins Harvey, interview by Gordon G. Henderson, August 5, 1965, Oral History of Mississippi: Contemporary Life and Viewpoint, Millsaps College; "Minutes of Meeting," CCHP, Box 55, Folder 3.

8. Clarie Collins Harvey, interview by Deborah Denard, July 2, 1976, MWANRC. $145 in 1961 equaled approximately $1,130 in 2014.

9. Clarie Collins Harvey, interview by Gordon G. Henderson, August 5, 1965, Oral History of Mississippi: Contemporary Life and Viewpoint, Millsaps College.

10. Clarie Collins Harvey, interview by Deborah Denard, July 2, 1976, MWANRC, 13.

11. "May 29, 1961, Central A. M. E. Church, Freedom Riders Association Minutes," 2–3, CCHP, Box 55, Folder 3.

12. "Womanpower Unlimited minutes," December 19, 1962, CCHP, Box 19, Folder 11.

13. Ibid. Others in attendance at this initial meeting included Maggie Little, Evangeline Byrd, Etha Mae Bratton, Virgia Ella B. Barnes, Annie Wells, Pearl Perkins, Mr. Haskins, and Rev. J. B. Brown.

14. Clarie Collins Harvey, interview by Deborah Denard, July 2, 1976, MWANRC.

15. Womanpower, *Womanpower and the Jackson Movement*, 8.

16. White, *Ar'n't I a Woman?*, 119.

17. Mants, "We Turned This Upside-Down Country Right Side Up," 128.

18. Dorothy Height, interview by author, June 9, 2003.

19. Weber, "The New President," 23.

20. Payne, *I've Got the Light of Freedom*, 47–56; Dittmer, *Local People*, 1–2, 49, 78.

21. Dittmer, *Local People*, 87.

22. For a thorough history of the Freedom Riders, see Arsenault, *Freedom Riders*.

23. Zinn, *SNCC*, 44, 48–51; Meier and Rudwick, *CORE*, 137–39; Carson, *In Struggle*, 36; Blumberg, *Civil Rights*, 76–78.

24. Arsenault, *Freedom Riders*, 271. This action stands in sharp contrast to the warm welcome offered them by Governor Haley Barbour in 2011 on the fiftieth anniversary of the Rides.

25. Sandra Nixon, interview by author, November 10, 2001.

26. Joan Trumpauer Mulholland, interview by author, November 10, 2001.

27. Inghram, *Freedom Riders Speak for Themselves*, 23.

28. Shirley Smith, quoted in Shannon, *Just Because*, 132–33.

29. David Loring Richards to Ladies, September 15, 1961, CCHP. Rosie Noel was the wife of A. J. Noel, one of the founders of the Jackson NAACP, and the mother of Gladys Noel Bates, who filed a suit against the state of Mississippi for the equalization of Black and white teachers' salaries in 1948.

30. See Payne, "Sexism Is a Helluva Thing," for a discussion of the privileging that scholars often attribute to male-dominated forms of activism, a valuation that is often determined by men themselves. Women tend to recognize the value in their activism and the significance of their contributions, regardless of whether or not they receive "credit."

31. Diane Nash, telephone interview by author, June 14, 2012.

Chapter 2. "You Could Just See Things Being Accomplished"

1. "Woman's Day Program," April 30, 1961, Sovereignty Commission Online, MDAH, SCR ID # 2-55-2-18-2-1-1.

2. Payne, *I've Got the Light of Freedom*, 177.

3. Around age seven, Harvey began using Clarie as her first name. Primary school tablets, CCHP, Box 14, Folder 4.

4. "Collins Papers Donated," in *The Jackson Advocate*, October 16, 1985, Collins Family Papers; Meridian Council for the Arts website http://www.meridianms.org /MeridianArtsCouncil/artwechsler1.htm.

5. Collins Family Papers, 1889–1978, "Biographical Notes," 3; McMillen, *Dark Journey*, 11,

6. Clarie Collins Harvey, interview by John Jones and John Dittmer, April 21, 1981; McMillen, *Dark Journey*, 193.

7. Collins Family Papers, Box 1, Folder 26.

8. It was common for Black colleges during this time to have high schools on campus to supplement the poor secondary public school options available to Black children.

9. Weber, "The New President," 21.

10. Sewell, *Mississippi Black History Makers*, 176–77; "Biographical Data," 1, CCHP, Box, 13, Folder 1.

11. It is important to note all of the founders of the Jackson NAACP—Collins, A. J. Noel, A. W. Wells, and John Dixon—were either entrepreneurs or employed by the federal government. This is another example of the role economic independence played in fostering individual's political activism. Also significant is that the daughters of these men were members of the first NAACP Youth Council in Mississippi. Dittmer, *Local People*, 29–30; Memorandum to Gladys Noel Bates, Gladys Wells Spates, Ester Dixon Lindon, March 11, 1985, CCHP, Box 56, Folder 5.

12. "Collins Papers Donated"; Blalock and Bishop, *Mississippi's Black Women*, 63; "Mrs. Mary Augusta Rayford Collins," n.d., CCHP, Box 11, Folder 16.

13. Clarie Collins Harvey, interview by John Jones and John Dittmer, April 21, 1981, Oral Histories Collection, MDAH.

14. Clarie Collins Harvey, "Civil Rights and the American Negro," unpublished essay, 6, CCHP, Box 19, Folder 15.

15. Clarie Collins Harvey, interview by Vicki Crawford, July 13, 1986, personal collection of Vicki Crawford.

16. See Ransby, *Ella Baker and the Black Freedom Movement*.

17. Dora Wilson, interview by author, September 7, 2011.

18. Clarie Collins Harvey, interview by John Jones and John Dittmer, April 21, 1981, Oral Histories Collection, MDAH.

19. "World Conference of Christian Youth," 337.

20. Jenness, *Twelve Negro Americans*, 117–18.

21. Clarie Collins Harvey, interview by Ruth Weber, n.d., CWUR.

22. Clarie Collins Harvey, interview by John Jones and John Dittmer, April 21, 1981, Oral Histories Collection, MDAH.

23. Harvey, "A Life Transformed," 182.

24. Ibid., 183.

25. Smith, *To Serve the Living*, 8, 59.

26. "Biographical Data, Emma Clarie Collins Harvey," 2, CCHP, Box 13, Folder 1.

27. Robert H. Miller to Mrs. C. Collins Harvey, August 1, 1956, CCHP, Box 1, Folder 14.

28. "Womanpower Unlimited Receipts," 1, CCHP, Box 63, Folder 7; *Milwaukee Sentinel*, October 7, 1961, 12, part 1.

29. A. M. E. Logan, interview by author, November 8, 2001.

30. Parker-Weaver, "Reflections on the Life of Mrs. A. M. E. Logan," February 10, 2011, *The Jackson Advocate* online, http://www.jacksonadvocateonline.com/?p=2012.

31. A. M. E. Logan, interview by Vicki Crawford, July 16, 1986, personal collection of Vicki Crawford.

32. A. M. E. Logan, interview by author, November 8, 2001.

33. A. M. E. Logan, interview by Vicki Crawford, July 16, 1986, personal collection of Vicki Crawford.

34. A. M. E. Logan, interview by author, November 8, 2001.

35. Frank Figgers, telephone interview by author, August 2013; Williamson, *Radicalizing the Ebony Tower*, 20–21.

36. Willis Logan, telephone interview by author, November 14, 2012. Willis Logan is the youngest of A. M. E. and Style Logan's four children, born after they relocated to Jackson.

37. Alferdteen Harrison quoted in McLaughlin, "A. M. E. Logan," February 7, 2011.

38. Ibid.

39. Jesse Morris, interview by author, July 24, 2012.

40. A. M. E. Logan, interview by author, November 8, 2001; Parker-Weaver, "Reflections."

41. A. M. E. Logan, interview by author, November 8, 2001; Ineva May-Pittman, telephone interview by author, November 27, 2012.

42. Shirley Logan Montague, interview by author, July 21, 2012.

43. A. M. E. Logan, interview by author, September 2000.

44. The minutes from Womanpower's organizing meeting list Logan as the executive director and her responsibilities are reflective of such a title. Subsequent organizational materials, such as letterhead and minutes, list Logan as administrative secretary.

45. Clarie Collins Harvey, interview by Deborah Denard, July 2, 1976.

46. Thomas Gaither, Panel Discussion on The Freedom Rides at the 1961 Freedom Riders' 40th Reunion, Jackson, Mississippi, November 10, 2001.

47. A. M. E. Logan, interview by author, November 8, 2001.

48. Mrs. Martin L. Harvey Memorandum to Mrs. Logan, June 6, 1961, 1, CCHP, Box 63; Hamlin, *Crossroads at Clarksdale*, 40, 55.

49. Hamlin, *Crossroads at Clarksdale*, 40.

50. Ransby, *Ella Baker and the Black Freedom Movement*, 130.

51. Ibid., 178.

52. Springer, *Living for the Revolution*, 2.

53. Thelma Sanders's resume, in author's possession.

54. W. R. "Bo" Brown, telephone interview by author, November 17, 2012. Brown is Thelma Sanders's brother.

55. Ibid.

56. In 1967, I. S. Sanders received the inaugural honorary doctorate from his alma mater.

57. Putnam, "Educator, Black Leader Sanders, 95, Dies in Jackson after a Lengthy Illness," 18.

58. Thelma Sanders, interview by Mildred M. Williams, June 5, 1975, Oral History Collections, MWANRC.

59. Ibid.

60. The Ebony Fashion Fair began in 1958 as a nonprofit public service project to raise money for charitable causes. "Local Chairman Pave Way for Ebony Fashion Fair," *Ebony*, Vol. 21, No. 11, September 1966, 136; Thelma Sanders, interview by Mildred M. Williams, June 5, 1975, Oral History Collections, MWANRC.

61. Clarie Collins Harvey, interview by John Jones and John Dittmer, April 21, 1981.

62. Boyd, "The Battle of McComb," 1398.

63. Lloyd, *Lives of Mississippi Authors*, 348.

64. Sherry Lucas, "Jessie Mosley," *Clarion-Ledger*, June 30, 1991, 2E, MDAH, Jessie Mosley Subject File; Jessie Mosley, interview by author, June 1, 2001.

65. *Mississippi State Federation of Colored Women's Clubs Year Bulletin*, 1954–55, 28, CCHP, Box 55, Folder 12.

66. Wilma Mosley Clopton, interview by Marlene McCurtis; Jessie Mosley, interview by author, June 1, 2001.

67. Gates, "JSU to Salute Museum Founder on 90th Birthday."

68. Evers, "Why I Live in Mississippi," 118.

69. Lawrence Guyot, interview by author, March 30, 2002.

70. In the context of the civil rights movement, the use of the phrase "beloved community," originated by nineteenth-century religious philosopher Josiah Royce, is typically associated with Martin Luther King Jr. or SNCC's concept of a community in which everyone's humanity is acknowledged and respected and people have the opportunity to live up to their fullest potential. Harvey frequently used the term in a similar fashion and its use for her likely stemmed from the religious values that propelled her activism.

71. Womanpower, *Womanpower and the Jackson Movement*, 6.

72. Clarie Collins Harvey, interview by Robert Penn Warren, February 9, 1964.

73. In 1944, twenty-seven-year-old Irene Morgan was beaten and arrested for refusing to give up her seat to whites on a Greyhound bus from Virginia to Baltimore. She was charged and found guilty of resisting arrest and violating segregation statutes. With the assistance of the NAACP, Morgan appealed the latter charge to the Supreme Court, which ruled that segregating interstate passengers violated the commerce clause. In response, the Journey of Reconciliation was planned to test the decision. For a detailed discussion, see Arsenault, *Freedom Riders*.

74. Grant, *Ella Baker*, 91–92.

75. Feldstein, "'I Wanted the Whole World to See,'" 273.

76. McGuire, *At the Dark End of the Street*, 107.

77. Bernice Johnson Reagon, quoted in Robnett, *How Long? How Long?*, 37.

78. Womanpower, *Womanpower and the Jackson Movement*, 6.

79. Clarie Collins Harvey, interview by Gordon G. Henderson, August 5, 1965, Oral History of Mississippi: Contemporary Life and Viewpoint, Millsaps College.

80. Collins, *Black Feminist Thought*, 39.

81. Piven and Cloward, *Poor People's Movements*, xxii.

82. Clarie Collins Harvey, interview by Robert Penn Warren, February, 9, 1964. In the 1970s Harvey took a leadership role in the organization including serving on the Auditing and International Trends and Services Committees. As a member, she worked alongside former Womanpower members Ruth O. Hubert, Edna Lovelace, Daisy Reddix, and Aurelia Young. *The Links, Inc. Yearbook*, 1972–73, CCHP, Box 53, Folder 14; Jackson (MS) Chapter, The Links, Incorporated, May 1, 1978–April 30, 1979, ANYP, Series 6, Box 3, Folder 6.

83. Harris, "From the Kennedy Commission to the Combahee River Collective," 285.

84. "Agenda, Womanpower Unlimited 1st Meeting Permanent Officers," August 17, 1961, CCHP, Box 63, Folder 14.

85. Womanpower, *Womanpower and the Jackson Movement*, 5. Organizational materials—newsletters, meeting agendas and programs, letterhead, and minutes—indicate that some positions were temporary. For example, Aurelia Young was listed as the assistant pianist in a 1961 newsletter; however the organization's 1963 publication, *Womanpower and the Jackson Movement*, does not list this position. Additionally

because the collection of these documents is incomplete, it is impossible to know precisely when particular positions were created and eliminated.

86. The newsletter was published under various titles—*Woo*, *WU*, *WU Newsletter*, and *Womanpower Unlimited Newsletter*. "Womanpower Unlimited Minutes," March 14, 1963, CCHP, Box 19, Folder 11.

87. "Womanpower Unlimited Meeting at Farish Street Baptist Church Sunday, July 16," *The Jackson Advocate*, Vol. XIV, No. 37, July 1961, 5, Microfilm, MDAH.

88. Clarie Collins Harvey, letter to Members, April 20, 1964, CCHP, Box 63, Folder 12.

89. "Minutes, Womanpower Unlimited Meeting," April 8, 1964, CCHP, Box 19, Folder 11; "Agenda, Womanpower Unlimited Meeting," June 1965, CCHP, Box 19, Folder 17.

90. Dorothy Stewart, telephone interview by author, September 10, 2011; "Membership List," WUC, Series IV: Programs, Box 1, Folder 2, 1961; Harvey, "Womanpower Continues to Benefit Community," 3.

91. Aura Gary, interview by author, May 30, 2001.

92. Collins, *Black Feminist Thought*, 100–102; Hine, "Rape and the Inner Lives of Black Women in the Middle West."

93. Womanpower, *Womanpower and the Jackson Movement*, 20–21.

94. "A Note about the Friends of SNCC Groups—What Do They Do?" undated, Michael J. Miller Civil Rights Collection, University of Southern Mississippi, Civil Rights in Mississippi Digital Archive, http://digilib.usm.edu/cdm/ref/collection /manu/id/4703.

95. *WU*, January 1966, CCHP, Box 63, Folder 17.

96. Honey Knopp, "Confidential Report on Mississippi Visitation," August 3–13, 1964, 1, CCHP, Box 73, Folder 14.

97. Honey Knopp to Clarie Collins Harvey, November 14, 1964, CCHP.

98. Giddings, *When and Where I Enter*, 173.

99. MSFCWC, *MSFCWC Bulletin, 1954–55*, 12.

100. "Womanpower Unlimited membership list," CCHP.

101. "Womanpower Unlimited receipts," CCHP, Box 63, Folder 7.

102. Clarie Collins Harvey to A. M. E. Logan, June 6, 1961, 1, CCHP.

103. Ineva May-Pittman, interview by Steven Classen, August 25, 1993.

104. A. M. E. Logan, interview by author, September 2000.

105. Medgar Evers's first office was on Farish Street before he relocated to the Masonic Temple on Lynch Street.

Chapter 3. "'Cause I Love My People"

1. Evers-Williams and Marable, *The Autobiography of Medgar Evers*, 233; A. L. Hopkins, "Investigation of Negro Sit-ins at the Jackson, Mississippi City Zoo," June 26, 1961, Sovereignty Commission Papers Online, MDAH, SRD ID # 2-55-9-37-2-1-1.

2. *Voice of the Jackson Movement Newsletter*, August 25, 1961, CCHP, Box 70, Folder

15; Christian Social Action for Better Community Living, undated, CCHP; Dittmer, *Local People*, 116–17.

3. *Woo*, No. 4, April 30, 1962, 1, CCHP, Box 63, Folder 17.

4. Jesse Morris, interview by Tom Dent, July 20, 1979; COFO, "Mississippi: Structure of the Movement, Present Operations, and Prospectus for This Summer," 1964, 2, Civil Rights Movement Veterans website, http://www.crmvet.org/docs/dochome .htm#docsmfdp, accessed August 24, 2013; Dittmer, *Local People*, 118.

5. SNCC, "COFO: What It Is, What It Does," 1964, 2, Civil Rights Movement Veterans website, http://www.crmvet.org/docs/dochome.htm#docsmfdp; Hamlin, *Crossroads at Clarksdale*, 102–3.

6. Founded in 1944, the Atlanta-based Southern Regional Council is dedicated to fighting racial injustice and promoting racial equality in the South.

7. Dittmer, *Local People*, 119–20; Payne, *I've Got the Light of Freedom*, 108; Lawson, *Black Ballots*, 261–66.

8. O'Brien, *We Shall Not Be Moved*, 81.

9. Salter, *Jackson, Mississippi*, 19.

10. SNCC's as well as COFO's first major campaigns in the state were voter registration efforts. Additionally, in the years leading up to the movement, NAACP branches in Mississippi had directed much of their activity toward these efforts. The development of local voters' leagues and the efforts of MSFCWC organizations also indicate that this was a priority among Black activists in the state.

11. John Dittmer, *Local People*, 25.

12. Morris, *The Origins of the Civil Rights Movement*, 101.

13. Brown, "To Catch the Vision of Freedom," 72, 82–83.

14. Giddings, *When and Where I Enter*, 129.

15. Terborg-Penn, *African American Women in the Struggle for the Vote*, 94; Giddings, *When and Where I Enter*, 121.

16. Cooper, "The Status of Woman in America," 139.

17. Giddings, *When and Where I Enter*, 129.

18. Although Black women maintained an earnest dedication to the suffrage movement since its inception, white women's loyalty to Black women's enfranchisement was not as steadfast. As the suffrage movement gained national momentum in the 1890s, many white suffragists, who had initially supported universal women's suffrage, discovered that it was more advantageous to their cause to disassociate themselves from Black women's political strivings. Hoping to generate greater support among white males and southern white women, northern suffragists began to discriminate against Black women and support means like "educated" suffrage to exclude Black women and expedite their own enfranchisement. Nonetheless, Black women maintained a commitment to suffragist issues giving necessary power to the movement as a whole.

19. Terborg-Penn, *African American Women in the Struggle for the Vote*, 151–56.

20. Higginbotham, "Clubwomen and Electoral Politics in the 1920s," 141.

21. An example of this power is evident in the 1915 election of Oscar de Priest for

alderman in Chicago. After enlisting the support of the Alpha Suffrage Club, De Priest was able to defeat two white candidates for the position.

22. Higginbotham, "Clubwomen and Electoral Politics," 142–43.

23. Mary Collins to Members of the Mississippi State Federation of Colored Women's Clubs, Inc., October 27, 1955, CCHP.

24. Womanpower Unlimited Newsletter, Vol. 1, No. 1, November 8, 1961, 1, CCHP, Box 63, Folder 17.

25. The Voter's League to Pastor and Congregation, January 19, 1962, CCHP, Box 63, Folder 1.

26. *Womanpower Unlimited Newsletter*, Vol. 1, No. 3, February 1962, CCHP, Box 63, Folder 17.

27. C. Collins Harvey to Attorney Wiley Branton, June 15, 1962, SRCA, 75–06–06–14.

28. Clarie C. Harvey to Mr. Wiley Branton, August 1, 1961, SRCA, 75–06–06–14.

29. Womanpower Unlimited, "Final Report Womanpower Unlimited," Voter Education Project, January 23, 1963, CCHP, Box 63, Folder 13.

30. Clarie Collins Harvey to Wiley Branton, June 13, 1962, SRCA, 75–06–06–14.

31. Bishop Carolyn Tyler Guidry, telephone interview by author, October 18, 2012. Guidry moved to California with her husband and five children in 1964. After a twelve-year career with a bank, she enrolled at the Los Angeles Bible School to pursue the ministry and in 2005 was elected as the second female bishop in the A. M. E. Church.

32. A. M. E. Logan, "Womanpower Unlimited Field Report—10–22—11–11–1962," 3–4, SRCA.

33. A. M. E. Logan, "Womanpower Unlimited Report," October 15, CCHP, Box 63, Folder 10.

34. A. M. E. Logan, "Fieldworker's Report," December 4, 2, CCHP, Box 63, Folder 10.

35. Logan, "Womanpower Unlimited Field Report—10–22—11–11–1962," 4.

36. A. M. E. Logan, "Fieldworker's Report," November 26, 1, CCHP, Box 63, Folder 10.

37. "Agenda: Voter Registration Workshop," September 8, 1962, SRCA. William Higgs, a Mississippi native, was one of the few white attorneys working on civil rights cases in Mississippi, such as James Meredith's integration of Ole Miss. He also served as an attorney for SNCC and the MFDP, from Washington, D.C., as he was forced to leave Mississippi due to his civil rights work.

38. A. M. E. Logan, "4th Report," 9/10–9/16/62, CCHP, Box 63, Folder 10.

39. A. M. E. Logan, "Fieldworker's Report," October 20, CCHP, Box 63, Folder 10.

40. Logan, "Field Report, 10–22–11–11–1962," 2.

41. "Affidavit of Cornelious M. Johnson," October 31, 1961, Medgar Evers Papers, Series 2, Box 2, Folder 5.

42. Medgar Evers to Clarence Mitchell, December 28, 1961, Medgar Evers Papers, Series 2, Box 2, Folder 18.

43. Womanpower, *Womanpower and The Jackson Movement*, 13.

44. Womanpower, "Final Report Womanpower Unlimited Voter Education Project," 3.

45. Clarie Collins Harvey, interview by Gordon G. Henderson, August 5, 1965.

46. C. Collins Harvey to Wiley Branton, August 1, 1962, SRCA.

47. "Monthly Meeting Womanpower Unlimited," March 14, 1963, CCHP, Box 63, Folder 3.

48. Logan, "Field Report, 10–22–11–11–1962."

49. Womanpower, "Final Report Womanpower Unlimited Voter Education Project," 1–2. In September 1962, after a protracted battle with state officials and politicians that began with his application for admission earlier that year, James Meredith enrolled in the University of Mississippi. Although federal forces were on hand to maintain order, a riot erupted on campus that left two dead and hundreds wounded, underscoring for many white resistance to integration.

50. Clarie Collins Harvey, interview by Gordon G. Henderson, August 5, 1965.

51. Leslie W. Dunbar and Wiley A. Branton, "Second Annual Report of the Voter Education Project of the Southern Regional Council, Inc. for the Fiscal Year April 1, 1963 through March 31, 1964," 9–10, CCHP, Box 60, Folder 2.

52. Womanpower, *Womanpower and the Jackson Movement*, 19.

53. Dittmer, *Local People*, 157–59.

54. Womanpower Unlimited minutes, December 19, 1962, CCHP, Box 63, Folder 3.

55. Hazel L. Whitney, telephone interview by author, September 22, 2012.

56. Ineva May-Pittman, telephone interview by author, November 28, 2012; Hazel Whitney, telephone interview by author, September 22, 2012.

57. Jeanes teachers originated in 1909 with an endowment established by (white) Quaker Anna T. Jeanes. The teachers trained and hired with these funds were employed to serve as countywide supervisors of industrial education for Blacks throughout the South. The Negro Rural School Fund, as it was officially called, provided much-needed resources to improve educational and professional opportunities for Black students and teachers. See Williams et al., *The Jeanes Story*, for a detailed history.

58. Thompson, *The History of The Mississippi Teachers Association*, 181.

59. Crawford, "'We Shall Not be Moved,'" 59–63; Thompson, *The History of the Mississippi State Federation of Colored Women's Clubs*, 239.

60. Scott Draine, telephone interview by author, September 23, 2012.

61. Doretha Wiley, "Homegoing Services for Dr. Pearl Montgomery Draine," February 14, 2009, in author's possession.

62. Dorothy Stewart, telephone interview by author, September 10, 2011.

63. Hunter Gray (John Salter), email to author, September 6, 2012.

64. http://hunterbear.org/medgar_w.htm, accessed September 6, 2012.

65. Shirley Montague, interview by author, July 21, 2012.

66. http://hunterbear.org/medgar_w.htm.

67. Dittmer, *Local People*, 159–60.

68. Classen, *Watching Jim Crow*, 84–85.

69. Salter, *Jackson, Mississippi*, 237–38; O'Brien, *We Shall Not Be Moved*, 231.

70. "N.A.A.C.P. Mass Meeting," June 21, 1963, CCHP, Box 56, Folder 6; "Community Mass Meeting Program," April 22, 1962, CCHP, Box 53, Folder 9. In the April 1962 meeting, Harvey shared the stage with nine male presenters.

71. *WOO*, Oct 1963, 1, CCHP, Box 63, Folder 17.

72. O'Brien, *We Shall Not Be Moved*, 231.

73. *Woo*, October–September 1964, 1, CCHP, Box 63, Folder 17.

74. For more detailed information on Freedom Summer, see Carson, *In Struggle*; McAdam, *Freedom Summer*; John Dittmer, *Local People*; Payne, *I've Got the Light of Freedom*; Moye, *Let the People Decide*; Hogan, *Many Minds, One Heart*.

75. Clarie Collins Harvey, "Mississippi Summer Project—Womanpower Unlimited, A Report to the United States Commission on Civil Rights," August 15, 1964, 7, CCHP, Box 63, Folder 12.

76. Jesse Morris, telephone interview by author, October 12, 2012; Charles Cobb, email to author, October 18, 2012; Dave Dennis, email to author, October 18, 2012.

77. Harvey, "Mississippi Summer Project," 3.

78. Raines, *My Soul Is Rested*, 274.

79. Ineva May-Pittman, telephone interview by author, November 27, 2012; Harvey, "Mississippi Summer Project," 5.

80. Unita Blackwell, telephone interview by author, April 1997. Blackwell was a SNCC staff member and an MFDP organizer and became the first Black mayor of Mayersville, Miss.

81. Rosie Redmond Holden, interview by Lawrence Goodwyn, June 1975.

82. Howard Romaine, email to author, August 8, 2012.

83. Harvey, "Mississippi Summer Project," 4.

84. "An S-O-S," September 10, 1964, WUC, Series I: Correspondence, Box 1, Folder 3.

85. Jesse Morris, telephone interview by author, June 19, 2013; Sovereignty Commission Online, MDAH, SCR ID# 2–166–3–37–9–1–1. The MCHR set up an office on Farish Street, down the block from the church, and brought a little more than a hundred health care workers to the state during the summer of 1964. For a detailed discussion, see Dittmer, *The Good Doctors*.

86. *Woo*, Vol. 4, No. 8, August 1964, CCHP, Box 63, Folder 17.

87. Sig Fusco to Mrs. Redmond, September 1, 1964, WUC; A. M. E. Logan, interview by author, November 8, 2001.

88. Harvey, "Mississippi Summer Project," 4–5.

89. "Civil Rights Fair," July 18, 1964, CCHP, Box 2, Folder 5.

90. Naeve, "Mississippi Box Project," 24.

91. Virginia Naeve to Clarie Collins Harvey, August 17, 1, CCHP, Box 56, Folder 4.

92. "A Report from the Vermont Civil Rights Fair," n.d. Donations were also made to civil rights projects in other states such as SDS in Kentucky, organic gardening and voter registration projects in Tennessee, and literacy and relief projects in North Carolina.

93. Alice Jackson-Wright, telephone interview by author, December 29, 2011. Jackson-Wright's poem discusses a Black child's desire for access to the best her state

has to offer and to that which she deserves as an American citizen. It is frequently cited as an example of the intellectual ability and potential of Black southern youth that Freedom Schools nurtured. The last line, "I shall have them or be dead," signifies the spirit of resistance the schools hoped to foster.

94. Sig Fusco to Mrs. Redmond, September 1, 1964, WUC.

95. Clarie Collins Harvey to Mrs. Harry G. Newman, October 24, 1964, CCHP, Box 2, Folder 7.

96. Dittmer, *Local People*, 228.

97. Womanpower Unlimited to Pastors, Churches, Clubs, Fraternities, Sororities, Fraternal Societies, Professional Groups, Members of WU's Chain of Friendship, Individuals and Others, n.d., CCHP.

98. *Woo* (January 1966), CCHP, Box 63, Folder 17; Aurelia Young, "The Period of the Sixties," 4, ANYP, Series 4, Box 3, Folder 2. Delta Sigma Theta Sorority, Inc. is a historical Black sorority founded in 1913 at Howard University to promote sisterhood and service. For more information see Giddings, *In Search of Sisterhood*.

99. Bolton, *The Hardest Deal of All*, 112–13.

100. *Woo*, Vol. 3, No 8, Aug. 1964, 2, CCHP, Box 63, Folder 17.

101. Jean Fairfax to Clarie Collins Harvey, October 14, 1964, CCHP, Box 2, Folder 7.

102. *WU Newsletter*, October 1, 1965, 2, CCHP, Box 63, Folder 17.

103. Clarie Collins Harvey to Mr. Seymour Herzog, September 1, 1964, CCHP, Box 2, Folder 7.

104. Irving Adler, "VIM Is a Great Success," *Vermont Civil Rights Union Bulletin*, June 1966, 2, CRMVC, MSA 307, Folder 19.

105. Jesse Morris, telephone interview by author, June 19, 2013.

106. The Vermont Civil Rights Union was formed in August 1964 by the Burlington NAACP and the Rutland National Conference of Christians and Jews, to "sponsor and support legislation and civil rights programs in Vermont." Karen Petersen, untitled paper, 7, CRMVC, MSA 307, Folder 14.

107. Untitled, September 30, 1965, CRMVC, MSA 307, Folder 18.

108. Ineva May-Pittman, telephone interview by author, November 27, 2012; Pearl Draine, Letter to the Editor, *Bennington Banner*, March 29, 1966, CRMVC, MSA 307; Letter to VIM Supporters, May 2, 1966.

109. Adler, "VIM Is a Great Success," 1.

110. Ibid.

111. Clarie Collins Harvey, interview by Gordon G. Henderson, August 5, 1965.

112. Jane Schutt, interview by Leesha Faulkner, October 3, 1994.

113. Ibid.; Jane Schutt, interview by Gordon G. Henderson, July 16, 1965.

114. United Church Women was organized in 1941 as United Council of Church Women from a meeting of women representing three interdenominational women's groups. In 1950, the group became part of the National Council of Churches of Christ as the General Department of United Church Women. In 1966, it became an autonomous group under the name "Church Women United." The organization will be referenced by its historically accurate name throughout the text.

115. Riehm, "Dorothy Tilly and the Fellowship of the Concerned," 41; Jane Schutt,

interview by John Jones and John Dittmer, February 2, 1981. Dorothy Tilly founded the Fellowship of the Concerned in 1949 as a way to mobilize primarily white women to address race relations in the South as part of their Christian duty. Tilly, the director of Women's Work for the Southern Regional Council at the time of the FOC's founding, led this eventually biracial, interdenominational group of women to challenge racial prejudice in their communities.

116. Jane Schutt, interview by Gordon G. Henderson, July 16, 1965.

117. Ibid.

118. Jane Schutt, interview by Leesha Faulkner, October 3, 1994, 4; Jane Schutt, interview by John Jones and John Dittmer, February 2, 1981.

119. Jane Schutt, interview by Gordon G. Henderson, July 16, 1965.

120. Ibid.

121. Shannon, *Just Because*, 115.

122. Ibid., 113.

123. Ibid., 116.

124. Jane Schutt, interview by Leesha Faulkner, October 3, 1994.

125. "Prayer Fellowship Letter," CCHP, Box 36, Folder 15.

126. See Jones, "'How Shall I Sing the Lord's Song?'" for a discussion of racial exclusivity in southern UCW chapters.

127. "Wider Prayer Fellowship List," 1965, CCHP, Box 36, Folder 15.

128. Ibid.

129. Jane Schutt, interview by Leesha Faulkner, October 10, 1994.

130. Ibid.

131. Instead of removing the charred cross, Schutt decorated it with Christmas ornaments. Dittmer, *Local People*, 195; Jane Schutt, interview by Leesha Faulkner, October 10, 1994; Ella Schutt McBride Hamilton (Mrs. Schutt's daughter), telephone interview by author, August 1, 2013.

132. Pearl Street Prayer Fellowship to Members of the Wider Fellowship, Summer 1964, CCHP.

133. Mrs. Kyle (Elizabeth) Haselden to Polly Cowan, August 30, 1965, 1, CWUR.

134. Verna Polk Curtis, telephone interview by author, November 18, 2011.

Chapter 4. "We Who Believe in Freedom"

1. "Women Strike for Peace," 3–4, March 1962, CCHP.

2. Swerdlow, "Women Strike for Peace," 193–95.

3. Grooms, "'Give Us a Missile Base,'" 395–96.

4. Ibid.; Eaton, "Women in Geneva," 47.

5. Swerdlow, *Women Strike for Peace*, 196.

6. Ibid., 197.

7. Clarie Collins Harvey, "The Day of the Petition," 2, CCHP.

8. Swerdlow, *Women Strike for Peace*, 197–98.

9. Clarie Collins Harvey, "Geneva, Switzerland," Thursday, April 5, 1962, 1–2, CCHP.

10. Swerdlow, *Women Strike for Peace*, 198.

11. Eaton, "Women in Geneva," 48.

12. Grooms, "'Give Us a Missile Base,'" 397.

13. Swerdlow, *Women Strike for Peace*, 197.

14. Eaton, "Women in Geneva," 47.

15. *WOO Newsletter*, no. 4, April 30, 1962, CCHP, Box 63, Folder 17.

16. Clarie Collins Harvey, "Women International Strike for Peace," n.d., 4, CCHP.

17. Harvey, "A Life Transformed," 182.

18. Clarence T. R. Nelson, "Several Highlights from the General Conference of the Methodist Church in Denver, Colorado," April 27–May 7, 1960, CCHP, Box 37, Folder 8.

19. General Board of Social Concerns of the Methodist Church, "The Social Creed of the Methodist Church," *Contact* 2, no. 1 (June 1, 1960): 5, CCHP, Box 36, Folder 9.

20. United States Department of Justice, "Re: Women's Peace Conference Sponsored by the Women's Strike for Peace and the Women for Peace Organizations, at Ann, Arbor, Michigan, June 8–10, 1962," Federal Bureau of Investigation New Orleans, La., July 30, 1962, 2, CCHP, Box, 14, Folder 1.

21. Clarie Collins Harvey, "Anderson Chapel Speech," March 15, 1959, CCHP, Box 20, Folder 19.

22. Womanpower, *Womanpower and the Jackson Movement*, 6.

23. Clarie Collins Harvey, interview by Gordon G. Henderson, August, 5, 1965, Oral History of Mississippi: Contemporary Life and Viewpoint, Millsaps College.

24. In January of 1963, Womanpower's Executive Board voted in favor of Harvey's proposal to pledge $5 for three months to the national WSP office. Not a small sum considering the plethora of civil rights projects locally that were in desperate need of funds. Womanpower Unlimited minutes, January 10, 1963, 2, CCHP, Box 63, Folder 3.

25. Anne Bloom, Mary Chandler, Ralph Russell, and Lawrence Scott also attended the meeting; however, the aforementioned women became the key women of the organization.

26. Swerdlow, *Women Strike for Peace*, 18.

27. Ibid., 17–18, 44–45.

28. Ibid., 30. This was an issue of great importance to the women personally as mothers concerned about the well-being of their children and also strategically as a way to gain support from other mothers/women, who, they believed, should have been concerned about the welfare of all children.

29. Ibid., 23–25.

30. Some chapters used Women International Strike for Peace (WISP) or Women for Peace.

31. "Women for Peace," n.d., CCHP, Box 64, Folder 5.

32. Eleanor Garst, Draft of Letter (for individual salvation and signature and note if desired) to accompany leaflet, September 22, 1961, WSPR, Series A1, Box 2, Folder 8.

33. Swerdlow, *Women Strike for Peace*, 48; Untitled article, 1966, WSPR Series A1, Box 3, Folder 2.

34. "Fact Sheet Women—Strike for Peace."

35. Swerdlow, *Women Strike for Peace*, 72.

36. Ibid., 47; Womanpower, *Womanpower and the Jackson Movement*, 6.

37. Swerdlow, *Women Strike for Peace*, 46, 106.

38. Ibid., 107.

39. Reagon, "My Black Mothers and Sisters," 82.

40. The D.C. chapter, for example, collaborated with CORE and LA WSP issued a statement in support of civil rights in May 1963, as a result of the hesitancy of the national organization to take a stance.

41. Swerdlow, *Women Strike for Peace*, 51.

42. Ibid., 90.

43. Boggs, *Living for Change*, 107.

44. Eunice Armstrong to Mrs. Schulz, June 6, 1962, WSPR, Series A3, Box 6, Folder 7; Boggs, *Living for Change*, 107; Estepa, "Taking the White Gloves Off," 91.

45. Swerdlow, *Women Strike for Peace*, 91–92.

46. Statement from Civil Rights Committee, From Second National Conference of WSP in Champaign-Urbana, Illinois, June 6–9, 1963, WSPR, Series A1, Box 3.

47. Swerdlow, *Women Strike for Peace*, 92.

48. Clarie Collins Harvey, interview by John Jones and John Dittmer, April 21, 1981.

49. Eunice Armstrong to Clarie Collins Harvey, February 26, 1964, CCHP, Box 1, Folder 20.

50. Gail Eaby, "Impressions & Reporting," WISP Conference, June 9–10, 1962—Ann Arbor, Michigan, WSPR, Series B1, Box 1, Folder 1.

51. The committee included E. C. Quaye, chair, Ghana; Heinrich Buchbinder, Switzerland; Ritchie Calder, United Kingdom; Josué de Castro, Brazil; and D. Chaman Lall, India. Boaten, *Conclusions of the Accra Assembly*, 1; Mayfield, *Selections from the Accra Assembly Papers*, vii. Frances Herring, "World without the Bomb," 2, CCHP, Box 52, Folder 13.

52. Quarm, *Diplomatic Offensive*, 1.

53. Armah, *Peace without Power*, 132.

54. Ibid., 136.

55. "Clarie Collins Harvey Goes to Peace Conference in Ghana," *The Jackson Advocate* 15, no. 34 (June 30 1962): 8.

56. Armah, *Peace without Power*, 136.

57. Herring, "World without the Bomb," 2.

58. Quoted in Herring, "World without the Bomb," 5.

59. Swerdlow, *Women Strike for Peace*, 91.

60. Eunice B. Armstrong to Mrs. Clarke, June 13, 1962, CCHP, Box 17, Folder 1.

61. Selma Sparks, telephone interview by author, December 15, 2011.

62. Ibid.

63. Armah, *Peace without Power*, 136; Mayfield, *Selections from the Accra Assembly*, 168–77.

64. Kwame Nkrumah, "Address of Osagyefo the President at the Opening of the Accra Assembly," 7, June 21, 1961, CCHP, Box 52, Folder 4.

65. Ibid., 3.

66. Harvey, "Women International Strike for Peace," 3.

67. Harvey, "Accra Impressions," *Women's Peace Movement Bulletin* 1, non. 8 (Sept. 20, 1962): 11, WSPR.

68. Boaten, *Conclusions of the Accra Assembly*, 124–24.

69. Clarie Collins Harvey, "World without the Bomb, Report and Interpretations," 1, CCHP, Box 52.

70. Ibid.

71. Frances Herring, "A New World Voice for Peace, in Palo Alto, California— W.I.S.P." August 1962, 2, WSPR, Series B2, Box 2, Folder 5.

72. Harvey, "Accra Impressions," 11; Harvey, " World without the Bomb," 2.

73. Clarie Collins Harvey, WSP Notebook, CCHP, Box 15, Folder 6.

74. Clarie Collins Harvey, interview by Robert Penn Warren, February 9, 1964, in Robert Penn Warren's "Who Speaks for the Negro: An Archival Collection."

75. Harvey, "Accra Impressions," 11.

76. Sparks, "A First Hand Report from the Accra Assembly," 4.

77. Ibid., 4–5.

78. Herring, "World without the Bomb."

79. For a discussion of WSP's efforts in this respect see Estepa, "Taking the White Gloves Off."

80. "Womanpower Unlimited minutes," March 14, 1963, 3, CCHP, Box 63, Folder 3.

81. Harvey served as one of four members of the local organizing committee.

82. "Women's Peace Pilgrimage to the Vatican," Mar. 18, 1963, WSPR, Series A4, Box 1, Folder 14.

83. Alice Pollard, "Women for Peace Release," April 15, 1963, WSPR, Series A4, Box 1, Folder 14.

84. Virginia Naeve and Alice Pollard, "Proposal: Pilgrimage to Rome for An Audience with Pope John on Peace Issues," February 23, 1963, 1, WSPR, Series A4, Box 1, Folder 14.

85. While not all WSPers were housewives, given the time period, even those who had professional careers were likely the primary individuals responsible for taking care of the children and other domestic chores. Thus, the appeal to women as housewives was hardly a foreign concept.

86. Alice Pollard, "Women for Peace Pilgrimage to Rome," April 30, 1963, WSPR Series A4, Box 1, Folder 14.

87. Pope John XXIII, "Comments by Pope John on His 'Pacem in Terris,'" *L'Osservatore Romano*, April 25, 1963, WSPR, Series A4, Box 1, Folder 14.

88. Women for Peace Pilgrimage telegram to President Kennedy, May 4, 1963, WSPR, Series A4, Box 1, Folder 14.

89. Alice Pollard, Press Release "Women for Peace Pilgrimage to Rome," May 4, WSPR, Series A4, Box 1, Folder 1.

90. Members of the Women for Peace Pilgrimage to Rome to Mr. Prime Minister, May 1, 1963, WSPR, Series A3, Box 5, Folder 5.

91. The Women for Peace Pilgrimage, April 1963—Geneva—Rome, "To: Central Committee of the World Council of Churches," 1–2, CCHP.

92. "International Peace Pilgrimage," April 20 to May 4, 1963, CCHP.

93. Independent Political Forum, Press Release, April 29, 1963, CCHP, Box 61, Folder 10.

94. Coretta Scott King, quoted in Dorothy Bernstein, "Report—May 7 et seq., Test Ban Lobby," 1, CCHP, Box 64, Folder 8.

95. Swerdlow, *Women Strike for Peace*, 93.

96. Ibid., 94–95.

97. Ibid., 205; Dorothy Bernstein, Harriet Shapiro, and Committee on Reports, "Report: The Hague Conference," 2, CCHP, Box 64, Folder 8.

98. Dora Wilson, interview by author, September 7, 2011.

99. Ibid.

100. Ibid.

101. Swerdlow, *Women Strike for Peace*, 211. While WSP still had a long way to go with respect to diversifying their membership and delegations, this trip seems to represent an attempt initiated by WSP to include both Black (Lorraine Thomas from Detroit, Lavinia Franklin from Washington, D.C., and Blanche Calloway Jones) and working-class women as they also sought out, for example, trade union representative, Sonia P. Kaross.

102. Virginia Naeve to Clarie Collins Harvey, June 3, 1964, CCHP, Box 1, Folder 20.

103. Swerdlow, *Women Strike for Peace*, 206.

104. Ibid., 210.

105. Bernstein et al., "Report," 4; Swerdlow, *Women Strike for Peace*, 212.

106. Bernstein et al., "Report," 6.

107. Ibid., 7.

108. Swerdlow, *Women Strike for Peace*, 214.

109. Dora Wilson went on to study at the Oberlin Conservatory of Music and later obtained a master's degree in music history from Washington University and a PhD in musicology from the University of Southern California. After teaching at California State Long Beach for many years, Dr. Wilson accepted a job at Ohio University in 1984 where she eventually became professor of music.

110. *Woo*, Vol. III, No. 8, August 1964, 1, CCHP, Box 63, Folder 17.

111. Womanpower, *Womanpower and the Jackson Movement*, 17; "Womanpower Unlimited minutes," March 14, 1963, 2, CCHP, Box 63, Folder 3.

112. Diane Nash, telephone interview by author, June 14, 2012.

113. "700 Attend Mass Meeting of Mothers," *Mississippi Free Press* 1, no. 24 (May 26, 1962): 4; Aurelia Young, Personal Journal, May 26, 1962, ANYP, Box 1; "Mrs. Bevel Speaks in Jackson," United States National Student Association, Civil Rights Bulletin, May 24, 1962, 1, James Lane Papers, George Mason University, Box 58, Folder 11.

114. Ibid.

115. Nash, "They Are the Ones Who Got Scared," 79–82. Many of her peers thought that Nash should not spend time in jail because she was pregnant. Nash explained that she was willing to uphold the jail, no bail strategy because any Black child born in Mississippi would be imprisoned, whether physically behind bars or not.

116. *Woo*, October 1963, 2, CCHP, Box 63, Folder 17.

117. *Womanpower Unlimited Newsletter*, Vol. III, No. 1, January 1964, 2, CCHP, Box 63, Folder 17.

118. *Woo*, Vol. III, No. 2, February 1964, 1, CCHP, Box 63, Folder 17.

119. Ibid., 1–2; *Woo*, Vol. IV, January–February 1965, 1, CCHP, Box 63, Folder 17.

120. *Womanpower Unlimited Newsletter*, Vol. IV, January–February 1965, 1, CCHP, Box 63, Folder 17.

121. *Woo*, Vol. III, No. 8, August 1964, 1, CCHP, Box 63, Folder 17.

Chapter 5. "Welcome, Ladies, to Magnolialand"

1. "Wider Prayer Fellowship List," 1965, CCHP.

2. The Council and NCNW will be used interchangeably to refer to the National Council of Negro Women.

3. Smith, "Closed Doors," 13.

4. Height, *Open Wide the Freedom Gates*, 180. Height's autobiography provides an important account of WIMS from the national perspective. See also Harwell, "Wednesdays in Mississippi."

5. Dorothy Height, interview by Holly Cowan Shulman, January 24, 2003, transcript in author's possession.

6. Height, *Open Wide the Freedom Gates*, 84.

7. Ibid., 157.

8. The National Women's Council for Civil Rights was established by President John F. Kennedy in 1963. Established in 1945, the Citizens' Committee for Children of New York is a locally based child advocacy organization focusing on issues such as health, housing, and education.

9. Ferebee was a pioneer in making health care accessible to Blacks. In the 1920s she established a clinic in Washington, D.C., to provide care for impoverished Blacks who lacked access to the city's segregated charitable clinic. She directed the Alpha Kappa Alpha's Mississippi Health Project during 1935–1942, which provided health care to poor Blacks in the rural South. Cowan began volunteering with NCNW in the early 1960s through the Taconic Foundation. Her own son traveled to Mississippi as a Freedom Summer volunteer. Holly Cowan Shulman, "Polly Spiegel Cowan: Civil Rights Activist, 1913–1976," Jewish Women's Archive http://jwa.org/weremember /cowan, September 1, 2011; Height, *Open Wide the Freedom Gates*, 157.

10. Height, *Open Wide the Freedom Gates*, 159–60.

11. Ibid., 160; Polly Cowan, *Preliminary Report — Women in Mississippi — WIMS* (Washington, D.C.: Educational Foundation of the National Council of Negro Women, 1964), 2, NCNWP WIMS, Series 19, Folder 281.

12. "WIMS Materials," Wednesdays in Mississippi: Civil Rights as Women's Work Breaking Down Human Barriers and Mobilizing Women, An Exhibit, website accessed September 1, 2011, http://www.history.uh.edu/cph/WIMS/.

13. Height, *Open Wide the Freedom Gates*, 162–63; "Inter-Organization Women's Committee Memo," March 15–16, 1964, MRP, Series 3, Box 2.

14. "Inter-Organization Women's Committee," March 14, 1964, NCNWP WIMS, Series 19, Folder 190.

15. Dorothy Height, interview by author, June 9, 2003.

16. Dorothy I. Height to Mrs. Martin Harvey, November 24, 1959, CCHP, Box, 1 Folder 15; "National Council of Negro Women Press Release," March 31, 1960, 3, CCHP, Box 62, Folder 19.

17. "Atlanta Consultation, March 15–16, 1964," 1, MRP, Series 3, Box 2.

18. Ibid.

19. "Interview with Dorothy Height," in *The Black Women Oral History Project*, 182.

20. Joiner, "Wednesdays in Mississippi," 32.

21. Alice Hamburg et al., "Proposal for a Women for Peace Delegation to the State of Mississippi," in *Peace Concern*, 1963, 1, CCHP, Box 2, Folder 6.

22. Mrs. C. Collins Harvey to Mrs. Alice Hamburg, August 21, 1963, CCHP, Box 1, Folder 19.

23. Polly Cowan, "Preface," May 28, 1964, NCNWP WIMS, Series 19, Folder 277; Polly Cowan, "YWCA," May 7, 1964, MRP, Series 3, Box 2.

24. Dorothy Height, interview by author, June 9, 2003; "Schedule for Team 3," NCNWP WIMS, Series 19, Folder 304; "Schedule for Team 6," NCNWP WIMS, Series 19, Folder 307.

25. Doris Wilson, interview by author, June 2004.

26. Ibid.

27. Dora Wilson, "Wednesdays in Mississippi" Panel, Sisters in the Struggle: Honoring Women Veterans of the Modern Civil Rights Movement Conference, Sarah Lawrence College, Bronxville, New York, March 8, 2003.

28. Ibid.

29. Dorothy Height, interview by Holly Cowan Shulman, October 16, 2002, transcript in author's possession.

30. Ann Hewitt, interview by Doris Ann Younger, May 15, 1997; Polly Cowan to Ann Hewitt, June 18, 1964, NCNWP WIMS, Series 19, Folder 72.

31. Ann Hewitt, interview by Doris Ann Younger, May 15, 1997.

32. Cowan, *Preliminary Report*, 5.

33. Ibid., 6.

34. "Schedule for Team 3," NCNWP WIMS, Series 19, Folder 304.

35. "Suggestions for WIMS Team Members' Reports," Summer 1964, MRP, Series 3, Box 2.

36. Polly Cowan, "Proposal," May 22, 1964, NCNWP WIMS, Series 19.

37. Cowan, *Preliminary Report*, 1.

38. Justine Randers-Pehrson, "Report of a Team Member: 'Wednesdays in Mississippi,'" July 20, 1964, 1, NCNWP WIMS, Series 19, Folder 304.

39. "Statement by Ruth Batson," April 23, 1965, RBP, Box 4, Folder 1.

40. Ruth Batson, "Wednesdays in Mississippi Report," RBP, Box 1.

41. Ibid.

42. Pearl Willen, "Report," 2, NCNWP WIMS, Series 19, Folder 303.

43. Although the women typically produced thorough reports of their trips and had an extensive debriefing, to protect the anonymity of the southern women names

were often omitted from the reports and transcripts from the 1964 trips making it difficult to uncover the identities of some of the local women.

44. Alice Ryerson, "Report on Trip to Mississippi," 1; Wednesdays in Mississippi, Boston Team Debriefing, Transcript, 7–8, NCNWP WIMS, Series 19, Folder 303.

45. Ryerson, "Report on Trip to Mississippi," 2.

46. Batson, "Wednesdays in Mississippi," 3.

47. Mrs. Edward Ryerson Jr. "Report on Trip to Mississippi," July 14–16, 1964, 6, NCNWP WIMS, Series 19, Folder 303.

48. Ibid., 9; Batson, "Wednesdays in Mississippi Report," 5.

49. "Schedule for Team #2," NCNWP WIMS, Series 19, Folder 303; Geraldine Kohlenberg, "Comments on the July 15th Wednesdays in Mississippi," 6, NCNWP WIMS, Series 19, Folder 303.

50. Batson, "Wednesdays in Mississippi Report."

51. Ibid.

52. Cowan, *Preliminary Report*, 19.

53. Team Debriefing, Washington-Maryland, July 21–22, Team No. 3, 25, NCNWP WIMS, Series 19, Folder 304.

54. Kohlenberg, "Comments on the July 15th," 1–2, NCNWP WIMS, Series 19, Folder 303.

55. Ibid., 6.

56. Ibid.; Geraldine Kohlenberg to Polly Cowan, October 12, 1964," 1, NCNWP WIMS, Series 19, Folder 303.

57. Notes, from Team 2, Boston to Canton, 1964, 4–5, NCNWP WIMS, Series 19, Folder 44.

58. Ibid., 7.

59. Clarie Collins Harvey, interview by Gordon G. Henderson, August 5, 1965.

60. Cowan, *Preliminary Report*, 6.

61. Randers-Pehrson, "Report of a Team Member," 3.

62. Margery Gross and Frances Tenenbaum, *Wednesdays in Mississippi, 1964–1965: Final Report* (Washington, D.C.: Educational Foundation of the National Council of Negro Women, 1965), NCNWP WIMS, Series 19, Folder 276.

63. Batson, "Wednesdays in Mississippi Report," 3.

64. "Schedule for Team #6, August 11–13," Wednesdays in Mississippi: Civil Rights as Women's Work Breaking Down Human Barriers and Mobilizing Women, An Exhibit website, accessed September 1, 2011, http://www.history.uh.edu/cph/WIMS/.

65. Jean Davis, interview by Polly Cowan, June 27, 2003, transcript in author's possession.

66. Miriam J. Ezelle to Mrs. Schutt, n.d., JSP, Series 2, Box 1.

67. Miriam Davis, "Report on Wednesday, August 12, 1964 in Mississippi," NCNWP WIMS, Series 19, Folder 307; Miriam Davis, interview by Holly Cowan Shulman, November 16, 2002, accessed August 24, 2013, http://www.history.uh.edu/cph/WIMS/.

68. Gerry Kohlenberg to Polly Cowan, 1, NCNWP WIMS, Series 19.

69. Sister Catherine John, "Report Questionnaire—Wednesdays in Mississippi," 1–2, NCNWP WIMS, Series 19, Folder 303.

70. Geraldine P. Woods, "Wednesdays in Mississippi Report," July 22, 1964, 3, NCNWP WIMS, Series 19.

71. Giddings, *In Search of Sisterhood*, 257.

72. *Woo*, October 1965, CCHP, Box 63, Folder 17.

73. "Materials Needed by COFO," September 1964, MRP, Series 3, Box 2.

74. Mildred Pitt Goodman interview, by Kojo Nnamdi, April 20, 2001, http://the kojonnamdishow.org/shows/2001–04–20/wednesdays-mississippi.

75. Florynce Kennedy to Mrs. I. S. Sanders, November 12, 1964, 1, NCNWP WIMS, Series 19, Folder 306.

76. Wednesdays in Mississippi: Civil Rights as Women's Work Breaking Down Human Barriers and Mobilizing Women, An Exhibit website, accessed September 1, 2011, http://www.history.uh.edu/cph/WIMS/.

77. Polly Cowan to Peggy Roach, November 25, 1964, MRP, Series 3, Box 2.

78. *WIMS Newsletter*, February 19, 1965, NCNWP WIMS, Series 19, Folder 233.

79. Ibid., 6.

80. Born in New York and raised in Virginia and California, Patt Derian moved to Jackson in 1960 with her physician husband, Paul, and their three children. Two years later she helped organize Mississippians for Public Education.

81. *WIMS Newsletter*, April 1965, MRP, Series 3, Box 2.

82. Polly Cowan to Pearl Draine, NCNWP WIMS, Series 19, Folder 60.

83. Gross and Tenenbaum, *Final Report*, 8.

84. John Perkins, "Jackson 'Head Start' Project Takes Shape," *Clarion Ledger*, May 26, 1965; Robert Ezelle Jr., son of WIMS hostess Miriam Ezelle and president of the Jackson Chamber of Commerce, chaired Head Start's steering committee.

85. See Greenberg, *The Devil Has Slippery Shoes*, for a detailed discussion of the CDGM.

86. WIMS Newsletter, April 1965, 1, NCNWP WIMS, Series 19, Folder 233.

87. Roscoe A. Boyer, "Special Training Institute on Problems of School Desegregation, Summer 1965, Final Report," 2, 10–13, NCNWP WIMS, Series 19, Folder 334.

88. Roscoe Boyer, "Excerpts from Letters from Mississippi Friends," 5, NCNWP WIMS, Series 19, Folder 201.

89. Gross and Tenenbaum, *Final Report*, 18–19.

90. Ellen Tarry, "Team Visit—Mississippi, July 21, 1965," 3, NCNWP WIMS, Series 19, Folder 310; Ann Hewitt, interview by Doris Ann Younger, May 15, 1997.

91. Mildred Pitt, "Three Days in Mississippi," 7, NCNWP WIMS, Series 19, Folder 314.

92. Dorothy Height, interview by Holly Cowan Shulman, October 16, 2002, 20; "Ann Hewitt," Wednesdays in Mississippi: Civil Rights as Women's Work Breaking Down Human Barriers and Mobilizing Women, An Exhibit website, accessed September 1, 2011, http://www.history.uh.edu/cph/WIMS/trip/AnnHewitt_excerpts.html.

93. "Second WIMS Conference Report," November 11–12, 1965, 1, MRP, Series 3, Box 2.

94. *WIMS Newsletter*, December 1966, 4–5, MRP, Series 3, Box 2.

95. "WIMS—Boston Project, Meeting at Ruth Batson's," February 10, 1966, RBP, Box 1.

96. Dorothy Height, interview by Holly Cowan Shulman, October 16, 2003; Height, *Open Wide the Freedom Gates*, 188, 190.

97. *Workshops in Mississippi Newsletter*, June 1968, RBP, Box 1.

98. Height, *Open Wide the Freedom Gates*, 89.

99. Ransby, *Ella Baker and the Black Freedom Movement*.

100. *WIMS Newsletter*, June 1968, NCNWP WIMS, Series 19, Folder 233.

101. Dorothy Height, interview by Holly Cowan Shulman, October 16, 2003; Height, *Open Wide the Freedom Gates*, 190.

102. *WIMS Newsletter*, February, 1966, 1, NCNWP WIMS, Series 19, Folder 233.

103. Edith Savage, telephone interview by author, August 18, 2010.

104. *WIMS Newsletter*, February 1966, 3.

105. Ibid., 2; Aurelia Young to Buddy Mayer, December 14, 1965, NCNWP WIMS, Series 19, Folder 60.

106. "Second WIMS Conference Report," 12, NCNWP WIMS, Series 19, Folder 56.

107. Trude W. Lash, "Memo to Polly Cowan," September 8, 1964, NCNWP WIMS, Series 19, Folder 306.

108. Excerpts from Letters from Mississippi Friends, 4, NCNWP WIMS, Series 19, Folder 201.

109. Florence Gooch to Susan Goodwillie, August 28, 1965, NCNWP WIMS, Series, 19, Folder 201.

110. Gladys Zales, "Journey into Fear: My Jackson Episode," NCNWP WIMS, Series 19, Folder 306.

111. Polly Cowan to Miriam Davis, January 11, 1966, NCNWP WIMS, Series 19, Folder 76.

112. Josie Johnson, telephone interview by author, February 2011.

113. Doris Wilson, "Wednesdays in Mississippi" Panel, Sisters in the Struggle Conference.

114. Josie Johnson, telephone interview by author, February 2011.

115. Marian Wright Edelman, the first black woman admitted to the Mississippi bar, was one of the legal contacts for Wednesdays Women.

Chapter 6. "When There Was a Need"

1. Two dates have been acknowledged as the beginning of The Box Project—1962 when Virginia Naeve sent her first box to a Southern family and 1963 when Naeve says that a formal system was implemented to facilitate multiple helper and recipient families. Therefore, the twenty-fifth anniversary celebration was held in 1988, twenty-five years from 1963, and the fiftieth was in 2012, 50 years from 1962.

2. Donna Goldman, telephone interview by author, November 27, 2012.

3. Naeve, "Mississippi Box Project," 24.

4. Naeve, "What Can We (I) Do," 3.

5. Naeve, "Mississippi Box Project," 24.

6. Serena Naeve (Virginia Naeve's daughter), email to author, November 18, 2012.

7. Virginia Naeve, telephone interview by author, February 20, 2012.

8. Naeve, "What Can We (I) Do," 3.

9. Naeve, "Children . . . and Ourselves," 10.

10. Naeve, "Mississippi Box Project," 24.

11. Ibid.

12. Naeve, "What can We (I) Do," 4.

13. Kevin Graffagnino (Myrtle Lane's son), telephone interview by author, March 5, 2012.

14. Naeve, "Mississippi Box Project," 24.

15. In 1969, of the 2,875 families being assisted by The Box Project, 2,500 were in Mississippi followed by 87 in Louisiana, 76 in North Carolina, and 50 in Alabama and Minnesota. Georgia was next with 25 families. *The Box Project Newsletter*, n.d., CCHP, Box 80, Folder 14.

16. Virginia Naeve, telephone interview by author, February 20, 2012.

17. Rosie Holden to Jackson, Mississippi, October 1968, WUC. Rosie Redmond married in the mid-1960s and became Rosie Holden.

18. Brandon Naeve, telephone interview by author, February 16, 2012.

19. Jane Burditt, "From Vermont to Mississippi: Breaking the Cycle of Poverty," *Southern Vermont*, June/July 1988, 21, Vermont Historical Society, CRVC, 1968–1996, MSA 307, Folder 15.

20. Virginia Naeve, telephone interview by author, February 20, 2012.

21. Naeve, "Mississippi Box Project," 25.

22. Howard and Bradley, "Homecoming," 103; Remsberg and Remsberg, "The Couple Who Cared," 17.

23. *Southern Box Project Newsletter*, November 1967, 3, CCHP, Box 80, Folder 14.

24. Ibid.

25. Ibid.

26. Naeve, "Mississippi Box Project," 24.

27. Quoted in Burditt, "From Vermont to Mississippi," 21.

28. *Southern Box Project Newsletter*, November 1967, 9.

29. Ibid.

30. Virginia Naeve, "Other News," in *Report on the Christmas Appeal and the Southern Package Project*, February 3, 1966, 2, CCHP, Box 2, Folder 14.

31. The Box Project, "For 25 Years" (Plainville, Conn.: The Box Project, 1987), 7, in author's possession.

32. Remsberg and Remsberg, "The Couple Who Cared," 24.

33. Naeve, "Report on the Christmas Appeal," 9.

34. *Southern Box Project Newsletter*, November 1967, 4.

35. Virginia Naeve, "Civil Rights S.O.S," n.d., CCHP, Box 80, Folder 14.

36. *Peace Concern*, Vol. 3, No. 8, August 1964, CCHP, Box 56, Folder 4.

37. Naeve, "Mississippi Box Project," 25.

38. Lane and Naeve also provided postage and labels for Liberty House to send its catalogs to donor families. *Southern Box Project Newsletter*, November 1967, 2.

39. "Help from a Prison," in *Southern Box Project Newsletter*, November 1967, 6.

40. MFDP to Box Project, January 4, 1966, quoted in "Report on Christmas Appeal," 10.

41. Pat Vail to Box Project, December 19, 1965, quoted in "Report on Christmas Appeal," 10.

42. Naeve, "What Can We (I) Do," 4.

43. The Box Project, "For 25 Years," 3.

44. *Southern Box Project Newsletter*, September 1968; *Box Project Newsletter*, April 1978, 1, CCHP, Box 80, Folder 14.

45. The Box Project, "For 25 Years," 3.

46. Virginia Naeve, "Mississippi: Impressions 22 years Later," 15, CCHP.

47. Jerry Howard and Margarite Bradley, "Homecoming," *New Age Journal*, 44, September/October 1988 CCHP, Box 80, Folder 14.

48. Donna Goldman, telephone interview by author, November 27, 2012.

49. *The Box Project Newsletter*, April 1978.

50. Virginia Naeve to Clarie Collins Harvey, August 17, 1964, 1, CCHP, Box 56, Folder 4.

51. Virginia Naeve to Clarie Collins Harvey, May 17, 1988, CCHP.

52. For a more detailed discussion of Project-C, see Morris, *Origins of the Civil Rights Movement;* and Eskew, *But for Birmingham.*

53. Lawton, "After the March Is Over," 158.

54. "Stein Reviews the Civil Rights Struggle," *Alabama Council Newsletter*, October 1971, RASP, Box 2, Folder 21.

55. Davis, "Remembering Carole, Cynthia, Addie Mae and Denise"; Harris, *Miracle in Birmingham,* 183.

56. Lawton, "After the March," 158.

57. Robert Stein, Theodore James Pinnock, and Walter Lawton, "A Proposal to Continue Enrichment Educational Programs for Youth and Adults in Selected Areas of Alabama and Mississippi, 1968," 2, RASP, Box 2, Folder 8.

58. Ibid., 3.

59. Ibid.

60. Clarie Collins Harvey to Sol Press, May 23, 1965, CCHP, Box 2, Folder 11.

61. Stein et al., "A Proposal," 6.

62. Womanpower, *Womanpower and the Jackson Movement,* 21.

63. (Mrs. Robert) Anita Stein to Mrs. Harvey, Oct. 24, 1964, CCHP. In April 25, 1963, after spending three days in Birmingham with Walter Lawton of the American Ethical Union, Robert Stein traveled to Jackson, Mississippi, with William Kunstler. Stein undertook this trip to obtain firsthand knowledge of the racial situation in the South for a civil rights workshop he was scheduled to conduct at the Encampment for Citizenship. Kunstler was in town to assist local attorney R. Jess Brown with the legal affairs surrounding the Jackson Nonviolent Movement's boycott of downtown Jackson businesses. Stein stayed with the Beittels on the campus of Tougaloo College during this trip. Robert Stein interview with Helen Stein, 1963, RASP, Box, 1, Folder 2; John Salter, email to author, October 31, 2012; Salter, *Jackson, Mississippi,* 96.

64. Clarie Collins Harvey and Pearl Draine to Mr. and Mrs. Stein, March 17, 1965, CCHP, Box 2, Folder 9; Robert M. Stein to Mrs. C. Collins Harvey, March 18, 1965, CCHP, Box 2, Folder 9.

65. Womanpower Unlimited, "Woman Power Unlimited Little Theater Speaks," 2–3, CCHP, Box 63, Folder 15.

66. Clarie Collins Harvey to Reverend, March 1968, CCHP.

67. "Camp Madison-Felicia: A Guide for Agencies," 1, RASP, Box 2, Folder 15.

68. Ibid., 2.

69. Ibid., 1.

70. Amy Tubbs, email to author, November 26, 2012.

71. Anthony Rose, correspondence with author, November 2012; Chris Butcher, correspondence with author, November 2012.

72. Steven Powell, telephone interview by author, November 7, 2012.

73. Doristine Parker Carey, interview by author, August 1, 2001.

74. Dwight Henry, interview by author, July 20, 2011.

75. Ibid.

76. Lawton, "After the March," 158.

77. Linda Marie Redmond Taylor, telephone interview by author, February 2012.

78. Loretta McGowan, interview by author, July 20, 2011; Ted Roberts, "My Summer Experience," *WU Newsletter*, October 1, 1965, Fall, 1, CCHP, Box, 63, Folder 17.

79. Doristine Parker Carey, interview by author, August 1, 2001; Clarie Collins Harvey, interview by John Jones and John Dittmer, April 21, 1981.

80. Counselors at Madison-Felicia, "Quotes from Evaluations and Questionnaires on camps attended by Southern Children Summer 1968," 1, RASP, Box 2, Folder 8.

81. Ibid.

82. Madison-Felicia Families, "Quotes from Evaluations and Questionnaires on Camps Attended by Southern Children Summer 1968," 1, RASP, Box 2, Folder 8.

83. Byron D'Andra Orey, telephone interview by author, October 16, 2012.

84. Steven Powell, telephone interview by author, November 7, 2012.

85. Amy Tubbs, email to author, November 27, 2012.

86. Linda Marie Redmond Taylor, telephone interview by author, February 2012; Byron D'Andra Orey, telephone interview by author, October 16, 2012.

87. Untitled Vicksburg newspaper, "Local Women Send Youngsters to Eastern Camp Site," Vol. 39, No 13, WUC, Series III: Subject Files, Box 1, Folder 6.

88. Womanpower, *Womanpower and the Jackson Movement*, 6. For a discussion of the Black Panther Party's survival programs, see Jones and Jeffries, "'Don't Believe the Hype': Debunking the Panther Mythology"; and Abron, "'Serving the People': The Survival Programs of the Black Panther Party."

Conclusion. Women's Power Transformed

1. Womanpower Unlimited, "Minutes of Special Task Force: Womanpower for Freedom," September 27, 1976, 2, CCHP, Box 63, Folder 4.

2. Fred L. Banks to Mrs. Martha Edens, September 24, 1976, CCHP, Box 63, Folder 2. For more on the NAACP boycott in Port Gibson, see Crosby, *A Little Taste of Freedom*.

3. Although an exact date is unclear, interviews with members and organizational documents have led me to conclude that the organization disbanded sometime during 1968.

4. Reverend John R. Washington, interview by author, November 9, 2001.

5. *Womanpower Unlimited Newsletter*, January 1966, CCHP, Box 63, Folder 17.

6. Clarie Collins Harvey, interview by Deborah Denard, July 2, 1976.

7. White, *Too Heavy a Load*, 195.

8. Lawrence Guyot, interview by author, March 30, 2002.

9. Clarie Collins Harvey, interview by Deborah Denard, July 2, 1976.

10. Jackson Section of National Council of Negro Women, Inc., undated flyer, CCHP.

11. Ibid.

12. Clarie Collins Harvey, interview by Deborah Denard, July 2, 1976.

13. Susie Noel and Rosie Holden, interview by Deborah Denard, June 29, 1976.

14. Clarie Collins Harvey, interview by Deborah Denard, July 2, 1976.

15. Jessie Mosley, interview by author, June 1, 2001.

16. White and Bishop, *Mississippi's Black Women*, 29.

17. Emma Moore, telephone interview by author, December 4, 2012. Moore was the Mississippi state convener for the NCNW at the time of the interview.

18. NCNW Jackson Section, Awards Information, in author's possession.

19. A. M. E. Logan, interview by Deborah Denard, July 16, 1986.

20. Loretta McGowan, interview by author, July 2011.

21. Shirley Montague, interview by author, July 21, 2012.

22. *Woo*, January 1964, CCHP, Box 63, Folder 17.

23. Some accounts say that the incident happened in an airport restaurant, while others give the site of the incident as an airport waiting room. Womanpower, *Womanpower and the Jackson Movement*, 10; *Womanpower Unlimited Newsletter*, Vol. 2, No. 1, December 1962, 2.

24. Statement given to FBI, November 24, 1965, CCHP.

25. Clarie Collins Harvey to Mr. A. W. Wood, President Sears Roebuck Company, May 17, 1968, CCHP, Box 2, Folder 8.

26. Shaw, *What a Woman Ought to Do and to Be*, 42.

27. Clarie Collins Harvey, "So Much More," August, 1, 1974, 6, CCHP, Box 67, Folder 5.

28. Clarie Collins Harvey, interview by Vicki Crawford, July 13, 1986.

29. Aura Gary, interview by author, May 30, 2001.

Epilogue. "This Woman's Work"

1. Shirley Montague, interview by author, July 21, 2012.

2. Ibid.

3. Fred L. Banks, quoted in "NAACP Mourns the Loss of A. M. E. Logan," February 10, 2011, http://www.naacp.org/press/entry/naacp-mourns-the-loss-of-a.m.e.-logan.

4. Stephanie Parker-Weaver, telephone interview by author, September 23, 2012.

5. Parker-Weaver, "Reflections on the Life of Mrs. A. M. E. Logan."

6. Shirley Logan Montague, interview by author, July 21, 2012.

7. Senators Horhn, Jones, Simmons, Jordan, Senate Concurrent Resolution 597 (As Adopted by Senate): A Concurrent Resolution Mourning the Passing and Commend-

ing the Life of Mrs. A. M. E. Logan, the "Mother of the Civil Rights Movement." Mississippi Legislature 2011 Regular Session, http://legiscan.com/gaits/text/156849.

8. Shirley Montague, interview by author, July 21, 2012.

9. Womanpower, *Womanpower Unlimited and the Jackson Movement*, 6.

10. Nancy Weaver, "After Houston, IWY Work Continues," *Clarion Ledger*, March 10, 1978, 1C, MDAH, Jessie Mosley Subject File.

11. Spruill, "The Mississippi Takeover," 287.

12. Ibid., 292–93, 302–5. In the spirit of Fannie Lou Hamer and the MFDP, who challenged the seating of the state's all-white delegation at the 1964 Democratic National Convention in Atlantic City, Mississippi feminists challenged the IWY delegation. Although they were unsuccessful in unseating the delegation, they were, along with other states that failed to meet the National IWY's diversity requirement, granted representation through an at-large delegation.

13. Norman, *Mississippi in Transition*, 260. Mosley was appointed by Governor William Winter to serve on the Mississippi Humanities Council (MHC) during 1981–1984. According to their website, "The MHC is a private nonprofit corporation funded by Congress through the National Endowment for the Humanities to provide public programs in traditional liberal arts disciplines to serve nonprofit groups in Mississippi. MHC sponsors, supports, and conducts a wide range of programs designed to promote understanding of our cultural heritage, interpret our own experience, foster critical thinking, encourage reasonable public discourse, strengthen our sense of community, and thus empower Mississippi's people with a vision for the future." http://www.mshumanities.org/index.php/about, accessed August 24, 2012.

14. Sherry Lucas, "Jessie Mosley," *Clarion-Ledger,* June 30, 1991, 2E, MDAH, Jessie Mosley Subject File.

15. Clarie Collins Harvey to Mrs. Nell Lockhart, March 7, 1979, CCHP, Box 7, Folder 2.

16. Lucas, "Jessie Mosley," E1.

17. Thelma Sanders, Biographical Sketch, 3, in author's possession; Blalock and Bishop, *Mississippi's Black Women*, 62.

18. The FCC turned the license over to a nonprofit, biracial group known as Communications Improvement, Inc. The FCC granted a permanent license to operate to TV-3 Inc. in 1980. TV-3 was a group formed by five competing companies who were seeking the right to operate the station. For a detailed discussion, see Classen, *Watching Jim Crow.*

19. Women for Progress was founded in 1978 as a nonprofit, nonpartisan community improvement organization of action-oriented, influential, and talented individuals, under the leadership of Womanpower member Dorothy Stewart. http://www.womenforprogress.net/home.html, accessed August 24, 2012.

20. Collier-Thomas, *Jesus, Jobs, and Justice,* 469.

21. Jane Schutt, "Nominating speech," CCHP, Box 79, Folder 19.

22. Thelma Adair, telephone interview by author, September 20, 2012.

23. Harvey, "A Life Transformed," 183.

24. Morris, "Clarie Collins Harvey."

25. Clarie Collins Harvey to Dr. Clay Lee, February 23, 1981, CCHP.

26. Connie Shanks-Knight, interview by author, July 25, 2012; Thelma Adair, "Celebrating the Life and Transition of Emma Augusta Clarie Collins Harvey," June 1, 1995, in author's possession.

27. Adair, "Celebrating the Life and Transition," 2.

28. Euvester Simpson, telephone interview by author, December 1, 2012.

BIBLIOGRAPHY

Manuscript Sources

Amistad Research Center, Tulane University, New Orleans, Louisiana

Clarie Collins Harvey Papers (CCHP)
Collins Family Papers
Tom Dent Papers

Atlanta University Center, Atlanta, Georgia

Southern Regional Council Archives (SRCA)

General Commission on Archives and History, United Methodist Church

Church Women United Records (CWUR)

Margaret Walker Alexander National Research Center (MWANRC), Jackson State University, Jackson, Mississippi

Oral History Collections

Womanpower Unlimited Collection (WUC)

Millsaps College, Jackson, Mississippi

Oral History of Mississippi: Contemporary Life and Viewpoint

Mississippi Department of Archives and History, Jackson, Mississippi (MDAH)

Jackson Advocate Microfilm
Oral Histories Collection
Jane Schutt Papers (JSP)

SOVEREIGNTY COMMISSION PAPERS ONLINE
Subject Files, mdah.state.ms.us/arrec/digital_archives/sovcom/
Aurelia Norris Young Papers (ANYP)

National Archives for Black Women's History, Washington, D.C.

National Council of Negro Women Papers, Wednesdays in Mississippi Collection
(NCNWP WIMS)

Radcliffe Institute, Schlesinger Library, Harvard University, Cambridge, Massachusetts

Ruth Batson Papers (RBP)

Schomburg Center for Research in Black Culture, New York, New York

Robert and Anita Stein Papers (RASP)

Swarthmore College Peace Collection, Philadelphia, Pennsylvania

Women Strike for Peace Records (WSPR)

Vermont Historical Society, Barre, Vermont

Civil Rights Movement in Vermont Collection (CRMVC)

Women and Leadership Archives, Loyola University Chicago, Chicago, Illinois

Margaret "Peggy" Roach Papers (MRP)

Interviews Conducted by Author

Adair, Thelma. Telephone interview. September 20, 2012.
Allen, Vera Polk Bailey. Telephone interview. October 26, 2011.
Brown, W. R. (Bo). Telephone interview. November 17, 2012.
Clark, Fred Douglass Moore, Sr. Jackson, Mississippi, November 10, 2001.
Curtis, Verna Polk. Telephone interview. November 18, 2011.
Dean, Kenneth. Telephone interview. September 11, 2012.
Draine, Scott. Telephone interview. September 23, 2012.
Figgers, Frank. Telephone interview. August 2013.
Graffagnino, Kevin. Telephone interview. March 5, 2012.
Gaither, Thomas. Jackson, Mississippi, November 2011.
Gary, Aura. Jackson, Mississippi, May 30, 2001.
Goldman, Donna. Telephone interview. November 27, 2012.
Guidry, Carolyn Tyler. Telephone interview. October 18, 2012.
Guyot, Lawrence. Washington, D.C., March 30, 2002.

Height, Dorothy. Washington, D.C., June 9, 2003.

Henderson, Taletha. Telephone interview. November 1, 2012.

Henry, Dwight. Jackson, Mississippi, July 20, 2011.

Henry, Maddye Lyne. Jackson, Mississippi, July 20, 2011.

Horhn, John. Jackson, Mississippi, July 27, 2012.

Horowitz, Charles. Telephone interview. November 6, 2001.

Howe, Florence. Telephone interview. January 12, 2012.

Jackson-Wright, Alice. Telephone interview. December 29, 2011.

Johnson, Josie. Telephone interview. February 2011.

Lafayette, Bernard. Telephone interview. January 5, 2001.

Logan, A. M. E. Jackson, Mississippi, September 2000; November 8, 2001.

Logan, Willis. Telephone interview. November 14, 2012.

May-Pittman, Ineva. Telephone interview. November 27, 2012; May 13, 2013.

McGowan, Loretta Henry. Jackson, Mississippi, July 20, 2011.

Montague, Shirley Logan. Jackson, Mississippi, July 21, 2012.

Moore, Emma. Telephone interview. December 4, 2012.

Morris, Jesse. Jackson, Mississippi, July 24, 2012.

Morris, Jesse. Telephone interview. October, 2012; June 19, 2013.

Mosley, Jessie. Jackson, Mississippi, June 1, 2001.

Mulholland, Joan Trumpauer. Jackson, Mississippi, November 10, 2001.

Nash, Diane. Telephone interview. June 14, 2012.

Naeve, Brandon. Telephone interview. February 16, 2012.

Naeve, Virginia. Telephone interview. February 20, 2012.

Nixon, Sandra. Jackson, Mississippi, November 10, 2001.

Orey, Byron D'Adra. Telephone interview. October 16, 2012.

Parker-Weaver, Stephanie. Telephone interview. September 22, 2012.

Powell, Steven. Telephone interview. November 7, 2012.

Rollins, Annette Collins. Jackson, Mississippi, July 27, 2012.

Savage, Edith. Telephone interview. August 18, 2010.

Shanks-Knight, Connie. Jackson, Mississippi, July 26, 2012.

Simpson, Euvester. Telephone interview. December 1, 2012.

Sparks, Selma. Telephone interview. December 15, 2011.

Stewart, Dorothy. Telephone interview. September 10, 2011.

Taylor, Linda Marie Redmond. Telephone interview. March 5, 2012.

Washington, John. Jackson, Mississippi, November 9, 2001.

Whitney, Hazel. Telephone interview. September 22, 2012.

Wilson, Dora. Athens, Ohio, September 7, 2011.

Wilson, Doris. Pittsburgh, Pittsburgh, June 29, 2004.

Interviews Conducted by Others

Clopton, Wilma Mosley. Interview by Marlene McCurtis. Transcript in author's possession.

Davis, Jean. interview by Holly Shulman. June 27, 2002. Location unidentified. Transcript in author's possession.

Goodman, Mildred Pitt. Interview with Kojo Nnamdi. *The Politics Hour*, WAMU, April 20, 2001.

Harvey, Clarie Collins. Interview by Robert Penn Warren. February 9, 1964, Robert Penn Warren's "Who Speaks for the Negro": An Archival Collection, http://who speaks.library.vanderbilt.edu/interview/clarie-collins-harvey.

Harvey, Clarie Collins. Interview by Gordon G. Henderson. August 5, 1965. Millsaps College, Oral History of Mississippi: Contemporary Life and Viewpoint.

Harvey, Clarie Collins. Interview by Ruth Weber. N.d. Church Women United Records.

Harvey, Clarie Collins. Interview by Peggye Thomas, Jackson, Mississippi, June 5, 1975. Margaret Walker Alexander National Research Center, Oral History Collection.

Harvey, Clarie Collins. Interview by Deborah Denard, Jackson, Mississippi, July 2, 1976. Margaret Walker Alexander National Research Center, Oral History Collection.

Harvey, Clarie Collins. Interview by John Jones and John Dittmer, April 21, 1981. Jackson, Mississippi, Mississippi Department of Archives and History.

Harvey, Clarie Collins. Interview by Vicki Crawford. Jackson, Mississippi, July 13, 1986. Personal collection of Vicki Crawford.

Height, Dorothy. Interview by Holly Cowan Shulman. Washington, D.C., October 16, 2002. Transcript in author's possession.

Hewitt, Ann. Interview by Doris Ann Younger, New York City, May 15, 1997. Church Women United Records.

Holden, Rosie. Interview by Lawrence Goodwyn, Jackson, Mississippi, June 1975. Margaret Walker Alexander National Research Center, Oral History Collection.

Logan, A. M. E. Interview by Vicki Crawford, Jackson, Mississippi, July 16, 1986. Personal collection of Vicki Crawford.

May-Pittman, Ineva. Interview by Steven D. Classen. Jackson, Mississippi, August 25, 1993. Transcript in author's possession.

Morris, Jesse. Interview by Tom Dent. Jackson, Mississippi, July 20, 1979. Tom Dent Papers, Amistad Research Center, Tulane University.

Mosley, Jessie B. Interview by Alferdteen Harrison. Jackson, Mississippi, February 10, 1994. Margaret Walker Alexander National Research Center, Oral History Collection.

Noel, Susie, and Rosie Holden. Interview by Deborah Denard. Jackson, Mississippi, June 1976. Margaret Walker Alexander National Research Center, Oral History Collection.

Sanders, I. S. Interview by Johnny Luckett. Jackson, Mississippi, May 5, 1974. Margaret Walker Alexander National Research Center, Oral History Collection.

Sanders, Thelma. Interview by Mildred M. Williams. Jackson, Mississippi, June 5, 1975. Margaret Walker Alexander National Research Center, Oral History Collection.

Schutt, Jane. Interview by Gordon Henderson. Jackson, Mississippi, July 16, 1965. Millsaps College, Oral History of Mississippi: Contemporary Life and Viewpoint.

Schutt, Jane. Interview by Deborah Denard. Jackson, Mississippi, July 3, 1976. Margaret Walker Alexander National Research Center, Oral History Collection.

Schutt, Jane. Interview by John Jones and John Dittmer. Jackson, Mississippi, February 2, 1981. Mississippi Department of Archives and History.

Schutt, Jane. Interview by Leesha Faulkner. Florence, Mississippi, October 3, 1994, October 10, 1994, Mississippi Oral History Program of the University of Southern Mississippi, http://digilib.usm.edu/cdm/ref/collection/coh/id/6235.

Newspapers and Other Serials

Clarion-Ledger
Ebony
Jackson Advocate
Mississippi Free Press

Articles and Books

Abron, JoNina M. "'Serving the People': The Survival Programs of the Black Panther Party." In *The Black Panther Party Reconsidered*, edited by Charles E. Jones, 177–92. Baltimore: Black Classic Press, 1998.

Allen, James. *Without Sanctuary: Lynching Photography in America*. Santa Fe: Twin Palm, 2000.

Aptheker, Bettina. "Directions for Scholarship." In *African American Women and the Vote, 1837–1965*, edited by Ann D. Gordon, 200–210. Amherst: University of Massachusetts Press, 1997.

Armah, Kwesi. *Peace without Power: Ghana's Foreign Policy, 1957–1966*. Accra: Ghana Universities Press, 2004.

Arsenault, Raymond. *Freedom Riders: 1961 and the Struggle for Racial Justice*. New York: Oxford University Press, 2006.

Barnett, Bernice McNair. "Invisible Southern Black Women Leaders in the Civil Rights Movement: The Triple Constraints of Gender, Race, and Class." *Gender & Society* 7, no. 2 (June 1993): 162–82.

Blalock, White Geneva Brown, and Eva Hunter Bishop, eds. *Mississippi's Black Women: A Pictorial Story of Their Contributions to the State and Nation*. Jackson: Mississippi Bicentennial Commission, 1976.

Blumberg, Rhoda Lois. *Civil Rights: The 1960s Freedom Struggle*. Boston: Twayne, 1984.

Boaten, F. E., ed. *Conclusions of the Accra Assembly: The Accra Assembly The World without the Bomb, 21st–28th June, 1962*. Ghana: Secretariat of the Accra Assembly, 1962.

Boggs, Grace Lee. *Living for Change: An Autobiography*. Minneapolis: University of Minnesota Press, 1998.

Bolton, Charles. *The Hardest Deal of All: The Battle over School Desegregation in Mississippi, 1870–1980*. Jackson: University Press of Mississippi, 2005.

Boyd, Malcolm. "The Battle of McComb." *Christian Century* 83 (1964): 1398.

Brown, Elsa Barkley. "To Catch the Vision of Freedom: Reconstructing Southern Black Women's Political History, 1865–1880." In *African American Women and the Vote, 1837–1965,* edited by Ann D. Gordon. Amherst: University of Massachusetts Press, 1997.

Burditt, Jane. "From Vermont to Mississippi: Breaking the Cycle of Poverty." *Southern Vermont* (June/July 1988): 19–21, 53–56.

Burks, Mary Fair. "Trailblazers: Women in the Montgomery Bus Boycott." In *Women in the Civil Rights Movement: Trailblazers & Torchbearers, 1941–1965,* edited by Vicki Crawford, Jacqueline Ann Rouse, and Barbara Woods, 71–83. Bloomington: Indiana University Press, 1990.

Burns, Stewart. *Daybreak of Freedom: The Montgomery Bus Boycott.* Chapel Hill: University of North Carolina Press, 1997.

Cannon, Katie G. "The Emergence of Black Feminist Consciousness." In *Feminist Interpretations of the Bible,* edited by Letty M. Russell, 30–40. Philadelphia: Westminster Press, 1985.

Carson, Clayborne. *In Struggle: SNCC and the Black Awakening of the 1960s,* 3rd ed. Cambridge, Mass.: Harvard University Press, 2000.

Chamberlain, Daphne R. "A. M. E. Logan." In *Mississippi Encyclopedia.* Jackson: University Press of Mississippi, forthcoming.

Classen, Steven D. *Watching Jim Crow: The Struggles over Mississippi TV, 1955–1969.* Durham, N.C.: Duke University Press, 2004.

Collier-Thomas, Bettye. *Jesus, Jobs, and Justice: African American Women and Religion.* New York: Alfred A. Knopf, 2010.

Collins, Patricia Hill. *Black Feminist Thought: Knowledge, Consciousness and the Politics of Empowerment.* New York: Routledge, 1991.

Cooper, Anna Julia. *A Voice from the South.* 1892; reprint, New York: Oxford University Press, 1987.

Crawford, Vicki. "Beyond the Human Self: Grassroots Activists in the Mississippi Civil Rights Movement." In *Women in the Civil Rights Movement: Trailblazers and Torchbearers, 1941–1965,* edited by Vicki Crawford, Jacqueline Ann Rouse, and Barbara Woods, 13–26. Bloomington: Indiana University Press, 1990.

Crosby, Emilye. *A Little Taste of Freedom: The Black Freedom Struggle in Claiborne County Mississippi.* Chapel Hill: University of North Carolina Press, 2005.

Davis, Angela Y. "Remembering Carole, Cynthia, Addie Mae and Denise." *Essence* 24, no. 5 (September 1993): 92–93, 126.

Dittmer, John. "The Politics of the Mississippi Movement, 1954–1964." In *The Civil Rights Movement in America,* edited by Charles Eagles, 65–96. Jackson: University of Mississippi Press, 1986.

———. *Local People: The Struggle for Civil Rights in Mississippi.* Champaign: University of Illinois Press, 1994.

———. *The Good Doctors: The Medical Committee for Human Rights and the Struggle for Social Justice in Health Care.* New York: Bloomsbury, 2009.

Eaton, Anne. "Women in Geneva." *Bulletin of the Atomic Scientists* (September 1962): 47–48.

Eskew, Glenn T. *But for Birmingham: The Local and National Movements in the Civil Rights Struggle*. Chapel Hill: University of North Carolina Press, 1997.

Estepa, Andrea. "Taking the White Gloves Off: Women Strike for Peace and 'the Movement,' 1967–73." In *Feminist Coalitions: Historical Perspectives on Second Wave Feminism in the United States*, edited by Stephanie Gilmore, 84–112. Urbana: University of Illinois Press, 2008.

Evers, Medgar (as told to Francis H. Mitchell). "Why I Live in Mississippi." In *The Autobiography of Medgar Evers: A Hero's Life and Legacy Revealed Through His Writings, Letters, and Speeches*, edited by Myrlie Evers-Williams and Manning Marable. Originally published in *Ebony*, November 1958.

Evers-Williams, Myrlie, and Manning Marable, eds. *The Autobiography of Medgar Evers: A Hero's Life and Legacy Revealed Through His Writings, Letters, and Speeches*. New York: Basic Civitas Books, 2008.

Farmer, James. *The Making of Black Revolutionaries*. Seattle: University of Washington Press, 1972.

Feldstein, Ruth "'I Wanted the Whole World to See': Race, Gender, and Constructions of Motherhood in the Death of Emmett Till." In *Not June Cleaver: Women and Gender in Postwar America, 1945–1960*, edited by Joanne Meyerowitz, 263–303. Philadelphia: Temple University Press, 1994.

Gates, Jimmie. "JSU to Salute Museum Founder on 90th Birthday." *Clarion Ledger*, November 26, 1993, n.p.

Garrow, David J., ed. *The Montgomery Bus Boycott and the Women Who Started It: The Memoir of Jo Ann Gibson Robinson*. Knoxville: University of Tennessee Press, 1997.

General Board of Social Concerns of the Methodist Church. "The Social Creed of the Methodist Church." *Contact* 2, no. 1 (June 1, 1960): 3–6.

Giddings, Paula. *When and Where I Enter: The Impact of Black Women in Race and Sex in America*. New York: William Morrow, 1984.

Gilkes, Cheryl Townsend. "Building in Many Places: Multiple Commitments and Ideologies in Black Women's Community Work." In *Women and the Politics of Empowerment*, edited by Ann Bookman and Sandra Morgen, 53–76. Philadelphia: Temple University Press, 1988.

Grant, Joanne. *Ella Baker: Freedom Bound*. New York: John Wiley & Sons, 1999.

Greenberg, Polly. *The Devil Has Slippery Shoes: A Biased Biography of the Child Development Group of Mississippi (CDGM)—a Story of Maximum Feasible Poor Parent Participation*. Reprint ed. Washington, D.C.: Youth Policy Institute, 1990.

Greene, Christina. *Our Separate Ways: Women and the Black Freedom Movement in Durham, North Carolina*. Chapel Hill: University of North Carolina Press, 2005.

Grooms, Mary. "'Give Us a Missile Base.'" *The Nation*, May 5, 1962, 395–97.

Hamlin, Françoise N. *Crossroads at Clarksdale: The Black Freedom Struggle in the Mississippi Delta after World War II*. Chapel Hill: University of North Carolina Press, 2012.

Harris, Duchess. "From the Kennedy Commission to the Combahee Collective: Black Feminist Organizing, 1960–80." In *Sisters in the Struggle: African-American Women in the Civil Rights–Black Power Struggle*, edited by Bettye Collier-Thomas and V. P. Franklin, 280–305. New York: New York University Press, 2001.

Harris, W. Edward. *Miracle in Birmingham: A Civil Rights Memoir, 1954–1965*. Indiana: Stonework Press, 2004.

Harvey, Clarie Collins. "Womanpower Continues to Benefit Community." *Mississippi Free Press*, November 16, 1963.

————. "A Life Transformed—Past & Future." *Journal of Ecumenical Studies* 16, no. 1 (Winter 1979): 182–83.

Harwell, Debbie Z. "Wednesdays in Mississippi: Uniting Women across Regional and Racial Lines, Summer 1964." *Journal of Southern History* 76, no. 3: 617–54.

Higginbotham, Evelyn Brooks. "Clubwomen and Electoral Politics in the 1920s." In *African American Women and the Vote, 1837–1965*, edited by Ann D. Gordon, 134–55. Amherst: University of Massachusetts Press, 1997.

Hill, Ruth Edmonds, ed. *The Black Women Oral History Project*. Arthur and Elizabeth Schlesinger Library on the History of Women in America, Radcliffe College. Westport, Conn.: Meckler, 1990.

Hine, Darlene Clark. "Rape and the Inner Lives of Black Women in the Middle West: Preliminary Thoughts on the Culture of Dissemblance." *Signs* 14 (Summer 1989): 912–20.

————. *Hine Sight: Black Women and the Re-Construction of American History*, 2nd printing. Bloomington: Indiana University Press, 1997.

Hogan, Wesley. *Many Minds, One Heart: SNCC's Dream for a New America*. Chapel Hill: University of North Carolina Press, 2009.

Holt, Len. *The Summer That Didn't End: The Story of the Mississippi Civil Rights Project of 1964*. 2nd ed. New York: Da Capo Press, 1992.

hooks, bell. *Feminist Theory: From Margin to Center*. Boston: South End Press, 1984.

Howard, Jerry, and Margarite Bradley. "Homecoming." *New Age Journal* 44 (September/October 1988): 40–44, 103–4, 107.

Inghram, Louise. *Freedom Riders Speak for Themselves*. Detroit, Mich.: News and Letters, 1961.

Irons, Jenny. "The Shaping of Activist Recruitment and Participation: A Study of Women in the Mississippi Civil Rights Movement." *Gender & Society* 21, no. 6 (December 1998): 692–709.

Jeffries, Hasan K. *Bloody Lowndes: Civil Rights and Black Power in Alabama's Black Belt*. New York: New York University Press, 2010.

Jenness, Mary. *Twelve Negro Americans*. Reprint ed. Freeport, N.Y.: Books for Libraries Press, 1977.

Joiner, Lottie. "Wednesdays in Mississippi: In 1964 Black and White Northern Women Joined Forces in the South." *Crisis* 109 (March–April 2002):31–37.

Jones, Cherisse R. "'How Shall I Sing the Lord's Song?': United Church Women Confront Racial Issues in South Carolina, 1940s–1960s." In *Throwing Off the Cloak of Privilege: White Southern Women Activists in the Civil Rights Era*, edited by Gail S. Murray, 131–52. Gainesville: University Press of Florida, 2004.

Jones, Charles E., and Judson L. Jeffries. "'Don't Believe the Hype': Debunking Panther Mythology." In *The Black Panther Party Reconsidered*, edited by Charles E. Jones, 25–55. Baltimore: Black Classic Press, 1998.

Joseph, Gloria. "Black Feminist Pedagogy and Schooling in Capitalist White America." In *Words of Fire: An Anthology of African American Female Thought*, edited by Beverly Guy-Sheftall. New York: New Press, 1995.

Lawson, Steven. *Black Ballots: Voting Rights in the South, 1944–1969*. Lanham, Md.: Lexington Books, 1999.

Lawton, Walter. "After the March Is Over." *Humanist* (September–October 1966):157–59.

Lee, Chana Kai. *For Freedom's Sake: The Life of Fannie Lou Hamer*. Urbana: University of Illinois Press, 2000.

Lloyd, James B. *Lives of Mississippi Authors, 1817–1967*. Jackson: University Press of Mississippi, 2009.

Locke, Mamie. "The Role of African-American Women in the Civil Rights Movement and Women's movements in Hinds County and Sunflower County, Mississippi." *Journal of Mississippi History* 53, no. 3 (1991): 229–39.

Lyells, Ruby E. Stutts. "A Look Ahead: What the Negro Wants." *Vital Speeches* (1949): 659–62.

Mants, Joann Christian. "We Turned This Upside-Down Country Right Side Up." In *Hands on the Freedom Plow: Personal Accounts by Women in SNCC*, edited by Faith S. Holsaert, Martha Prescod, Norman Noonan, Judy Richardson, Betty Garman Robinson, Jean Smith Young, and Dorothy M. Zellner, 128–40. Urbana: University of Illinois Press, 2010.

Mayfield, Julian, ed. *Selections from the Accra Assembly Papers*. Ghana: Secretariat of the Accra Assembly, 1962.

McAdam, Doug. *Political Process and the Development of Black Insurgency, 1930–1970*. Chicago: University of Chicago Press, 1982.

———. *Freedom Summer*. New York: Oxford University Press, 1990.

McGuire, Danielle. *At the Dark End of the Street: Black Women, Rape, and Resistance: A New History of the Civil Rights Movement from Rosa Parks to the Rise of Black Power*. New York: Vintage, 2010.

McLaughlin, Lacey. "A. M. E. Logan." Jackson Free Press online, February 7, 2011, jacksonfreepress.com/news/2011/feb/07/ame-logan.

McMillen, Neil R. *Dark Journey: Black Mississippians in the Age of Jim Crow*. Urbana: University of Illinois Press, 1989.

Meier, August, and Elliott Rudwick. *CORE: A Study in the Civil Rights Movement*. Urbana: University of Illinois Press, 1973.

Morris, Aldon. *The Origins of the Civil Rights Movement: Black Communities Organizing for Change*. New York: New Press, 1984.

Morris, Tiyi M. "Local Women and the Civil Rights Movement in Mississippi: Re-Visioning Womanpower Unlimited." In *Groundwork: Local Black Freedom Movements in America*, edited by Jeanne Theoharis and Komozi Woodard, 193–214. New York: New York University Press, 2005.

———. "Black Women Activists in Mississippi During the Civil Rights Era, 1954–1974." In *Southern Black Women in the Modern Civil Rights Movement*, edited by Bruce A. Glasrud and Merline Pitre, 137–52. College Station: Texas A&M University Press, 2013.

———. "Clarie Collins Harvey: The Transformative Vision of a World Citizen." *Journal of African American Studies* 17, no. 3 (September 2013): 275–89.

Moye, J. Todd. *Let the People Decide: Black Freedom and White Resistance Movements in Sunflower County, Mississippi, 1945–1968*. Chapel Hill: University of North Carolina Press, 2004.

Naeve, Virginia. "What Can We (I) Do." *MANAS* 18, no. 28 (July 14, 1965): 1–4.

———. "Children . . . and Ourselves: Unchurched Religious Education." *MANAS* 18, no. 48 (December 1, 1965): 9–11.

———. "Mississippi Box Project or Person-to-Person Help: How We Started." *Fellowship* 32, no. 5 (May 1966): 24–26.

Nash, Diane. "They Are the Ones Who Got Scared." In *Hands on the Freedom Plow: Personal Accounts by Women in SNCC*, edited by Faith S. Holsaert, Martha Prescod Norman Noonan, Judy Richardson, Betty Garman Robinson, Jean Smith Young, and Dorothy M. Zellner, 76–83. Urbana: University of Illinois Press, 2010.

Norman, Cora. *Mississippi in Transition: The Role of the Mississippi Humanities Council*. Knoxville: University of Tennessee Press, 2009.

O'Brien, M. J. "We Shall Not Be Moved: The Jackson Woolworth's Sit-In and the Movement It Inspired." Jackson: University of Mississippi Press, 2013.

Oshinsky, David. *Worse Than Slavery: Parchman Farm and the Ordeal of Jim Crow*. New York: Free Press, 1997.

Parker-Weaver, Stephanie. "Reflections on the Life of Mrs. A. M. E. Logan." Jackson Advocate online, February 10, 2011, jacksonadvocateonline.com/?p=2012.

Payne, Charles. *I've Got the Light of Freedom: The Organizing Tradition and the Mississippi Freedom Struggle*. Berkeley: University of California Press, 1995.

———. "Sexism Is a Helluva Thing: Rethinking Our Questions and Assumptions." In *Civil Rights History from the Ground Up: Local Struggles, a National Movement*, edited by Emilye Crosby, 319–29. Athens: University of Georgia Press, 2011.

Piven, Frances Fox, and Richard Cloward. *Poor People's Movements: Why They Succeed and How They Fail*. New York: Vintage Books, 1979.

Porter, Dorothy B. "The Organized Educational Activities of Negro Literary Societies, 1828–1846." *Journal of Negro Education* 5, no. 4 (October 1936): 555–76.

Putnam, Judy. "Educator, Black Leader Sanders, 95, Dies in Jackson after a Lengthy Illness." *Clarion-Ledger*, December 30, 1980, 18.

Quarm, S. E. *Diplomatic Offensive: An Overview of Ghana's Diplomacy under Dr. Kwame Nkrumah Ghana*. Ghana: Afram, 1997.

Raines, Howell. *My Soul Is Rested: The Story of the Civil Rights Movement in the Deep South*. New York: G. P. Putnam's Sons, 1977.

Ransby, Barbara. *Ella Baker and the Black Freedom Movement: A Radical Democratic Vision*. Chapel Hill: University of North Carolina Press, 2005.

Reagon, Bernice Johnson. "My Black Mothers and Sisters or Beginning a Cultural Autobiography." *Feminist Studies* 8, no. 1 (Spring 1982): 81–96.

———. "African Diaspora Women: the Making of Cultural Workers." *Feminist Studies* 12, no. 1 (1986):77–90.

Remsburg, Charles, and Bonnie Rembsburg. "The Couple Who Cared." *Good Housekeeping*, October 1974, 16, 20, 24.

Riehm, Edith Holbrook. "Dorothy Tilly and the Fellowship of the Concerned." In *Throwing Off the Cloak of Privilege: White Southern Women Activists in the Civil Rights Era*, edited by Gail S. Murray, 23–48. Gainesville: University Press of Florida, 2004.

Robnett, Belinda. *How Long? How Long?: African American Women in the Struggle for Civil Rights*. New York: Oxford University Press, 1997.

Royster, Jacqueline Jones, ed. *Southern Horrors and Other Writings: The Anti-Lynching Campaign of Ida B. Wells, 1892–1900*. New York: Bedford/St. Martin's, 1996.

Salter, John R., Jr. *Jackson, Mississippi: An American Chronicle of Struggle and Schism*. Reprint ed. Malabar, Fla.: Robert E. Krieger, 1987.

Sewell, George Alexander. *Mississippi Black History Makers*. Jackson: University Press of Mississippi, 1977.

Shannon, Margaret. *Just Because: The Story of the National Movement of Church Women United in the U.S.A. 1941 through 1975*. Corte Madera, Calif.: Omega Books, 1977.

Shaw, Stephanie J. *What a Woman Ought to Do and to Be: Black Professional Workers during the Jim Crow Era*. Chicago: University of Chicago Press, 1996.

Silver, James W. *Mississippi: The Closed Society*. New York: Harcourt, Brace, 1964.

Smith, Elaine M. "'Closed Doors': Mary McLeod Bethune on Civil Rights." In *Sisters in the Struggle: African-American Women in the Civil Rights–Black Power Struggle*, edited by Bettye Collier-Thomas and V. P. Franklin, 11–20. New York: New York University Press, 2001.

Smith, Suzanne E. *To Serve the Living: Funeral Directors and the African American Way of Death*. Cambridge, Mass.: Harvard University Press, 2010.

Sparks, Selma. "A First Hand Report from the Accra Assembly 'The World without the Bomb.'" *Liberator* 2, no. 7 (July 1962): 4–5.

Springer, Kimberly. *Living for the Revolution: Black Feminist Organizations, 1968–1980*. Durham, N.C.: Duke University Press, 2005.

Spruill, Marjorie Julian. "The Mississippi Takeover: Feminists, Antifeminists and the International Women's Year Conference of 1977." In *Mississippi Women: Their Histories, Their Lives*, vol. 2, edited by Martha Swain, Elizabeth Anne Payne, and Marjorie Julian Spruill, 287–313. Athens: University of Georgia Press, 2010.

Swerdlow, Amy. *Women Strike for Peace: Traditional Motherhood and Radical Politics in the 1960's*. Chicago: University of Chicago Press, 1993.

Terborg-Penn, Rosalyn. *African American Women in the Struggle for the Vote, 1850–1920*. Bloomington: Indiana University Press, 1998.

Thompson, Cleopatra D. *The History of The Mississippi Teachers Association*. Washington, D.C.: NEA Teachers Rights, 1973.

———. *The History of the Mississippi State Federation of Colored Women's Clubs, 1903–1990*. Jackson: Mississippi State Federation of Colored Women's Clubs, 1990.

Thornton, Bonnie Dill. "'The Means to Put My Children Through': Child Rearing Goals and Strategies among Black Female Domestic Servants." In *The Black Woman*, edited by La Frances Rodgers-Rose, 107–23. Newbury Park, Calif.: Sage, 1980.

Webb, Kenneth B., and Susan H. Webb. *Summer Magic: What Children Gain from Camp*. New York: Association Press, 1953.

Weber, Ruth. "The New President: A Face to the Rising Sun." *Church Woman* (June–July 1971): 20–27.

White, Deborah Gray. "Mining the Forgotten: Manuscript Sources for Black Women's History." *Journal of American History* 70, no. 1 (1987): 237–42.

Williams, Mildred M., Kara Vaughn Jackson, Madie A. Kiney, Susie W. Wheeler, Rebecca Davis, Rebecca A. Crawford, Maggie Forte, and Ethel Bell. *The Jeanes Story: A Chapter in the History of American Education, 1908–1968*. Jackson: University Press of Mississippi, 1979.

Williamson, Joy Ann. *Radicalizing the Ebony Tower: Black Colleges and the Black Freedom Struggle in Mississippi*. New York: Teachers College Press, 2008.

Womanpower Unlimited, *Womanpower and the Jackson Movement*. Jackson, Miss.: N.p., 1963.

"World Conference of Christian Youth." *Christian Education* 22, no. 5 (June 1939): 336–42.

Zinn, Howard. *SNCC: The New Abolitionists*. Boston: Beacon Press, 1965.

Dissertations and Unpublished Manuscripts

Crawford, Vicki. "'We Shall Not be Moved': Black Female Activists in the Mississippi Civil Rights Movement, 1960–1965." PhD Diss., Emory University, 1987.

Morris, Tiyi. "Black Women's Civil Rights Activism in Mississippi: The Story of Womanpower Unlimited." PhD Diss., Purdue University, 2002.

Petersen, Karen. Untitled paper on Vermont in Mississippi. Vermont Historical Society, Civil Rights Movement in Vermont Collection, n.d.

INDEX

Harvey, Martin L. Jr., 29, 30, 117
Haughton, M. G., 62, 80, 82
Head Start, 67, 137, 138, 139, 163, 172, 208n84. *See also* Child Development Group of Mississippi
Hearn, Katie Harrell, 132–33
Height, Dorothy, 18; friendship with Harvey, 117; reason for not establishing a chapter of NCNW in Jackson, 172; work with Wednesdays in Mississippi, 114, 115, 116, 120, 121, 122, 138, 139, 144
Henry, Aaron, 11, 54, 74
Henry, Dwight, 165
Henry, Maddye Lyne, 51, 165, 166, 167, 175
Herring, Frances, 94, 97, 101
Hewitt, Ann, 110, 113, 123, 130, 139
Hinds Community Council, 79
Hubert, Ruth Oates, 10, 39, 50, 193n82
humanism, 50, 90, 108, 122, 171, 172, 186

Independent Political Forum, 86, 103
integration, 11, 56, 76, 77, 80, 82, 128, 165; desegregation of facilities, 15, 21, 22, 135, 160, 197n49; Thelma Sanders's arrest 175
Inter-organizational Women's Committee, 117, 124
interracial communication, 109, 110, 118, 138, 154
interracial cooperation, 49, 71, 80, 82, 83, 113, 114, 172; and Wednesdays in Mississippi, 112–13, 123, 127, 132, 138–39, 143, 144
Interracial Vacations Camping Project, 138, 147, 161–68. *See also* Camp Madison-Felicia
intersectionality, 1, 2, 4, 5, 41, 90, 101, 186, 187n5; multiple oppressions 3, 5, 99, 100

Jackson, Alice (Wright), 74–75, 198n93
Jackson, Miss., 1, 2, 4, 7, 14, 19, 27–34 *passim*, 37, 82, 84, 151, 162; Freedom Riders in, 15–17, 22, 24; Freedom Summer activities in, 72, 73, 75; public schools in, 67, 77–78, 165, 167; voter education and registration, 11, 61, 63; Wednesdays in Mississippi activism in, 121, 130, 131, 132, 137, 138, 139, 142, 143; youth activism in, 20, 54, 55–56
Jackson Movement, 31, 33, 49, 52, 53, 55–56, 61, 66–70, 80, 145, 179
Jackson Nonviolent Movement (JNM), 47, 53, 54, 55, 139
Jackson State College, 20, 32, 141, 181, 182; WU members affiliated with, 2, 16, 39, 50, 51, 67, 68, 84
Johnson, Janet, 157
Johnson, Josie, 143, 144
Jones, Lillie Bell, 39, 68, 120, 124, 136
J. P. Campbell College, 32, 34, 46, 60, 109

Kennedy, Florynce, 134
Kennedy, John F., 21, 22, 86, 88, 102–3, 104, 208n8; Kennedy administration, 55, 69
Kennedy, Robert F., 21, 22
King, Coretta Scott, 95, 104, 108; assistance to The Box Project, 147–48, 149, 150, 160
King, Jeannette, 83, 113
King, Martin Luther, Jr. 33, 56, 161, 193n70
Knight, Mary, 150
Knopp, Fay Honey, 49, 78, 83, 103
Kohlenberg, Geraldine "Gerry," 128, 131, 133

labor, 8, 57, 97, 100, 189n5
Lane, Myrtle, 79, 150, 156
Lash, Trude, 142
Lawton, Walter, 161, 211n63
leadership, 3–4, 5, 10, 12, 28, 40–45 *passim*, 63, 84, 109, 176, 185; bridge leaders, 13, 36, 82, 114, 170; reinterpretation of women's activism, 41; roles in male dominated civil rights organizations, 3, 5, 41, 42, 43, 44, 50, 51, 92

United States Commission on Civil Rights, 71; Mississippi Advisory Committee to, 81, 83, 133

Vermont in Mississippi (VIM), 78–80, 150
violence, 7, 12, 38, 65, 103, 119; brutality against Biloxi "wade in" activists, 20; brutality against Freedom Riders, 21, 22; harassment, 26, 126, 143; lynching, 7–8; police brutality, 62, 63, 81, 115, 161, 193n73
Vivell, Diane, 112, 121, 122, 123
voting rights, 7, 8–9, 57, 81, 185; and clubwomen, 10, 57–59, 195n18; disenfranchisement, 7, 19, 56, 58, 62, 63; and Freedom Vote, 54, 69; Jackson Voter Education Coordinating Committee, 59–60; voter education, 14, 57, 59; Voter Education Project (VEP), 55, 59, 60, 62, 65; voter registration, 10, 11, 12, 14, 19, 33, 34, 40, 46, 58–59, 61–62, 70, 115, 147, 159, 180, 195n10, 196n37; voting registration in exchange for clothing, 157

Wednesdays in Mississippi (WIMS, Wednesdays Women), 82, 83–84, 105, 112–45, 151, 172, 181, 209n115; emergence of, 120–27; fear of reprisals, 116, 139; interracial structure of, 121–23; local and national activism, 133, 138, 139, 144; transformation of, 136; Workshops in Mississippi, 140, 181
white supremacy, 5, 8, 12, 20, 30, 116, 180; domination, 7, 8, 19, 20
Willen, Pearl, 128, 131
Williams, Ilza, 125, 127, 142
Williams, Mildred, 66, 67
Wilson, Dagmar, 90, 91, 94, 107
Wilson, Delores, 94, 107
Wilson, Dora, 28, 104, 107, 204n109; background, 105–6
Wilson, Doris, 112, 121, 128, 131, 143, 144; background, 122–23
Womanpower Unlimited (WU), 1, 3, 7,

10, 12, 13, 14, 31, 33, 34, 38, 39, 68, 150, 179; adopting families in need, 77–78; class status of WU activists, 51–52, 66; collaboration with civil rights organizations, 41, 46, 47, 48, 55, 56, 59, 95, 107, 169, 170; cosponsorship and leadership of the interracial camping project, 162–63, 164, 166, 167–68; economic status of members, 25, 50–51; emergence of WU, 15–17, 18; formal affiliation with NCNW, 172–74; Freedom Riders, 16, 17, 21–24, 35, 46, 51, 53, 91, 139, 177; legacy of, 174–77; linking social movements, 90 107–8, 111, 138; organizational structure, 40, 41, 44, 45, 46, 51, 52, 91, 193n85; peace activism, 89–90, 93, 108–9, 110; support of and collaboration with other activists 35, 47, 50, 75, 84, 91, 119–20; support of Freedom Summer project, 70, 71, 75, 177; support of The Box Project, 147, 151, 152, 168; sustaining the movement, 75–76, 84, 169, 170, 171; vision and purpose, 40–41; voter registration campaign, 53, 56, 58–65, 70, 71, 103, 170, 197n49; Wednesdays in Mississippi, 121, 124, 125, 131, 136, 137, 145, 201n24; Womanpower for Freedom Task Force, 169; Womanpower's Council of Women's Organizations, 69; Womanpower Unlimited disbands, 173, 212n; Women Strike for Peace, 95, 104–7, 1113; work with youth, 134, 162, 167
Women Strike for Peace (WSP), 49, 50, 74, 85–107, 111, 119, 150; beginnings of WSP, 90–95; Committee for a Sane Nuclear Policy (SANE), 91; exclusion of race from WSP activism, 93–95, 97, 101, 202n40, 204n101; four-point proposal for Vatican Pilgrimage, 101–2; the Hague trip, 104–7; LA WSP, 92, 94, 95; march to the Palais des Nations, 87; marginalization of female

peace activists in male dominated organizations, 91, 92; and Nkrumah's plenary address, 97–98; 17-Nation Disarmament Conference, 85–88; similarities and differences between WU and WSP, 91–93; strike to protest nuclear arms, 91; support for The Box Project, 156; use of motherhood imagery, 91, 102, 201n28, 203n85; Women for Peace Vatican Pilgrimage, 101–4; NATO Women's Peace Force conference and protest march, 105; World without the Bomb Conference, 95–101

Woo (WU newsletter), 46, 77, 78, 176
Woods, Geraldine, 133, 134
Workshops on Race, 109–10
World Council of Churches (WCC), 101, 103, 184

Young, Aurelia, 16, 50, 51, 125, 141, 193n82, 193n85
Young Women's Christian Association (YWCA) 27, 28, 35, 39, 49, 68, 116, 117, 120, 122, 123, 128, 136, 139, 144

Zales, Gladys, 112, 143

POLITICS AND CULTURE IN THE TWENTIETH-CENTURY SOUTH